MW01708107

NELSON

Primary Maths for Caribbean Schools

2nd edition

ERROL FURLONGE

Consultant editor Peter Clarke

JUNIOR BOOK 3

First published in 1997 by:
Stanley Thornes (Publishing) Ltd

Second edition published in 2005 by:
Nelson Thornes Ltd
Delta Place
27 Bath Road
CHELTENHAM
GL53 7TH
United Kingdom

06 07 08 09 10/ 10 9 8 7 6 5 4 3 2

A catalogue record for this book is available from the British Library

ISBN 0 7487 9627 4

Page make-up and Illustration by IFA Design Limited, Plymouth, Devon, UK.

Printed and bound in Great Britain by Scotprint

Contents

Acknowledgements

The author acknowledges the assistance and co-operation of all the practising teachers who responded to the questionnaire relating to the use of the series, and those who willingly discussed and advised on the contents of the course.

1 Numbers to 10 000

Review of numbers to 999

What numbers are represented in the following diagrams?

1. 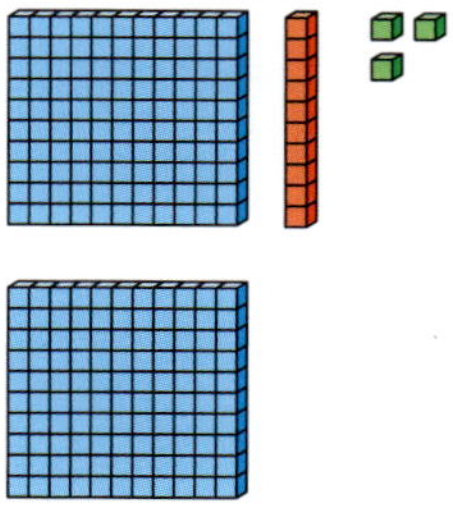

2. 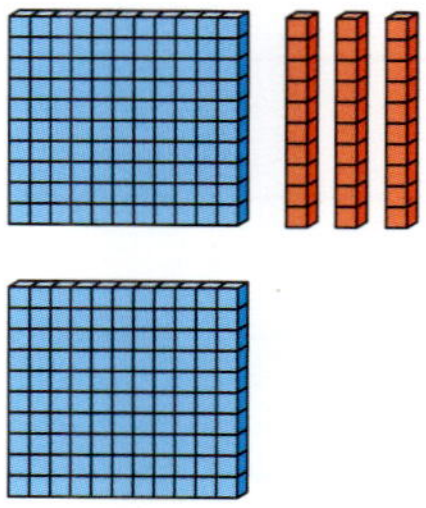

3. 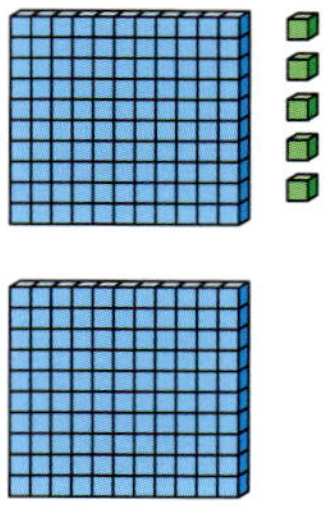

Write these numbers in words.

4. 1 2 3 **5.** 1 0 1 **6.** 1 1 0

7. 2 0 2 **8.** 2 2 0 **9.** 2 1 2

10. 3 3 0 **11.** 4 0 4 **12.** 5 9 0

Write numerals for the following.

13. one hundred and fifteen **14.** one hundred and fifty

15. one hundred and five **16.** three hundred and thirteen

17. three hundred and three **18.** five hundred and fifty

19. six hundred and sixty-one **20.** nine hundred and ninety

What is the value of the digit underlined in the following numbers?

21. 2 1 $\underline{2}$ **22.** $\underline{9}$ 0 9 **23.** 1 $\underline{7}$ 7

24. 3 $\underline{3}$ 0 **25.** 1 $\underline{1}$ 1 **26.** 2 $\underline{0}$ 1

Write these numbers in expanded form.

347 = 300 + 40 + 7

27. 6 4 2 **28.** 2 2 1 **29.** 3 1 3

30. 1 0 2 **31.** 1 2 0 **32.** 2 1 0

What are the next five numbers in each of the following patterns?

33. 100, 105, 110, ____ ____ ____ ____ ____

34. 200, 210, 220, ____ ____ ____ ____ ____

35. 320, 340, 360, ____ ____ ____ ____ ____

36. 400, 425, 450, ____ ____ ____ ____ ____

37. 500, 550, 600, ____ ____ ____ ____ ____

38. 200, 300, 400, ____ ____ ____ ____ ____

Write the numbers which are ringed on the number lines below.

39.

40.

41.

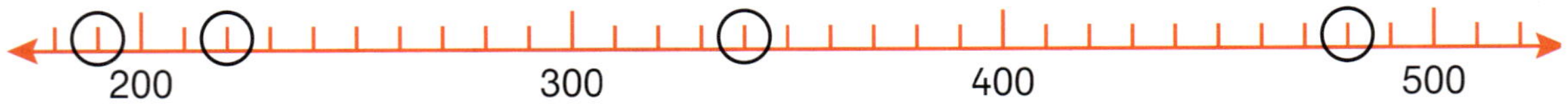

Write the correct sign, < or >, between the following pairs of numbers to make true statements.

42. 24 ☐ 42 **43.** 53 ☐ 35 **44.** 47 ☐ 74

45. 151 ☐ 115 **46.** 202 ☐ 220 **47.** 313 ☐ 303

48. 404 ☐ 440 **49.** 510 ☐ 501 **50.** 905 ☐ 950

What are the largest and smallest numbers that you can make using each set of 3 digits?

51. 3, 4, 2 **52.** 6, 5, 7 **53.** 2, 3, 1

The abacus

We can use an abacus to show numbers in the same way as we use our blocks and squares.

In the picture on the right each red bead represents ten, and each green bead represents one.

You can think of the red bead as a 10-cent coin. You can change it for 10 green beads. The green bead is like the one cent coin.

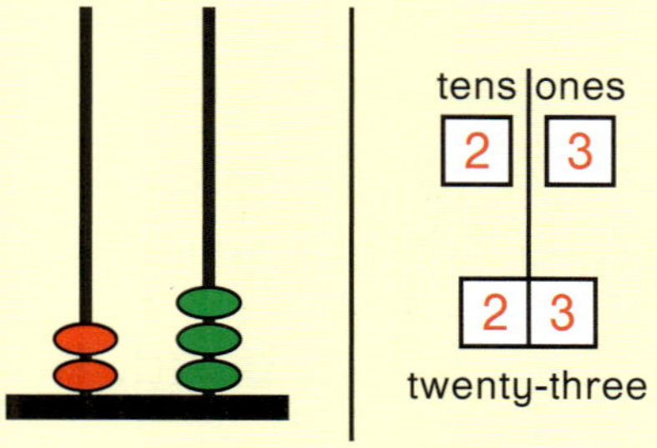

Write the numbers shown below in numerals and words.

1. 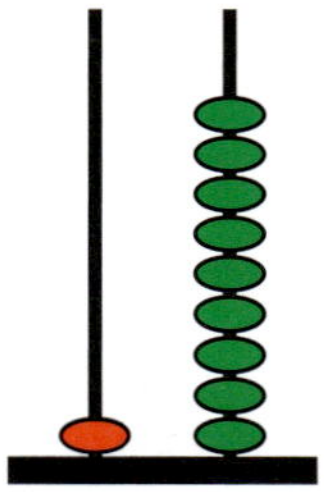

2. 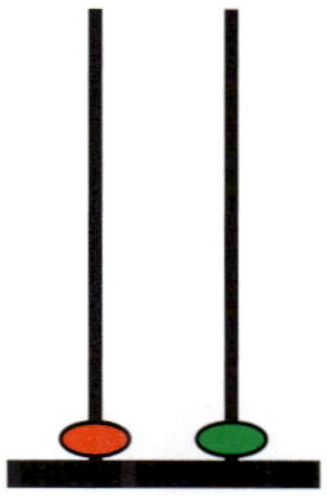

3. 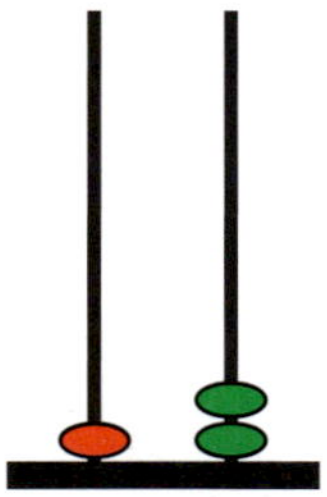

4. 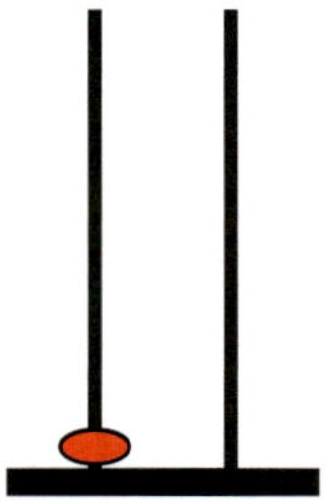

5. 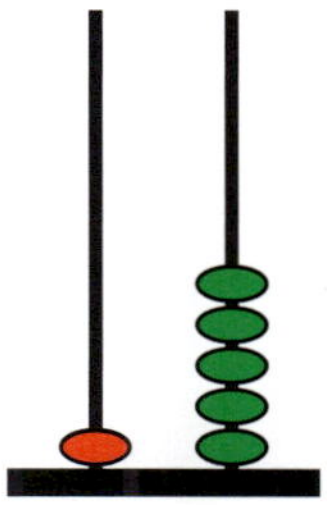

6. 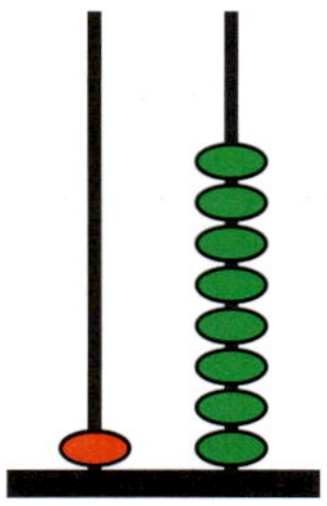

7. 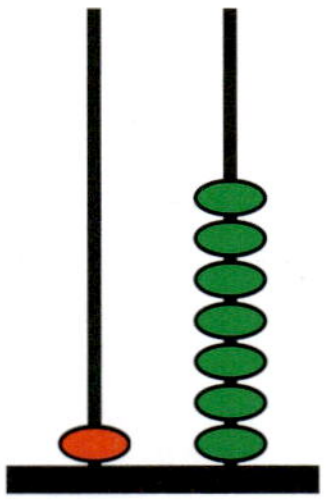

8. 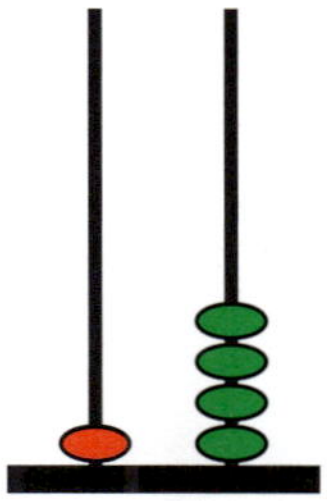

9. 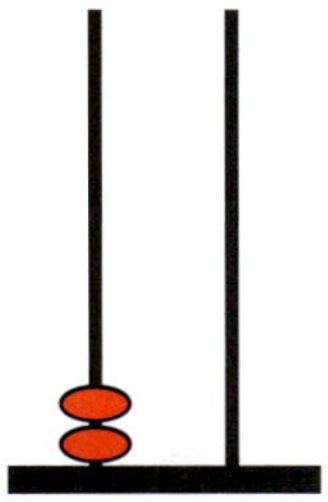

Two-digit numbers on the abacus

Now use your abacus.
Use green beads for **ones** (or units). Use red beads for **tens**.
Take out 20 green beads. These count for **ones**.
Put them in tens. How many tens?
There are 2 tens. So we need 2 red beads.
These count for tens.

Add 1 green bead: how many beads now?
We have 2 tens and 1 one.
This is 21 (twenty-one).

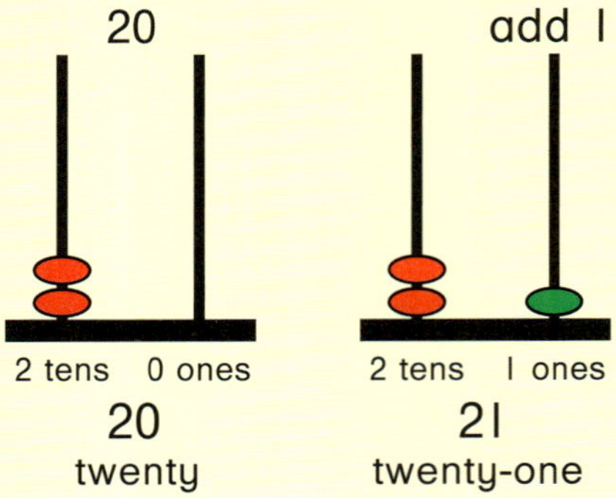

Write the number of tens and ones shown on each abacus below. Then write the numeral and number name for each number.

1. 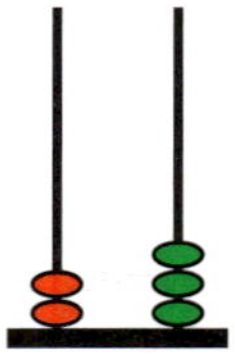

2. 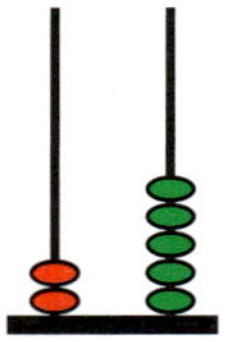

3. 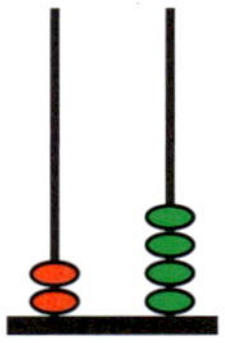

4. 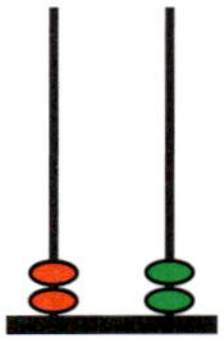

5. 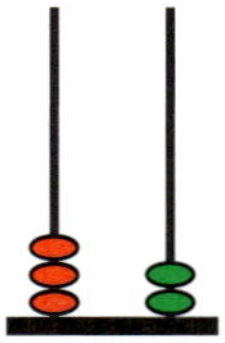

6. 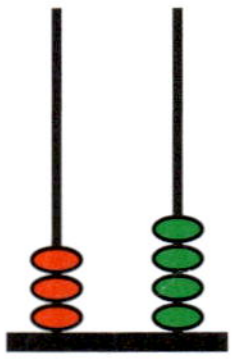

7. 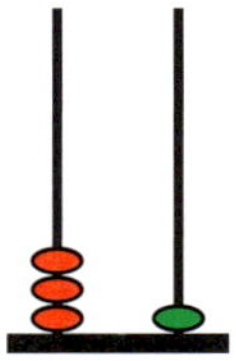

8. 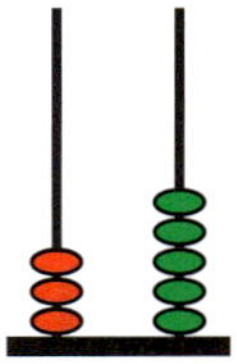

9. 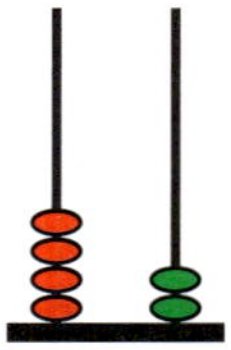

10. 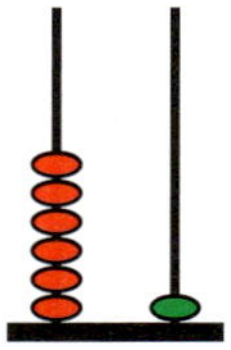

11. 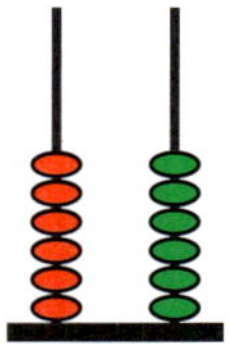

12. 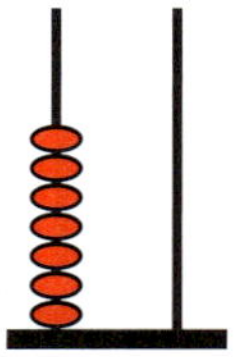

Three-digit numbers on the abacus

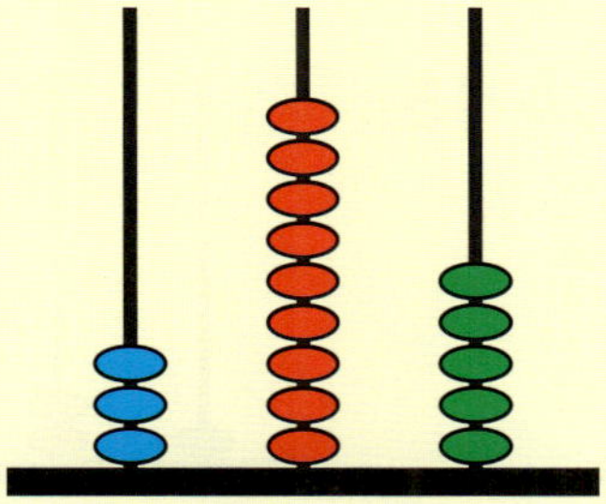

3 hundreds 9 tens 5 ones
395
three hundred and ninety-five

Write the numbers shown below in numerals and words.

1. 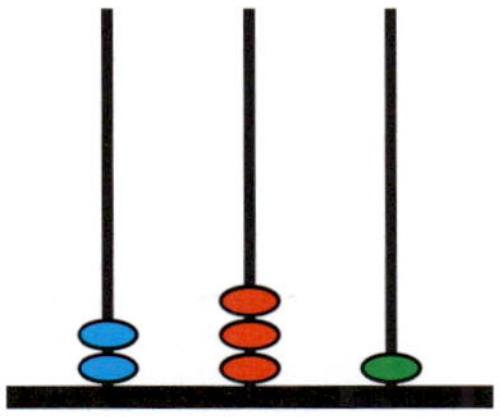

2. 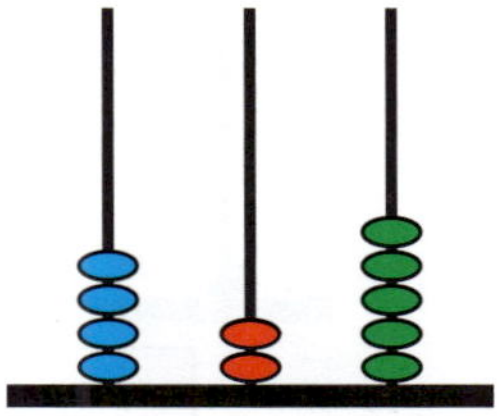

3. 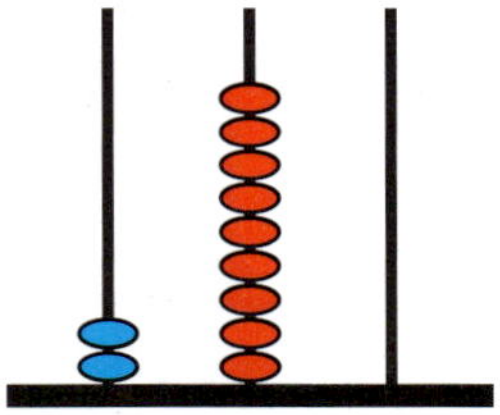

4. 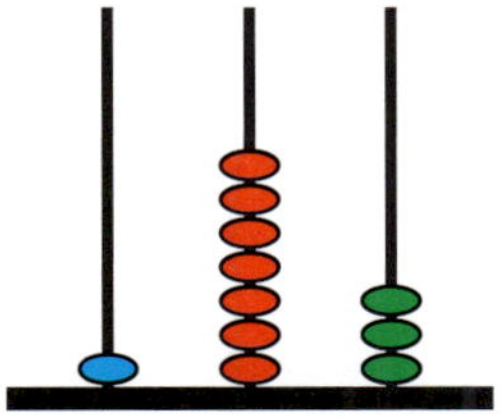

5. 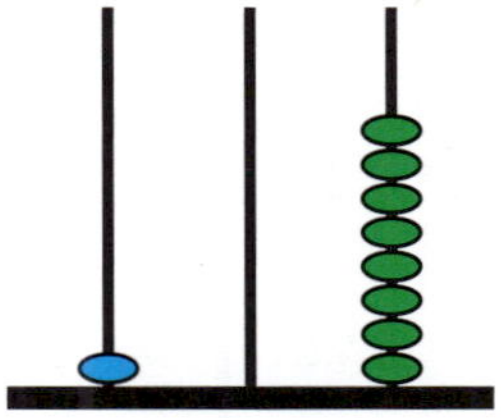

6. 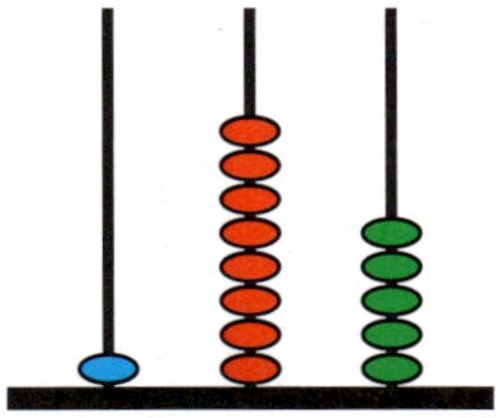

7. 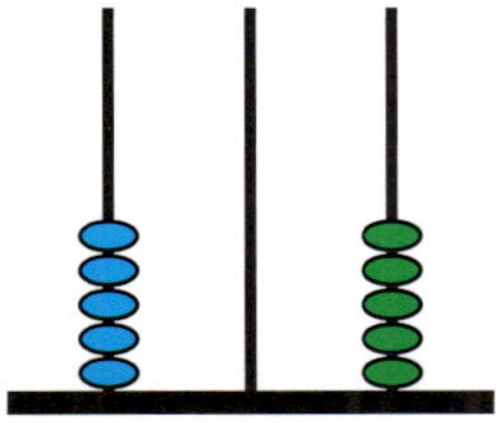

8. 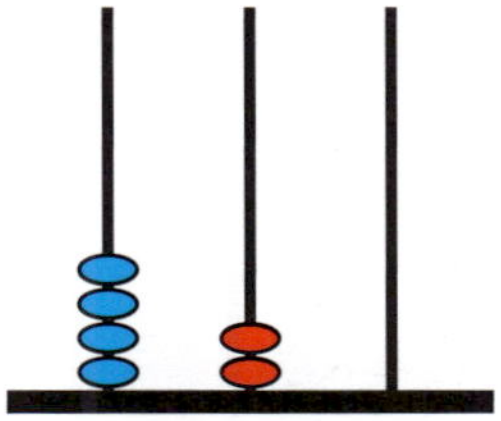

9. 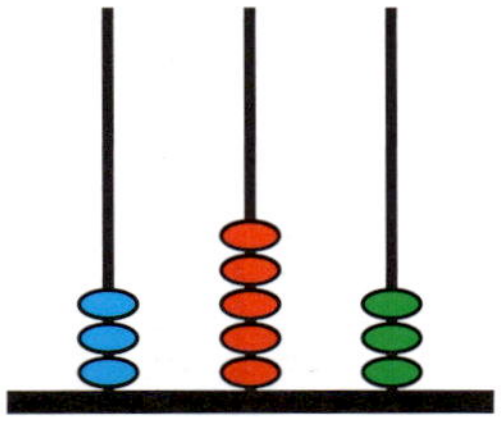

10. 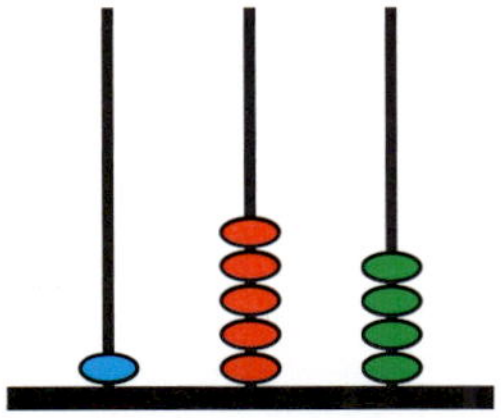

11. 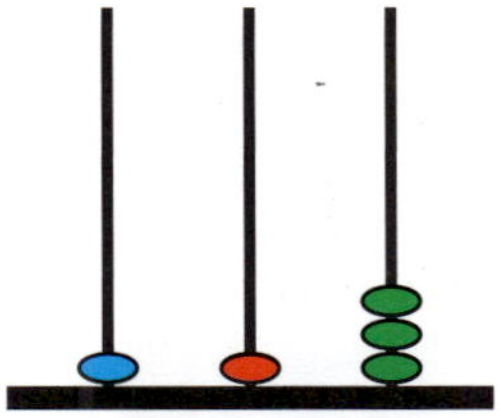

12. 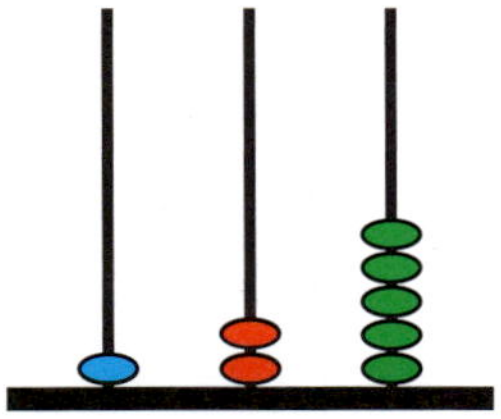

Beads are missing in some of the abacuses. Numbers are missing in others.
Draw the missing beads or write the missing numbers.

13.

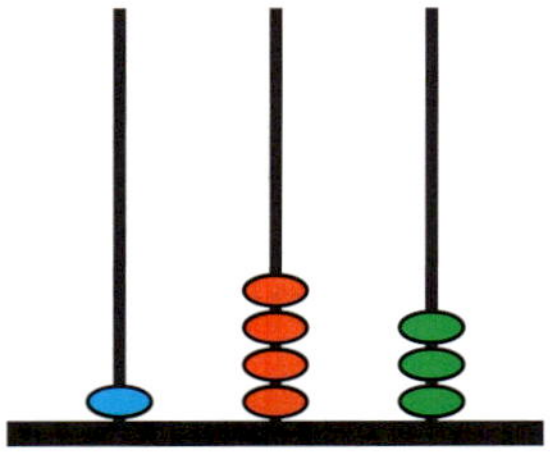

147

14.

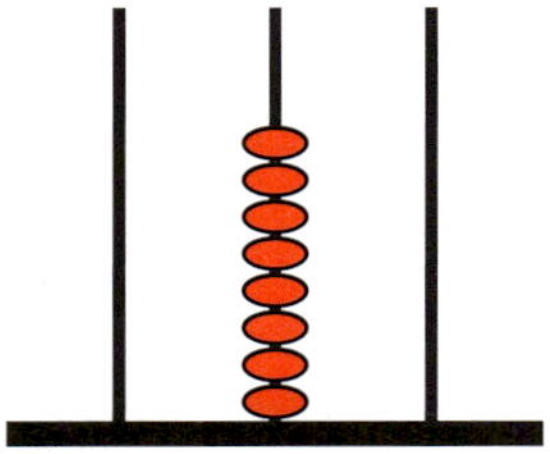

181

15.

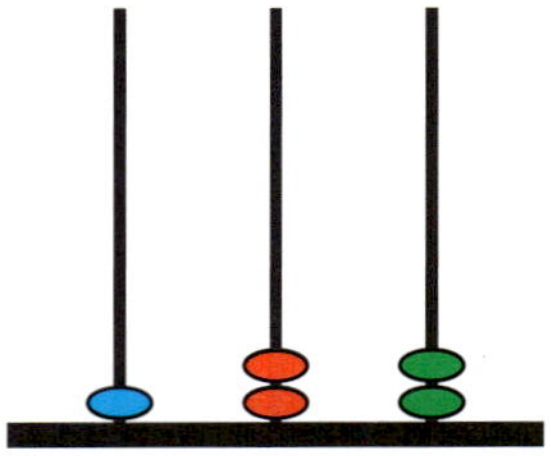

__2__

16.

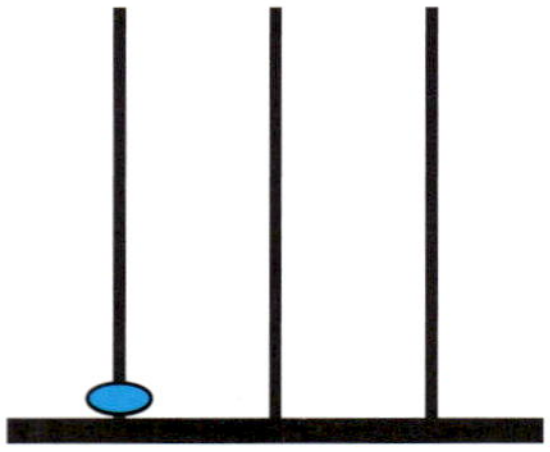

172

17.

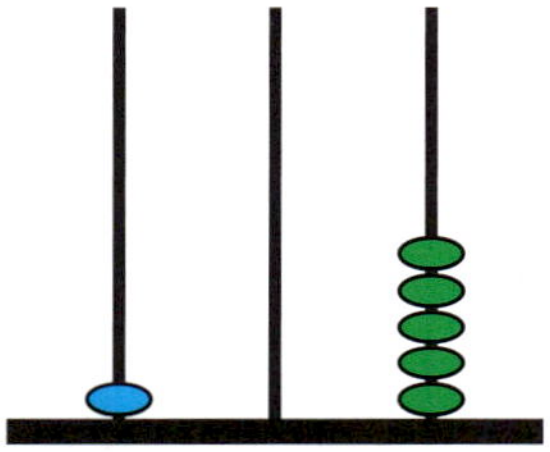

__0__

18.

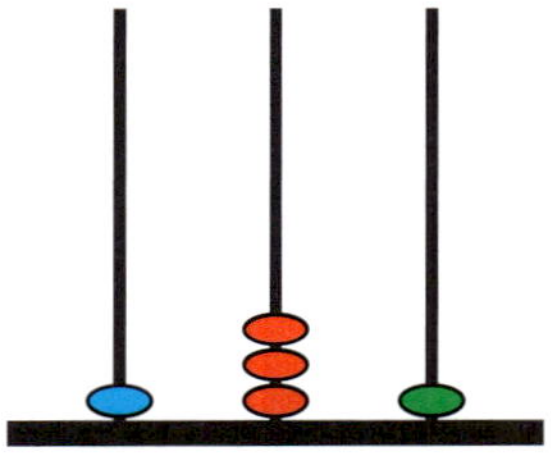

154

19.

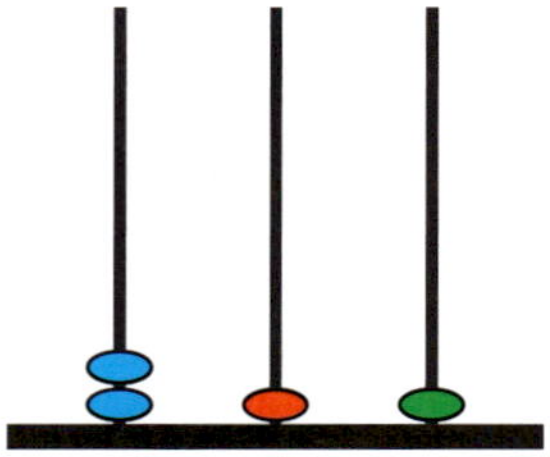

2__ __

20.

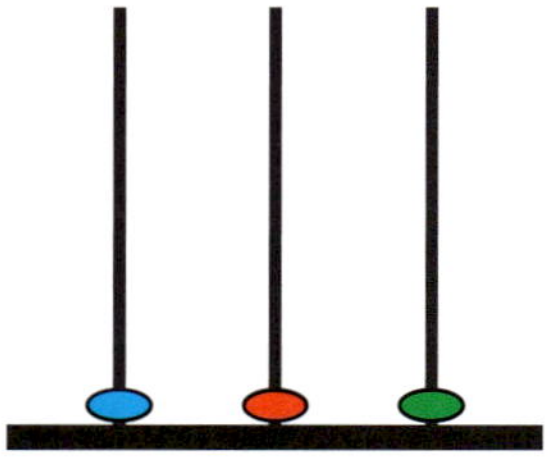

165

21.

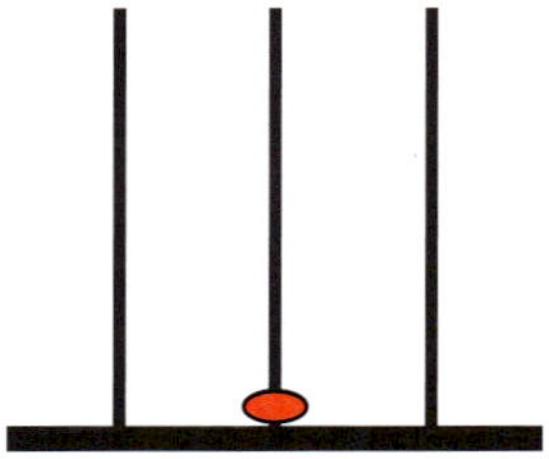

136

22.

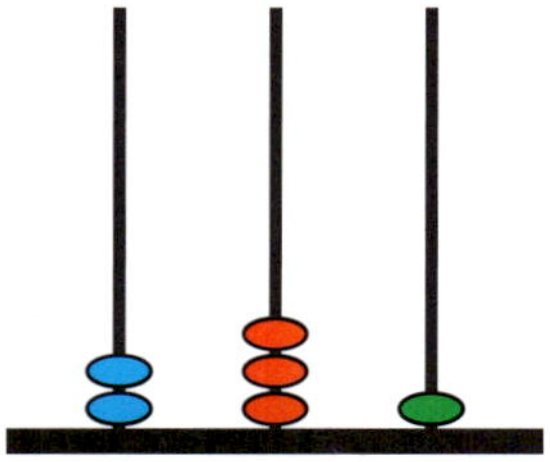

243

23.

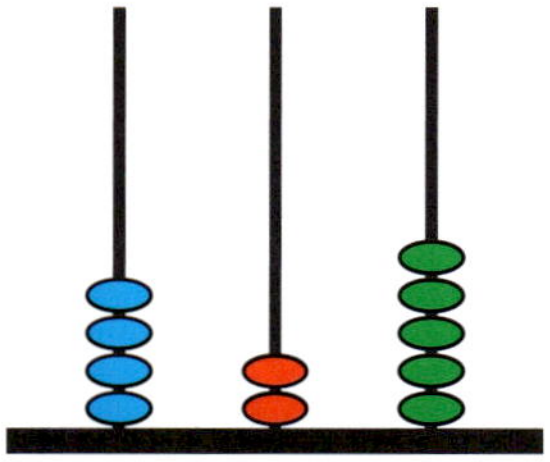

436

24.

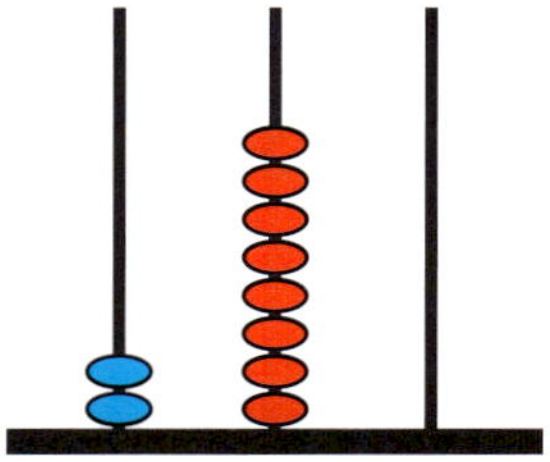

__8__

The number 1000

Let us count on from nine hundred and ninety:
nine hundred and ninety, nine hundred and ninety-one, nine hundred and ninety-two...
Write the numbers as you count: 990, 991, 992, ...
What is the largest three-digit number we can write?
The abacus picture below shows the addition of 999 + 1.

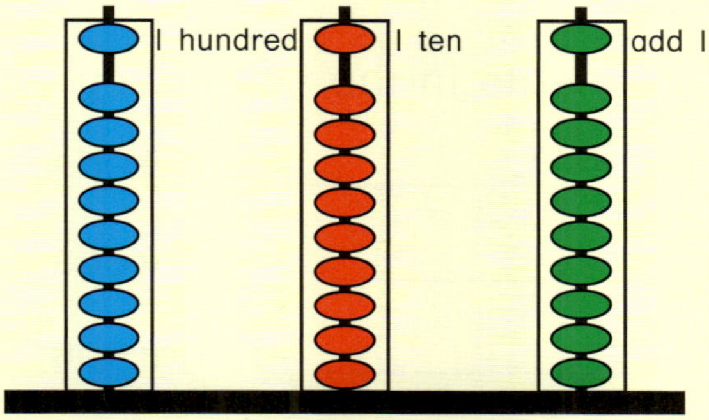

	hundreds	tens	units
	9	9	9
+			1
1	0	0	0

The next counting number after 999 is 1000, the number one thousand.

1000 is the same as 10 hundreds.

We can also use our blocks to show 1000.

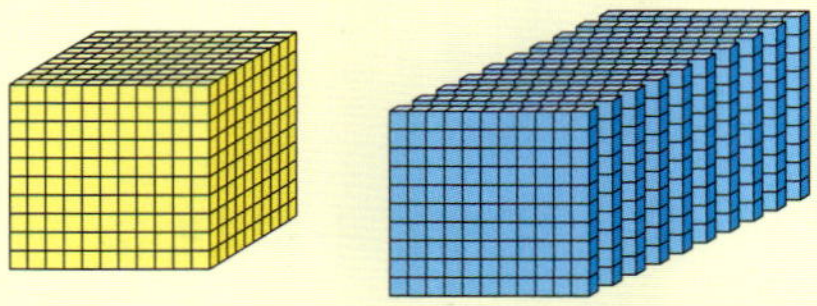

The 1000 block is made up of 10 one-hundred blocks.

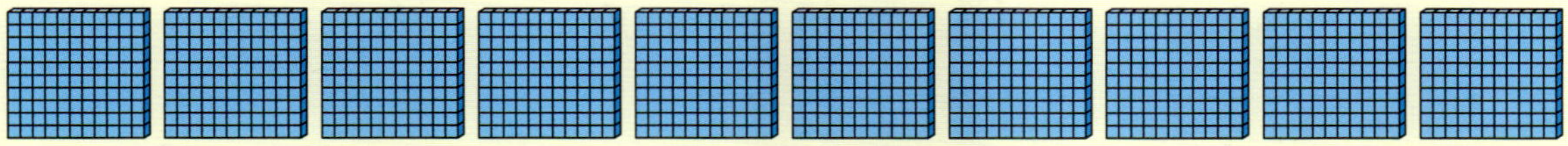

Thousands and hundreds

Look at the pictures below.

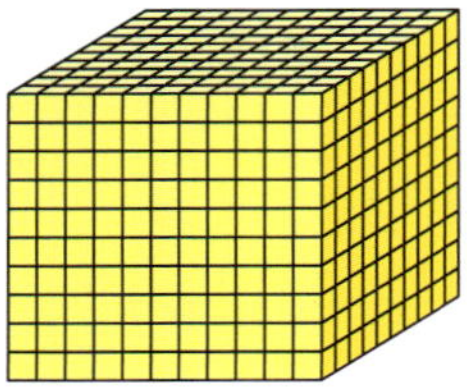

one thousand = ten hundreds = 1000

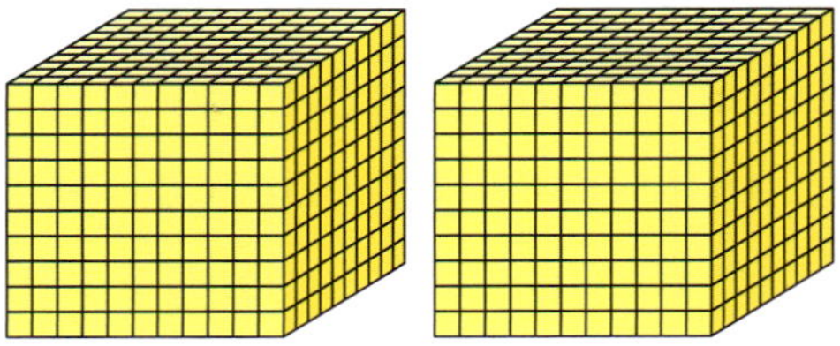

two thousands = twenty hundreds = 2000

Complete these statements in the same way.

1. three thousands = __________ hundreds = _____

2. four thousands = __________ hundreds = _____

3. five thousands = __________ hundreds = _____

4.–7. Continue to nine thousands.

Look at these pictures.

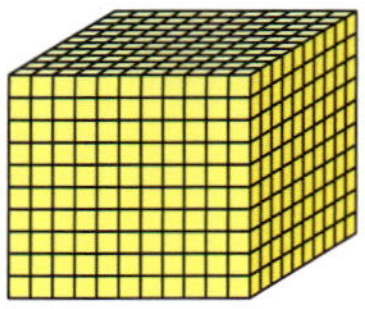

add

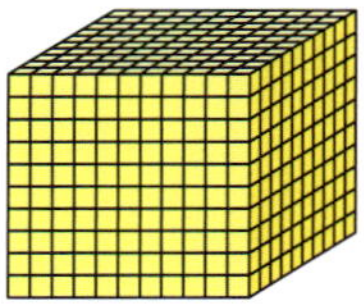

1000 add 1000
= 2000

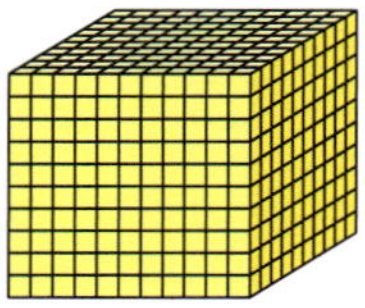

add

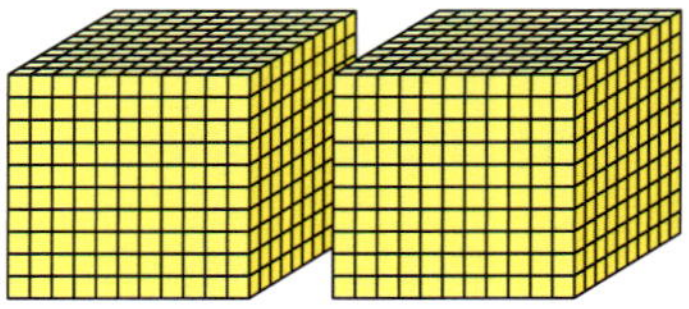

1000 add 2000
= 3000

Write answers to the following:

8. 1000 + 3000 **9.** 1000 + 4000 **10.** 1000 + 5000

11. 2000 + 3000 **12.** 2000 + 4000 **13.** 2000 + 5000

14. 3000 + 4000 **15.** 3000 + 5000 **16.** 3000 + 6000

17. What is 1000 + 9000?

18. What other additions of thousands will give you this number?

Now look at these pictures.

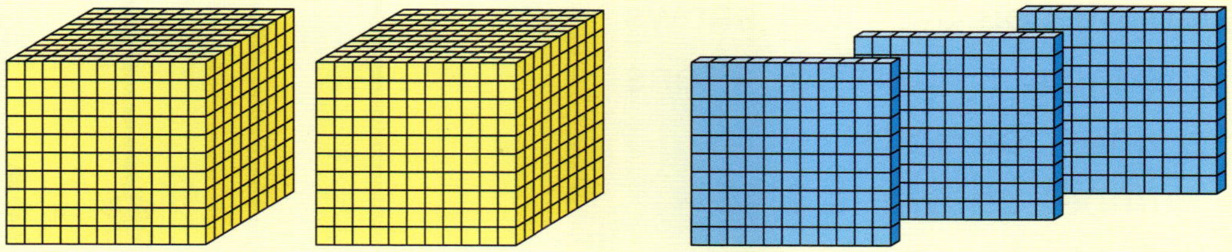

2 thousands plus 3 hundreds

20 hundreds plus 3 hundreds

23 hundreds

2300

twenty-three hundreds = 2300

We read the number 2300 as two thousand, three hundred.

Write numerals for the following:

19. eighteen hundreds

20. thirty-five hundreds

21. forty-two hundreds

22. seventy-four hundreds

23. nineteen hundreds

24. sixty-six hundreds

25. ninety-nine hundreds

26. ninety hundreds

Write these numbers in words:

1800 is one thousand, eight hundred

27. 1500

28. 3600

29. 5300

30. 9100

31. 8800

32. 1600

33. 9500

34. 4800

35. 7200

36. 6100

37. 8000

38. 3000

Four-digit numbers on the abacus

The abacus on the right shows 2 thousands, 1 hundred, 4 tens and 5 ones (or units).
The number shown is 2145 – two thousand, one hundred and forty-five.

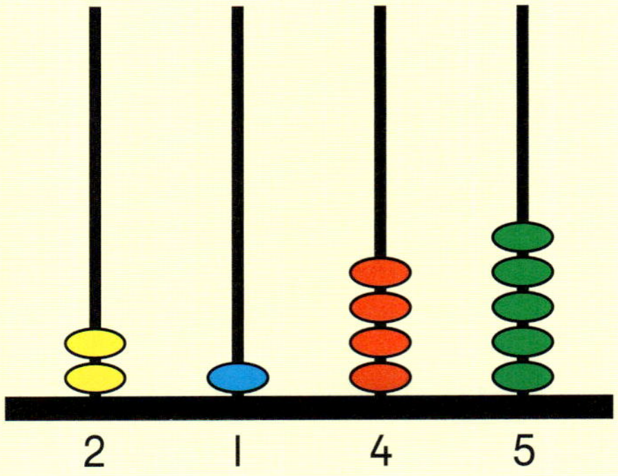

Write the number of thousands, hundreds, tens and ones in the numbers shown on each abacus.
Write the numeral and the number name for each number.

1.

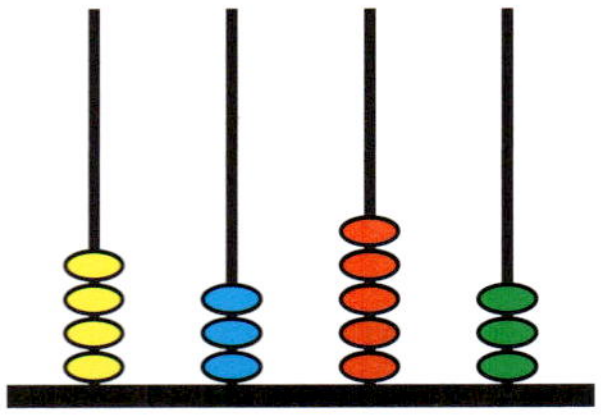

2.

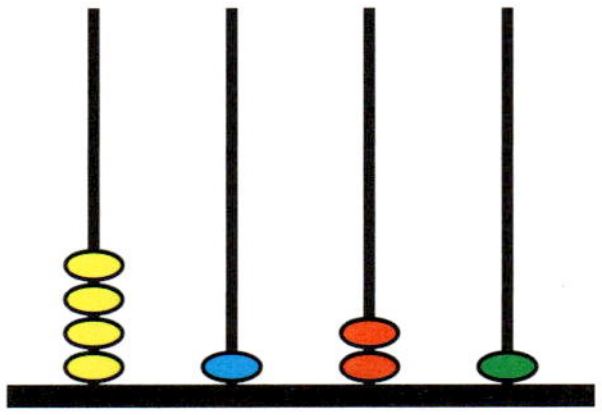

3.

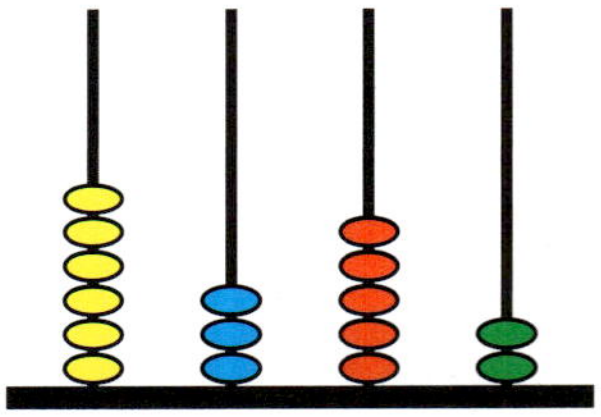

4.

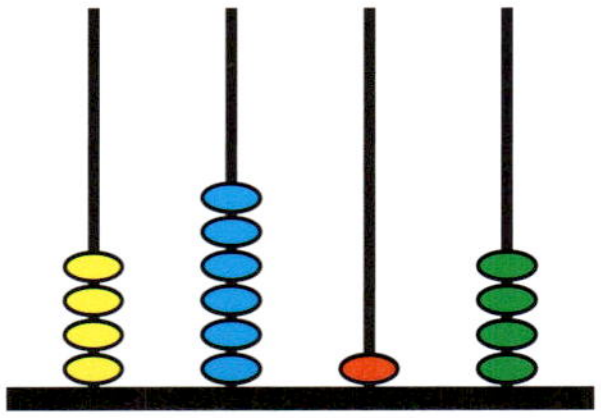

5.

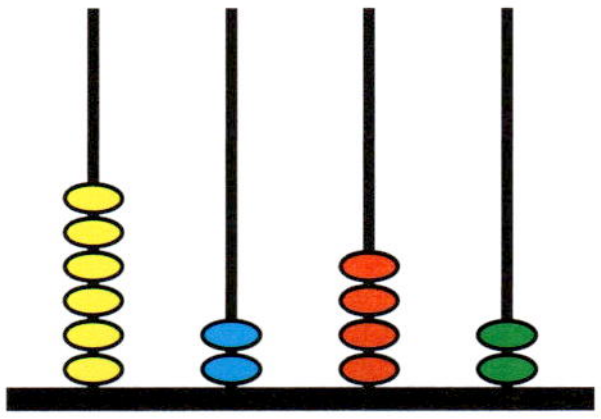

6.

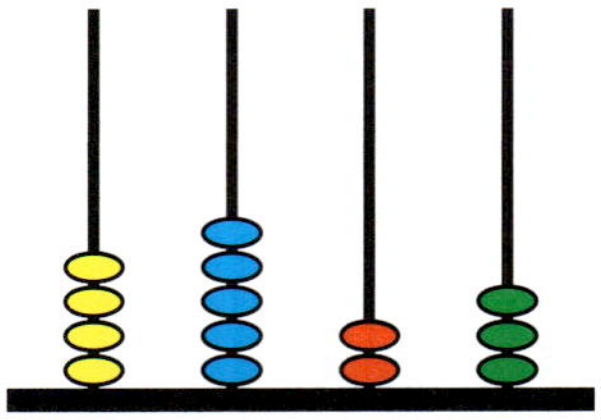

7.

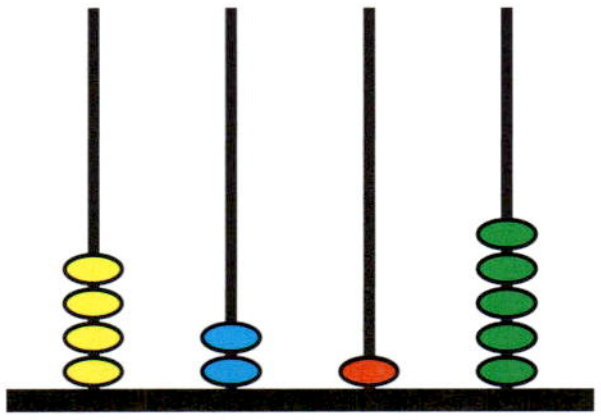

8.

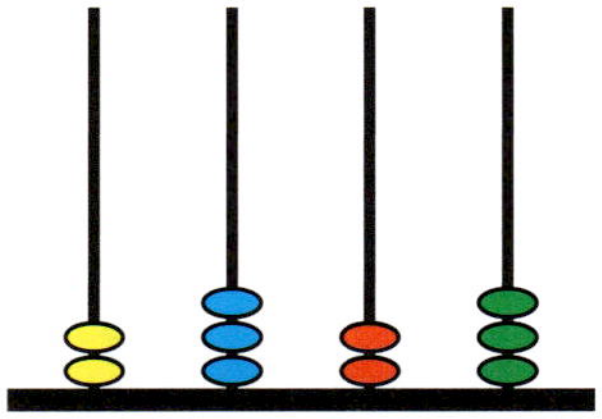

9.

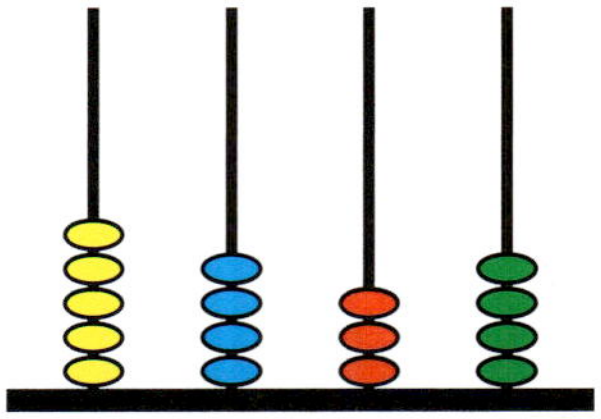

Place holder zero

Look at the abacuses on the right.

In the top abacus there are no hundreds.
There are 6 thousands, 0 hundreds, 4 tens and 2 units. The number is 6042 – six thousand and forty-two.

In the bottom abacus there are 2 thousands, 0 hundreds, 0 tens and 3 units (or ones). The number is 2003 – two thousand and three.

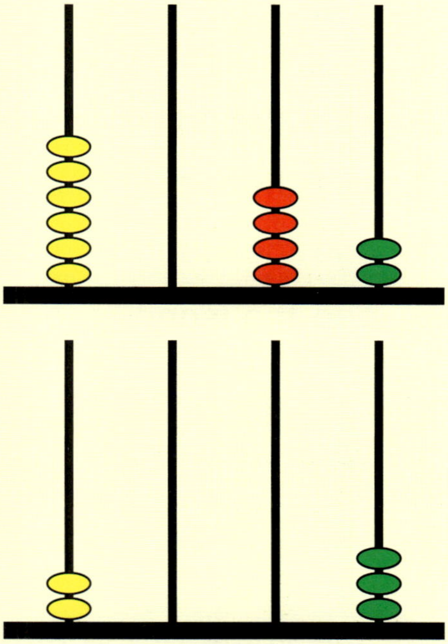

Copy the table below and complete it by writing the number names.

	Th	H	T	U	Number name
1.	3	4	5	6	three thousand, four hundred and fifty-six
2.	2	6	1	7	
3.	9	8	0	5	
4.	5	0	1	9	
5.	2	0	0	3	
6.	4	5	0	0	
7.	6	0	6	0	
8.	5	0	5	0	

Write numerals for the following:

9. three thousand, five hundred and thirty

10. six thousand, seven hundred and eight

11. nine thousand and two

12. one thousand, one hundred and eleven

13. one thousand and one

14. one thousand, one hundred and ten

Write out these numbers in words.

15. 5500 **16.** 8008 **17.** 1011

18. 3103 **19.** 6016 **20.** 1002

Give the value of the digit underlined.

21. $51\underline{1}5$ **22.** $8\underline{2}01$ **23.** $3\underline{3}03$ **24.** $\underline{1}111$

25. $621\underline{6}$ **26.** $10\underline{1}1$ **27.** $7\underline{7}77$ **28.** $70\underline{7}0$

Write numerals for these words.

five thousand, six hundred and seventy-two	5672

29. one thousand, six hundred and thirty-four

30. two thousand, two hundred and fifty-six

31. six thousand, nine hundred and twenty-one

32. five thousand, two hundred and fifty

Expanded notation

Look at these numbers written in the expanded form.

Number	Th	H	T	U	Expanded form
347		3	4	7	(3 × 100) + (4 × 10) + (7 × 1) = 300 + 40 + 7
2347	2	3	4	7	(2 × 1000) + (3 × 100) + (4 × 10) + (7 × 1) = 2000 + 300 + 40 + 7
4029	4	0	2	9	(4 × 1000) + (2 × 10) + (9 × 1) = 4000 + 20 + 9
4209	4	2	0	9	(4 × 1000) + (2 × 100) + (9 × 1) = 4000 + 200 + 9

Write these numbers in expanded form.

1. 1782 **2.** 4424 **3.** 6336 **4.** 9219
5. 4290 **6.** 6708 **7.** 5092 **8.** 4040
9. 1010 **10.** 1110 **11.** 1001 **12.** 1111
13. 3021 **14.** 5005 **15.** 3030 **16.** 3303
17. 4105 **18.** 2112 **19.** 7201 **20.** 5050

The number 2347 = 2000 + 300 + 40 + 7
= 2 thousands plus 347
also 2347 = 2300 + 40 + 7 and 2347 = 2340 + 7
= 23 hundreds plus 47 = 234 tens plus 7

So it is easy to write four-digit numbers as thousands plus a remainder, or as hundreds plus a remainder, or as tens plus a remainder.
We only have to look at the place value of the digits.

Write these numbers as thousands plus a remainder and as hundreds plus a remainder.

21. 1842 **22.** 2307 **23.** 3014 **24.** 4009
25. 5210 **26.** 6010 **27.** 2555 **28.** 1010

Arranging numbers in order

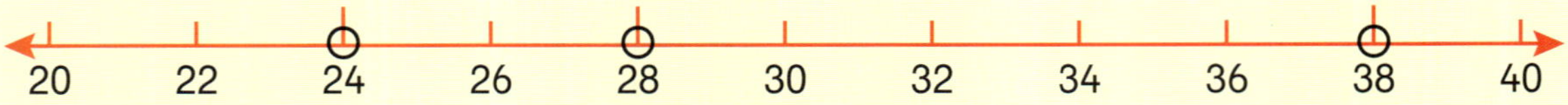

We can show on our number line that 24 is less than 28 ($24 < 28$).

Comparing the units digits in 24 and 28, we can see that 4 units is less than 8 units ($2\mathbf{4} < 2\mathbf{8}$).

We can also show that 28 is less than 38 ($28 < 38$). Comparing the tens digits in 28 and 38, we can see that 2 tens is less than 3 tens ($\mathbf{2}8 < \mathbf{3}8$).

Now look at this number line.

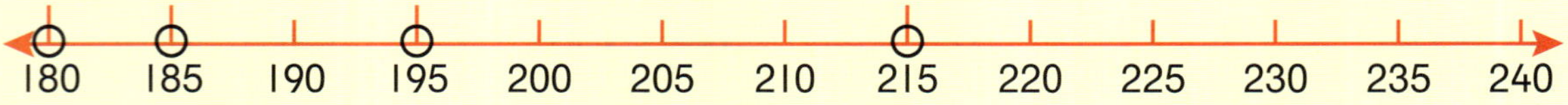

We see that:	$180 < 185$	$185 < 195$	$195 < 215$
	$0 < 5$	$8 < 9$	$1 < 2$

We can compare the size (magnitude) of numbers by comparing the magnitude of the digits beginning from the left.

Thus $3264 < 3268 < 3298 < 3376$

Our number line will show this.

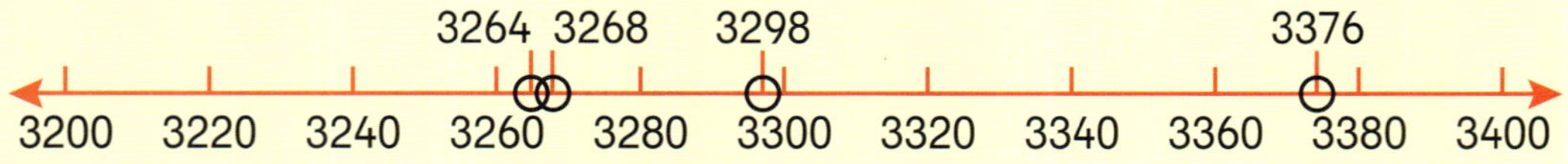

We can also use the greater than sign ($>$) to compare the numbers.

We can write $3376 > 3298 > 3268 > 3264$

Put in the correct sign, $>$ or $<$, between each pair of numbers.

5261 $>$ 5216

1. 1412 ☐ 1313 **2.** 2543 ☐ 2563 **3.** 4301 ☐ 4309

4. 6010 ☐ 6001 **5.** 9310 ☐ 8310 **6.** 1001 ☐ 1010

Arrange the following sets of numbers in descending order (largest to smallest).

1512 1425 1409 1615 – 1615 1512 1425 1409

7. 1413 1627 1842 1371 **8.** 2330 3220 4855 3765

9. 6076 3764 5345 4295 **10.** 4890 4000 4090 4009

Arrange the following sets of numbers in ascending order (smallest to largest).

1314 1221 1554 1464 – 1221 1314 1464 1554

11. 2740 3142 2991 3099 **12.** 6710 5419 7412 3838

13. 1030 1060 1022 1075 **14.** 9090 9009 9990 9900

What is the largest number you can make using each set of digits given?

1, 8, 3, 0 – 8310

15. 5, 6, 1, 8 **16.** 7, 1, 2, 6 **17.** 1, 5, 0, 9 **18.** 4, 2, 9, 3

19. 3, 4, 2, 7 **20.** 5, 0, 9, 2 **21.** 8, 1, 6, 3 **22.** 7, 1, 0, 4

Rounding numbers to the nearest 10 and 100

Remember:
When we write numbers to the nearest 10, or to the nearest 100, we say we **round** the number to the nearest 10, or we round the number to the nearest 100.

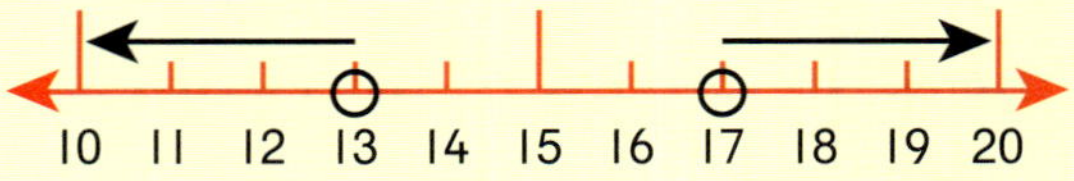

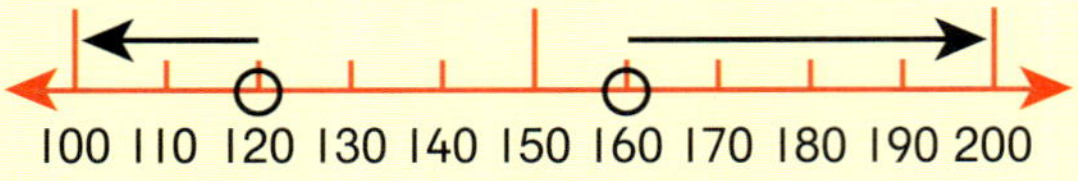

The numbers move upwards or downwards, as you see in the number lines above.
We say that we round upwards or downwards, or we round up or down.

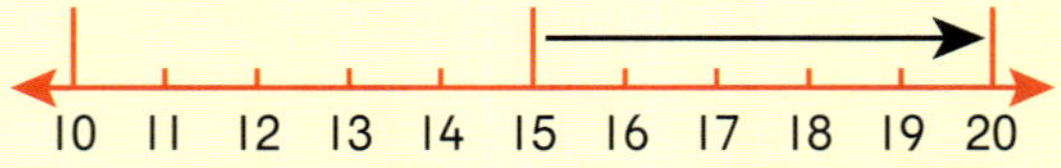

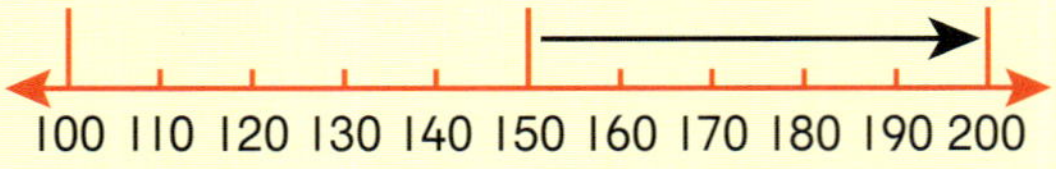

Remember: 15 to the nearest 10 becomes 20,
and 150 to the nearest 100 becomes 200.

In other words, the midway number is always rounded upwards.

Round these numbers to the nearest 10.

1. 36 **2.** 19 **3.** 64 **4.** 55 **5.** 21

6. 48 **7.** 65 **8.** 73 **9.** 8 **10.** 92

Round these numbers to the nearest 100.

11. 149 **12.** 234 **13.** 312 **14.** 650 **15.** 806

16. 450 **17.** 749 **18.** 751 **19.** 210 **20.** 916

Round up or down.

21. 16 to the nearest 10

22. 140 to the nearest 100

23. 550 to the nearest 100

24. 545 to the nearest 100

25. 32 to the nearest 10

26. 305 to the nearest 100

27. 350 to the nearest 100

28. 24 to the nearest 10

29. 95 to the nearest 10

30. 95 to the nearest 100

Rounding numbers gives us a quick way to check answers to calculations. For example,

186 + 201 + 131 ≈ (is approximately equal to)
200 + 200 + 100, that is 500

The exact answer is 518.

Give approximate and exact answers for these calculations:

31. 166 + 210 + 112

32. 231 + 391 + 109

33. 599 – 201

34. 322 – 188

35. 292 + 141 + 70

36. 515 – 319

37. 164 + 349 + 56

38. 72 + 124 + 282 + 158

39. 412 – 195

40. 825 – 285

41. 632 – 164

42. 66 + 94 + 38 + 172

43. 54 + 101 + 99

44. 295 + 32 + 105

45. 542 – 288

46. 609 – 290

47. 420 + 275 + 49

48. 422 – 188

Assessment 1

Write the numeral and the number name for each of the numbers shown below.

1.

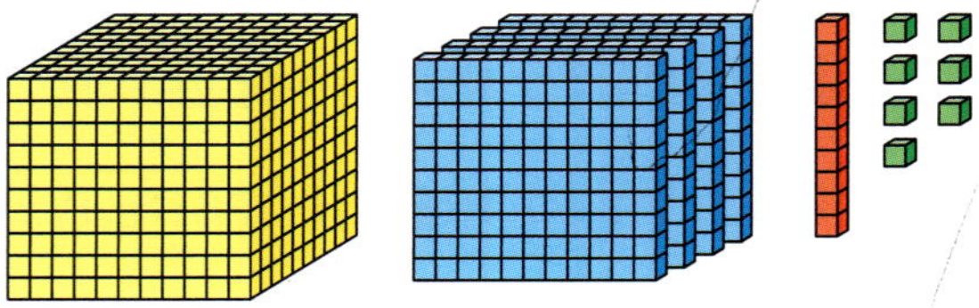

2.

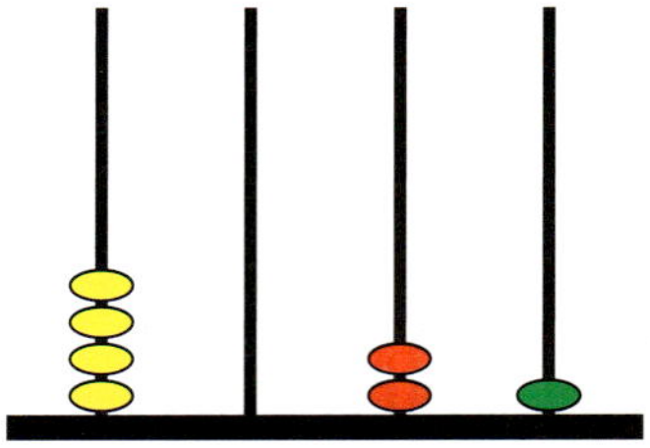

Write numerals for these numbers.

3. one thousand, six hundred and fifty

4. seven thousand, one hundred and seven

5. six thousand and two

Write these numbers in words.

6. 3487 **7.** 6045 **8.** 5001

Give the value of the red digits.

9. 2118 **10.** 6436 **11.** 5418

Write these numbers in expanded form.

12. 4612 **13.** 1508 **14.** 9031

15. Write the number 1929 as hundreds plus a remainder.

16. Write the number 3451 as thousands plus a remainder.

17. Arrange these numbers in ascending order (smallest first).

6139 5812 6290 5064 6142

Round these numbers to the nearest hundred.

18. 419 **19.** 810 **20.** 580

2 Addition and subtraction

Reviewing basic addition facts

In this exercise you can use your calculator to check your answers.
Copy and complete the following calculations.

```
  21      42      23      56
+ 32    + 54    + 65    + 33
----    ----    ----    ----

----    ----    ----    ----
```

Now check your answers using a calculator.
Make up some problems of your own.
Check your answers using a calculator.

Copy and complete these calculations.

```
1.   39      2.   48      3.   27      4.   56
   + 48         + 67         + 86         + 45
   ----         ----         ----         ----

   ----         ----         ----         ----

5.  145      6.  212      7.   29      8.  116
     66          180          105          274
  + 237        +  79        + 378        +  93
  -----        -----        -----        -----

  -----        -----        -----        -----

9.  245     10.  219     11.   44     12.  187
     78          174          167          294
    162           38           63           26
  +  94        +  22        + 205        + 178
  -----        -----        -----        -----

  -----        -----        -----        -----
```

13. $$\begin{array}{r} 4\,4\,5 \\ 1\,2\,8 \\ +\,2\,5\,3 \\ \hline \\ \hline \end{array}$$

14. $$\begin{array}{r} 2\,0\,7 \\ 1\,3\,5 \\ +\quad 6\,5 \\ \hline \\ \hline \end{array}$$

15. $$\begin{array}{r} 6\,3\,4 \\ 6\,5 \\ +\quad 7\,6 \\ \hline \\ \hline \end{array}$$

16. $$\begin{array}{r} 4\,6 \\ 2\,3\,7 \\ +\quad 8\,5 \\ \hline \\ \hline \end{array}$$

Now check your answers using a calculator.

Work out the missing numbers in these calculations.

17. $$\begin{array}{r} \square\,2\,\square \\ +\,3\,\square\,8 \\ \hline 5\,7\,5 \\ \hline \end{array}$$

18. $$\begin{array}{r} 4\,\square\,8 \\ +\,\square\,3\,7 \\ \hline 6\,9\,\square \\ \hline \end{array}$$

19. $$\begin{array}{r} 2\,5\,\square \\ +\,4\,\square\,8 \\ \hline \square\,8\,6 \\ \hline \end{array}$$

20. $$\begin{array}{r} \square\,9\,6 \\ +\,4\,0\,\square \\ \hline 8\,\square\,0 \\ \hline \end{array}$$

21. $$\begin{array}{r} 1\,\square\,9 \\ +\,\square\,1\,\square \\ \hline 3\,2\,4 \\ \hline \end{array}$$

22. $$\begin{array}{r} \square\,2\,3 \\ +\,1\,4\,\square \\ \hline 4\,\square\,1 \\ \hline \end{array}$$

23. $$\begin{array}{r} 1\,5\,\square \\ +\,5\,\square\,8 \\ \hline \square\,3\,2 \\ \hline \end{array}$$

24. $$\begin{array}{r} \square\,5\,2 \\ +\,1\,\square\,9 \\ \hline 5\,3\,\square \\ \hline \end{array}$$

Answer these questions.

25. 245 + 83 + 124

26. Find the sum of 64, 209 and 328.

27. What is the total of 325, 46 and 9?

28. Add together 73, 208 and 16.

29. 175 + 203 + 321 =

30. 219 + 147 + 358 =

Now check your answers using a calculator.

Addition of four-digit numbers without regrouping

3254 + 1423

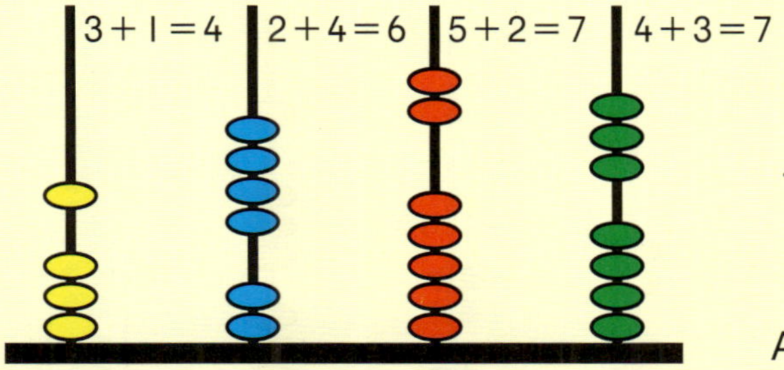

	Thousands	Hundreds	Tens	Ones
	3	2	5	4
+	1	4	2	3
	4	6	7	7

$$\begin{array}{r} 3254 \\ +\,1423 \\ \hline 4677 \end{array}$$

Add the ones
Add the tens
Add the hundreds
Add the thousands

3254 + 1423
= 4677

Copy and complete these calculations.

1. $\begin{array}{r} 4135 \\ +\,2814 \\ \hline \\ \hline \end{array}$ **2.** $\begin{array}{r} 2506 \\ +\,431 \\ \hline \\ \hline \end{array}$ **3.** $\begin{array}{r} 1617 \\ +\,3242 \\ \hline \\ \hline \end{array}$ **4.** $\begin{array}{r} 2811 \\ +\,4167 \\ \hline \\ \hline \end{array}$

5. $\begin{array}{r} 1512 \\ 341 \\ +\,6034 \\ \hline \\ \hline \end{array}$ **6.** $\begin{array}{r} 2008 \\ 141 \\ +\,3850 \\ \hline \\ \hline \end{array}$ **7.** $\begin{array}{r} 6340 \\ 1057 \\ +\,602 \\ \hline \\ \hline \end{array}$ **8.** $\begin{array}{r} 1414 \\ 5083 \\ +\,462 \\ \hline \\ \hline \end{array}$

Now check your answers using a calculator.

Work out the missing numbers in these calculations.

9. $\begin{array}{r} 2\square 54 \\ 4\square 1 \\ +\,103\square \\ \hline \square 788 \\ \hline \end{array}$ **10.** $\begin{array}{r} \square 162 \\ \square 04 \\ +\,50\square 2 \\ \hline 679\square \\ \hline \end{array}$ **11.** $\begin{array}{r} 4\square 04 \\ \square 415 \\ +\,14\square 0 \\ \hline 789\square \\ \hline \end{array}$ **12.** $\begin{array}{r} 4\square 12 \\ 67\square \\ +\,51\square 4 \\ \hline \square 999 \\ \hline \end{array}$

Now check your answers using a calculator.

Addition of four-digit numbers – regrouping ones

2132 + 2238

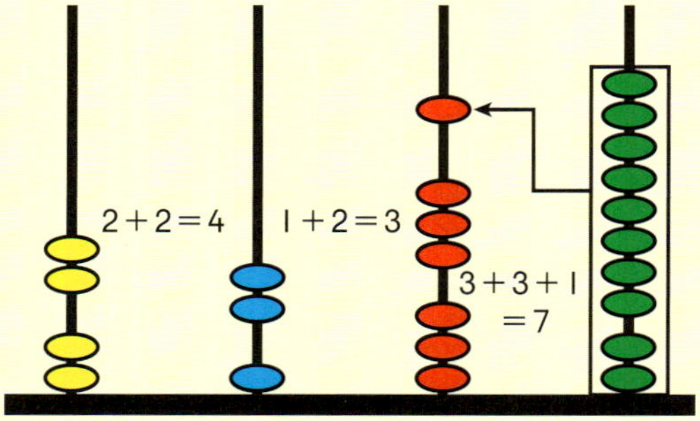

Thousands	Hundreds	Tens	Ones
2	1	3	2
+ 2	2	3	8
4	3	7 ← [1]	0

2132 + 2238
= 4370

2+8=10
10 = 1 ten 0 ones

```
     1
  2 1 3 2
+ 2 2 3 8
  -------
  4 3 7 0
```

Add the ones
Add the tens
Add the hundreds
Add the thousands

Copy and complete theses calculations.

1. 312 + 1464 + 4117

2. 1438 + 232 + 3215

3. 2115 + 146 + 3523

4. 419 + 2312 + 1264

5. 2348 + 215 + 1128

6. 5126 + 347 + 1224

7. 3417 + 1129 + 231

8. 546 + 2124 + 338

9. 4326 + 135 + 1327

10. 3310 + 269 + 1119

11. 1427 + 2246 + 127

12. 1684 + 109 + 108

Now check your answers using a calculator.

Addition of four-digit numbers – regrouping tens and ones

2239 + 3173

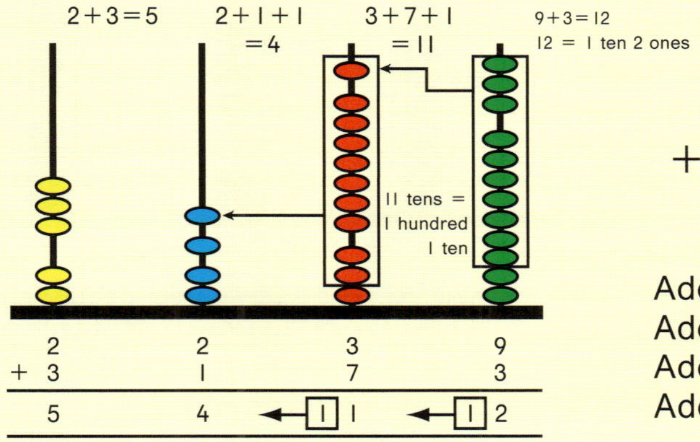

$$\begin{array}{r} {}^{}2\,{}^{1}2\,{}^{1}3\,9 \\ +\ 3\,1\,7\,3 \\ \hline 5\,4\,1\,2 \end{array}$$

Add the ones
Add the tens
Add the hundreds
Add the thousands

2239 + 3173 = 5412

Copy and complete these calculations.

1. 217 + 1358 + 272

2. 4085 + 379 + 1221

3. 1637 + 294 + 2025

4. 550 + 689 + 1194

5. 697 + 1114 + 187

6. 2684 + 179 + 2303

7. 4178 + 239 + 1168

8. 5168 + 212 + 1479

9. 1459 + 386 + 2175

10. 4001 + 3998 + 1027

11. 5508 + 199 + 1088

12. 4061 + 279 + 1108

Now check your answers using a calculator.

Regrouping in adding four-digit numbers

2534 + 2667

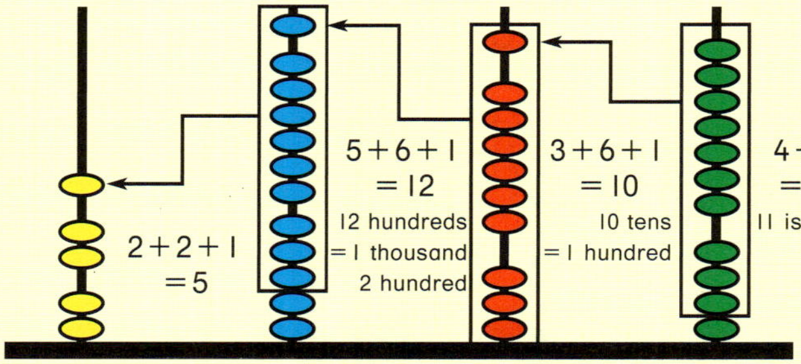

$$\begin{array}{r} {}^{1}2\,{}^{1}5\,{}^{1}3\,4 \\ +\ 2\,6\,6\,7 \\ \hline 5\,2\,0\,1 \end{array}$$

2	5	3	4
2	6	6	7
5	← 1 2	← 1 0	← 1 1
5	2	0	1

Add the ones
Add the tens
Add the hundreds
Add the thousands

2534 + 2667
= 5201

Copy and complete these calculations.

1. 2131 + 1423 + 5224 = ____

2. 4645 + 1652 + 1163 = ____

3. 1295 + 1779 + 3648 = ____

4. 1101 + 1001 + 1110 = ____

5. 2462 + 1897 + 744 = ____

6. 4090 + 2095 + 315 = ____

7. 402 + 4005 + 1210 = ____

8. 5800 + 609 + 991 = ____

Work out the missing numbers in these calculations.

9. 313□ + 22□4 + 3□43 = □589

10. 21□9 + 534□ + 1□35 = □956

11. 2□68 + 285□ + 32□7 = □101

12. 6□89 + 45□ + 6□8 = □050

Now check your answers using a calculator.

Rounding to the nearest 1000

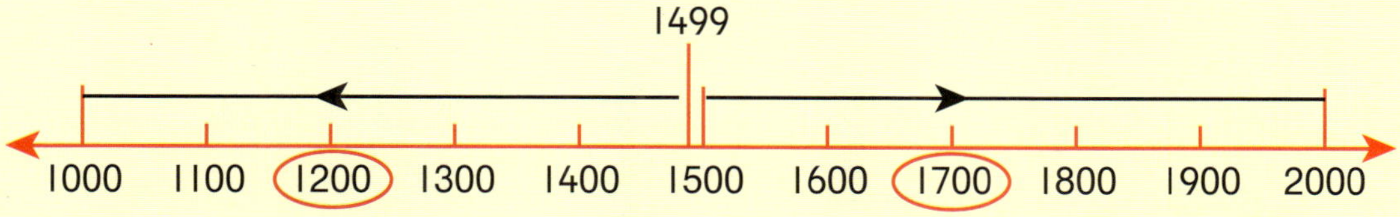

Look at the number line above.

The numbers 1200 is nearer to 1000 than to 2000, so we round 1200 down to 1000.

Using the same rule we round 1700 up to 2000.

The midway number is always rounded up, so 1500 must be rounded up to 2000.

The number line shows:

- all the numbers from 1500 up to 2000 are rounded up to 2000
- all the numbers from 1499 down to 1000 are rounded down to 1000.

Round these numbers to the nearest 1000.

1. 1120 **2.** 1543 **3.** 1050 **4.** 1500 **5.** 1001

6. 4200 **7.** 5300 **8.** 8500 **9.** 6660 **10.** 7712

Give approximate and exact answers for these calculations.

11. 3537 + 2090 + 4488 **12.** 2401 + 1813 + 5019

13. 1836 + 3986 + 3875 **14.** 3820 + 1180 + 920

15. 1464 + 1506 + 2009 **16.** 250 + 1791 + 1110

17.	**18.**	**19.**	**20.**
1010	1650	305	1440
495	2790	1562	900
+ 3760	+ 250	+ 749	+ 6492
____	____	____	____

Revising subtraction of two-digit and three-digit numbers

Copy and complete these calculations.

1. $\begin{array}{r} 51 \\ -\ 19 \\ \hline \\ \hline \end{array}$ **2.** $\begin{array}{r} 62 \\ -\ 18 \\ \hline \\ \hline \end{array}$ **3.** $\begin{array}{r} 73 \\ -\ 15 \\ \hline \\ \hline \end{array}$ **4.** $\begin{array}{r} 96 \\ -\ 19 \\ \hline \\ \hline \end{array}$

5. $\begin{array}{r} 212 \\ -\ 94 \\ \hline \\ \hline \end{array}$ **6.** $\begin{array}{r} 415 \\ -\ 267 \\ \hline \\ \hline \end{array}$ **7.** $\begin{array}{r} 820 \\ -\ 344 \\ \hline \\ \hline \end{array}$ **8.** $\begin{array}{r} 705 \\ -\ 248 \\ \hline \\ \hline \end{array}$

9. $\begin{array}{r} 657 \\ -\ 135 \\ \hline \\ \hline \end{array}$ **10.** $\begin{array}{r} 482 \\ -\ 148 \\ \hline \\ \hline \end{array}$ **11.** $\begin{array}{r} 728 \\ -\ 295 \\ \hline \\ \hline \end{array}$ **12.** $\begin{array}{r} 108 \\ -\ 57 \\ \hline \\ \hline \end{array}$

Now check your answers using a calculator.

Work out the missing numbers in these calculations.

13. $\begin{array}{r} \square 8 \square \\ -\ 2 \square 3 \\ \hline 444 \\ \hline \end{array}$ **14.** $\begin{array}{r} 5 \square 7 \\ -\ \square 1 \square \\ \hline 435 \\ \hline \end{array}$ **15.** $\begin{array}{r} 872 \\ -\ \square 4 \square \\ \hline 7 \square 1 \\ \hline \end{array}$ **16.** $\begin{array}{r} 764 \\ -\ \square 3 \square \\ \hline 6 \square 4 \\ \hline \end{array}$

17. $\begin{array}{r} 41 \square \\ -\ \square 94 \\ \hline 2 \square 1 \\ \hline \end{array}$ **18.** $\begin{array}{r} 65 \square \\ -\ 2 \square 6 \\ \hline \square 04 \\ \hline \end{array}$ **19.** $\begin{array}{r} 4 \square 3 \\ -\ \square 1 \square \\ \hline 191 \\ \hline \end{array}$ **20.** $\begin{array}{r} 6 \square 5 \\ -\ \square 8 \square \\ \hline 346 \\ \hline \end{array}$

21. $\begin{array}{r} \square 47 \\ -\ 18 \square \\ \hline 3 \square 2 \\ \hline \end{array}$ **22.** $\begin{array}{r} 3 \square \square \\ -\ \square 48 \\ \hline 238 \\ \hline \end{array}$ **23.** $\begin{array}{r} \square 7 \square \\ -\ 342 \\ \hline 1 \square 9 \\ \hline \end{array}$ **24.** $\begin{array}{r} \square \square 2 \\ -\ 176 \\ \hline 22 \square \\ \hline \end{array}$

Now check your answers using a calculator.

Subtraction of four-digit numbers

5896 − 2431

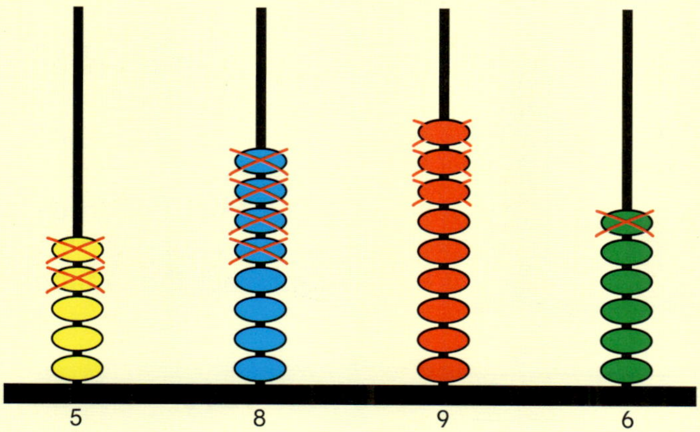

5	8	9	6
− 2	4	3	1
3	4	6	5

$$\begin{array}{r} 5896 \\ -\,2431 \\ \hline 3465 \\ \hline \end{array}$$

Subtract ones
Subtract tens
Subtract hundreds
Subtract thousands

5896 − 2431 = 3465

Copy and complete these calculations.

1. $\begin{array}{r} 4286 \\ -\,1042 \\ \hline \\ \hline \end{array}$ **2.** $\begin{array}{r} 5974 \\ -\,2431 \\ \hline \\ \hline \end{array}$ **3.** $\begin{array}{r} 6258 \\ -\,2142 \\ \hline \\ \hline \end{array}$ **4.** $\begin{array}{r} 7584 \\ -\,2311 \\ \hline \\ \hline \end{array}$

5. $\begin{array}{r} 9428 \\ -\,3101 \\ \hline \\ \hline \end{array}$ **6.** $\begin{array}{r} 6284 \\ -\,1131 \\ \hline \\ \hline \end{array}$ **7.** $\begin{array}{r} 5987 \\ -\,2437 \\ \hline \\ \hline \end{array}$ **8.** $\begin{array}{r} 6677 \\ -\,1122 \\ \hline \\ \hline \end{array}$

9. $\begin{array}{r} 8496 \\ -\,1374 \\ \hline \\ \hline \end{array}$ **10.** $\begin{array}{r} 8764 \\ -\,2413 \\ \hline \\ \hline \end{array}$ **11.** $\begin{array}{r} 7492 \\ -\,2040 \\ \hline \\ \hline \end{array}$ **12.** $\begin{array}{r} 4245 \\ -\,2004 \\ \hline \\ \hline \end{array}$

Now check your answers using a calculator.

Subtraction of four-digit numbers – regrouping ones

3342 − 1218

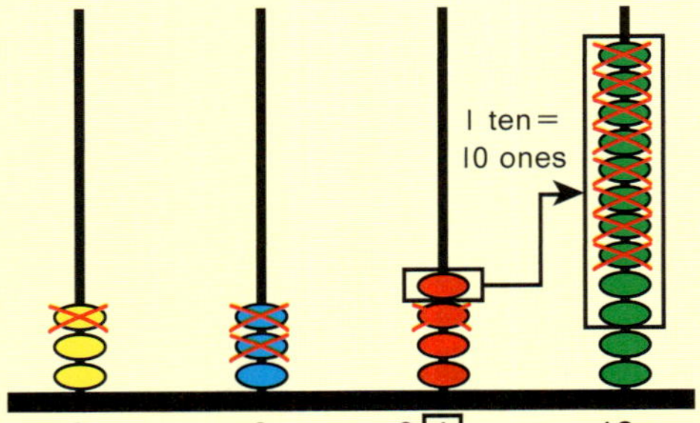

3	3	3 [4]	12
− 1	2	1	8
2	1	2	4

Subtract ones
12 − 8 = 4
Subtract tens
3 − 1 = 2
Subtract hundreds
3 − 2 = 1
Subtract thousands
3 − 1 = 2

$$\begin{array}{r} 3\,3\,\overset{3}{\not4}\,{}^{1}2 \\ -\ 1\,2\,1\,8 \\ \hline 2\,1\,2\,4 \end{array}$$

3342 − 1218 = 2124

Check the answer by adding back or using a calculator.

Copy and complete these calculations.

1. 6446 − 2127

2. 3855 − 1428

3. 1543 − 448

4. 6040 − 1029

5. 4663 − 1247

6. 3951 − 1816

7. 1768 − 1149

8. 2330 − 1121

9. 4781 − 2359

10. 2674 − 1248

11. 7482 − 3008

12. 5840 − 2617

Now check your answers using a calculator.

Subtraction of four-digit numbers – regrouping tens and ones

2423 − 1148

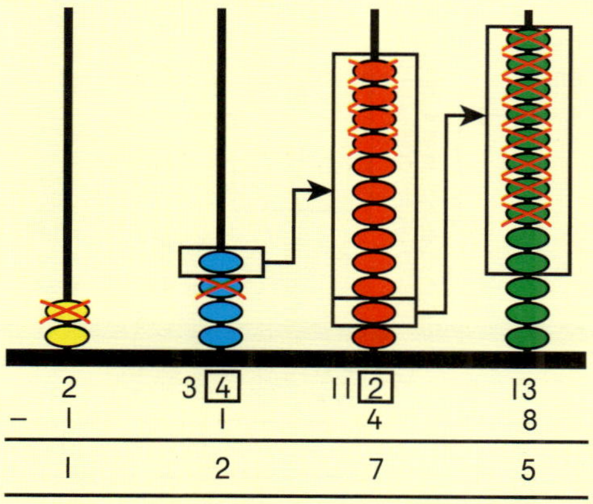

Subtract ones
13 − 8 = 5
Subtract tens
11 − 4 = 7
Subtract hundreds
3 − 1 = 2
Subtract thousands
2 − 1 = 1

```
    3 11 13
  2 4  2  3
− 1 1  4  8
  1 2  7  5
```

2423 − 1148 = 1275

Check the answer by adding back or using a calculator.

Copy and complete these calculations.

1. 3824 − 1648

2. 4921 − 1665

3. 5610 − 4374

4. 3912 − 1675

5. 4823 − 1579

6. 5516 − 399

7. 8810 − 3573

8. 4632 − 2348

9. 7820 − 5294

10. 3612 − 1474

11. 5342 − 1268

12. 9813 − 4464

Now check your answers using a calculator.

Subtraction of four-digit numbers – regrouping

3654 – 1768

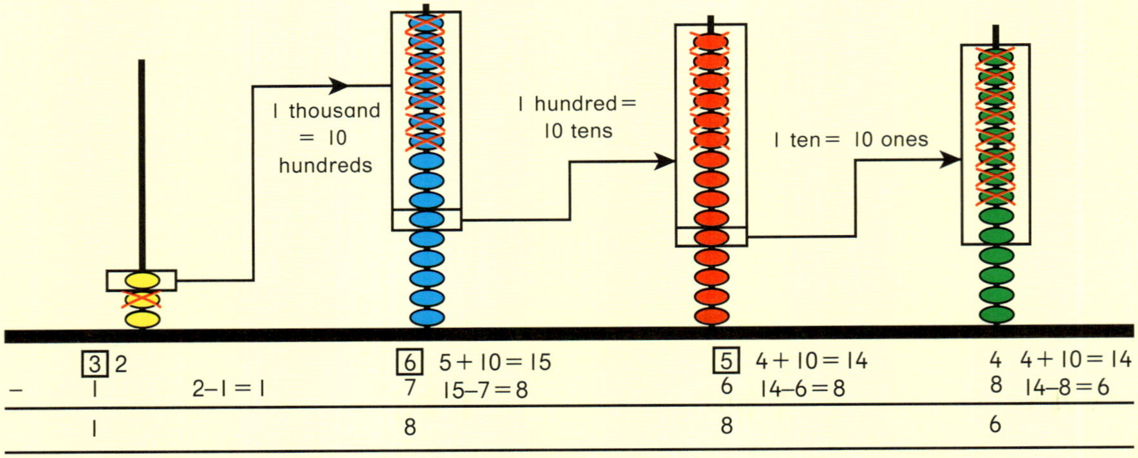

Once you have gone through the steps correctly your working page should look like this.
You should always check your answers by adding back, or using a calculator.

	Th	H	tens	ones
	2 ~~3~~	15 5 ~~6~~	14 4 ~~5~~	1 ~~4~~
–	1	7	6	8
	1	8	8	6

Copy and complete these calculations.

1. 1235 – 123 = ____

2. 6573 – 4352 = ____

3. 5656 – 1537 = ____

4. 3879 – 1696 = ____

Work out the missing numbers in these calculations.

5. 5□3□ – 24□6 = □216

6. 68□□ – □557 = 5□92

7. □2□8 – 129□ = 3□46

8. 4□□1 – 271□ = □434

Subtraction from 100

Lenny had 100 marbles. He gave 24 to Ravi. How many did he have left?

We must subtract 24 from 100 to get our answer.

	hundreds	tens	ones
	1	0	0
−		2	4

We have 0 tens and 0 ones. We must first change 1 hundred to 10 tens.

	tens	ones
	10	0
−	2	4

We still have 0 ones. We must change 1 ten to 10 ones.

	tens	ones
	9	10
−	2	4
	7	6

We can now subtract. The answer is 76.

Here are the steps on the abacus.

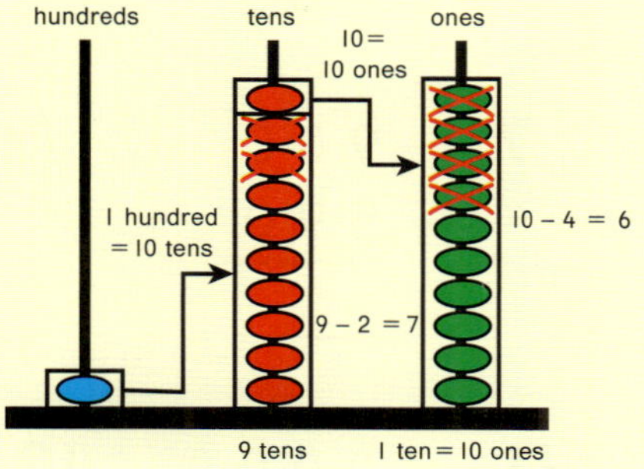

	~~1~~	⁹~~0~~	¹0
−		2	4
		7	6

$10 - 4 = 6$

$9 - 2 = 7$

Work out the answers to these calculations. The steps in Question 1 have been put in to help you.

1.

	hun.	tens	ones
	1	0	0
−		3	5

	tens	ones
	10	0
−	3	5

	tens	ones
	9	10
−	3	5

	hun.	tens	ones
	1	0	0
−		3	5

2. $100 - 28$

3. $100 - 54$

4. $100 - 48$

5. $100 - 29$

Subtraction from multiples of 100 and 1000

We must use the same steps when we subtract from 200, 300 and so on, up to 1000.

$$\begin{array}{r} \overset{4}{\cancel{5}}\,\overset{1\,9}{\cancel{0}}\,\overset{1}{0} \\ -\;2\,1\,8 \\ \hline 2\,8\,2 \\ \hline \end{array} \qquad \begin{array}{r} \cancel{1}\,\overset{1\,9}{\cancel{0}}\,\overset{1\,9}{\cancel{0}}\,\overset{1}{0} \\ -\;\;3\,4\,5 \\ \hline 6\,5\,5 \\ \hline \end{array}$$

Copy and complete these calculations.

1. $\begin{array}{r} 100 \\ -\;25 \\ \hline \end{array}$ **2.** $\begin{array}{r} 200 \\ -\;172 \\ \hline \end{array}$ **3.** $\begin{array}{r} 300 \\ -\;146 \\ \hline \end{array}$ **4.** $\begin{array}{r} 500 \\ -\;259 \\ \hline \end{array}$

5. $\begin{array}{r} 800 \\ -\;444 \\ \hline \end{array}$ **6.** $\begin{array}{r} 700 \\ -\;203 \\ \hline \end{array}$ **7.** $\begin{array}{r} 900 \\ -\;590 \\ \hline \end{array}$ **8.** $\begin{array}{r} 600 \\ -\;233 \\ \hline \end{array}$

9. $\begin{array}{r} 1000 \\ -\;152 \\ \hline \end{array}$ **10.** $\begin{array}{r} 2000 \\ -\;205 \\ \hline \end{array}$ **11.** $\begin{array}{r} 3000 \\ -\;310 \\ \hline \end{array}$ **12.** $\begin{array}{r} 4000 \\ -\;555 \\ \hline \end{array}$

13. $\begin{array}{r} 1100 \\ -\;194 \\ \hline \end{array}$ **14.** $\begin{array}{r} 2200 \\ -\;647 \\ \hline \end{array}$ **15.** $\begin{array}{r} 3300 \\ -\;439 \\ \hline \end{array}$ **16.** $\begin{array}{r} 4400 \\ -\;575 \\ \hline \end{array}$

Now check your answers using a calculator.

Word problems

Work out the answers to these word problems. Show all your working.

1. On the first 4 days of a Test Match the runs scored were 296, 328, 280 and 302.
   (a) What was the total number of runs scored on the 4 days?
   (b) If the Test Match lasted for 5 days and the total score for the 5 days was 1410 runs, how many runs were scored on the fifth day?

2. On 3 days a gardener sold 620 kg, 584 kg and 1008 kg of tomatoes.
   (a) How much did he sell altogether?
   (b) Find the difference between the sale of tomatoes on the first and third days.

3. A publisher printed 5500 magazines and sold 3245. How many were unsold?

4. On the 4 days of the Red Stripe Cup cricket match between Jamaica and Trinidad and Tobago the attendance was 2010, 1425, 1220 and 2146. What was the total attendance to the nearest thousand?

5. Out of a batch of 1000 pens 844 were sent to schools. How many were left from the batch?

6. Ten thousand tickets for a football match were put on sale. Only 8524 were sold before the match. How many tickets were unsold?

Assessment 2

1. Add the following numbers: 54, 1029, 268 and 3502.

2. Write the answer to this calculation to the nearest 1000.

   4809 + 1125 + 2730 ≈

3. Work out the missing numbers:

$$\begin{array}{r} 4\,\square\,6\,2 \\ 4\,8\,\square \\ +\;2\,5\,\square\,3 \\ \hline \square\,7\,9\,0 \\ \hline \end{array}$$

4. 3218 − 1440 =

5. 1000 − 256 =

6. Work out the missing numbers:

$$\begin{array}{r} \square\,3\,\square\,7 \\ -\;1\,2\,9\,\square \\ \hline 1\,\square\,2\,7 \\ \hline \end{array}$$

7. By how much does 4203 exceed 1615?

8. If I pay $1995 for a TV set I save $229 on the regular price. What is the regular price of the set?

9. On Friday 1520 people attended the calypso show, on Saturday 2264, and on Sunday 975. How many people altogether attended the shows on Friday, Saturday and Sunday?

10. A dealer ordered 5000 toy cars. He found 236 of them to be broken. How many were not broken?

11. A truck delivered 240 cases of soft drinks on Monday, 185 on Tuesday and 175 on Wednesday. How many cases were delivered altogether? Approximately how many hundred cases were delivered?

3 Solid shapes

Faces of solids

Copy and complete the table below.

	Name of solid	Number of flat surfaces	Number of curved surfaces	Shape of flat surfaces

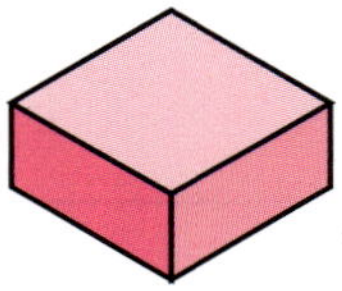				

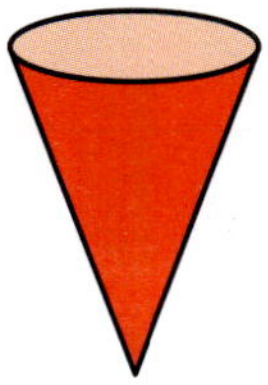				

3-D shapes – faces, edges and vertices

You will need: a cube shape.

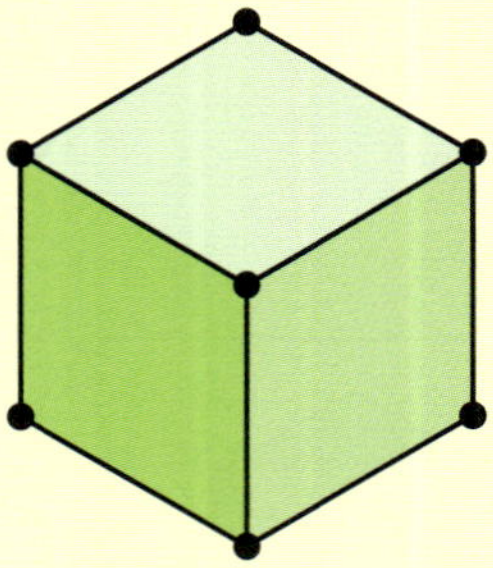

Look at this drawing of a cube and the solid cube on your desk.
How many faces of the cube do you see in the drawing?
How many faces does your cube have?
How many edges do you see in the drawing? How many edges are hidden?
The points where the edges meet are called **vertices**.
How many vertices do you see in the drawing?
How many vertices does your cube have?

Copy and complete the table below. Write the number of faces, edges and vertices in these shapes.

	Number of faces	Number of edges	Number of vertices
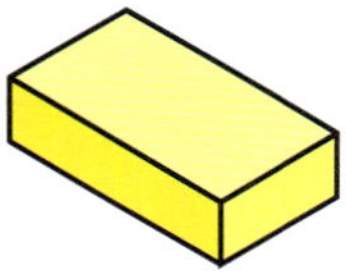			
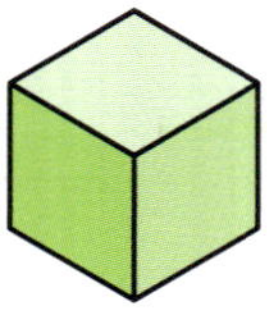			
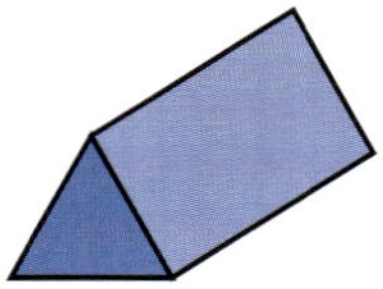			
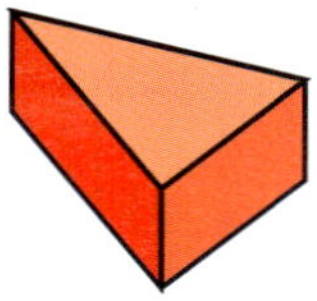			

Nets

Carefully draw and label this shape.

Cut out the shape and fold along the dotted lines.
What shape have you made?

This shape is called the **net** of a cube.

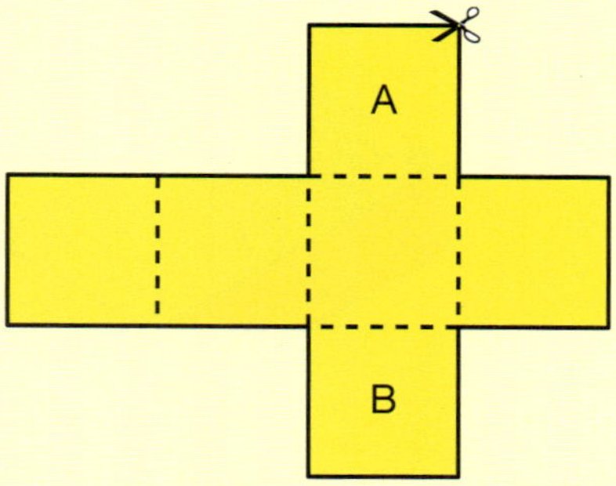

Now move squares A and B to different positions and draw new nets.
What shapes do you have when you cut and fold?

Here is one of the new positions of the squares:

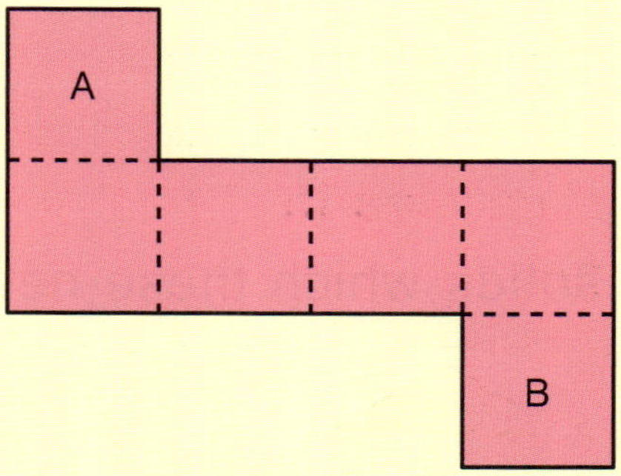

Look at the shape on the right.
It is made up of 3 pairs of rectangles.
Can you pick out the pairs which are the same?

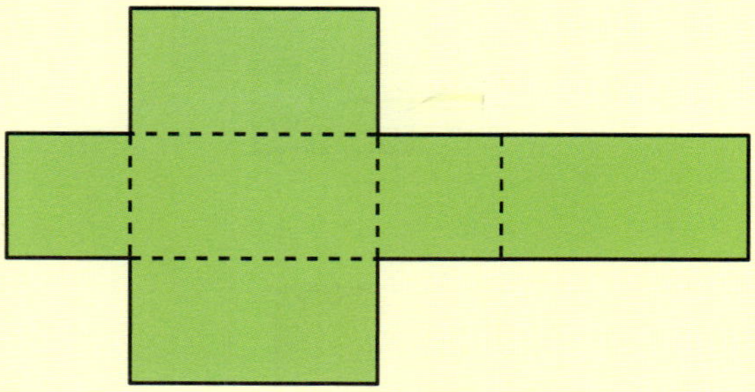

Copy the rectangles and then draw the shape.
Cut out the shape and fold along the dotted lines.

This shape is the net of a cuboid.

Faces and nets of solids

Draw the solids shown below and their faces.

1.

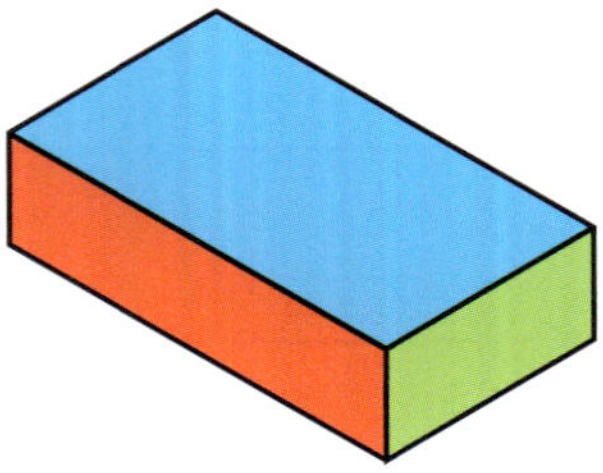

2.

3.

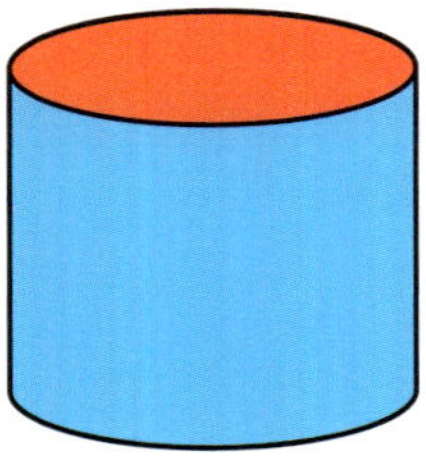

4.

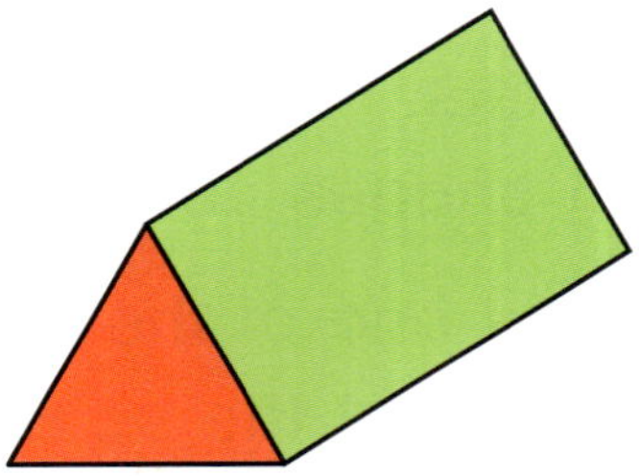

Draw the solids which these nets represent.

5.

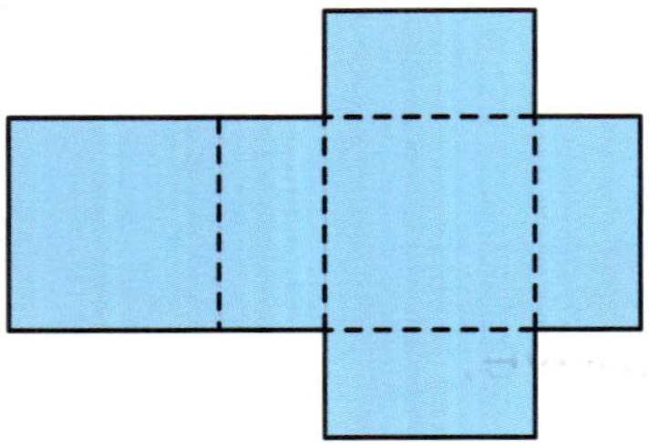

6.

7.

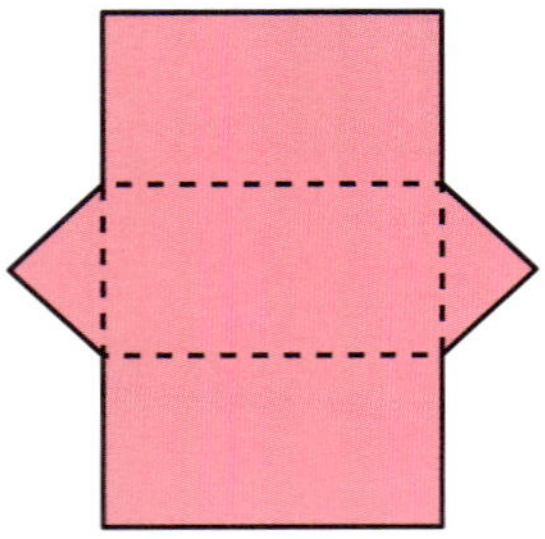

8.

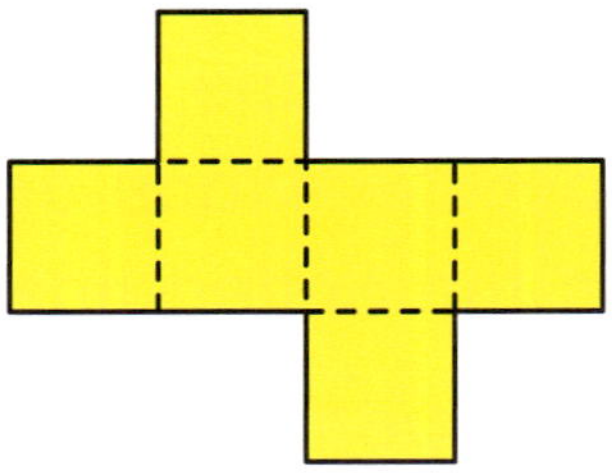

Constructing cubes and cuboids

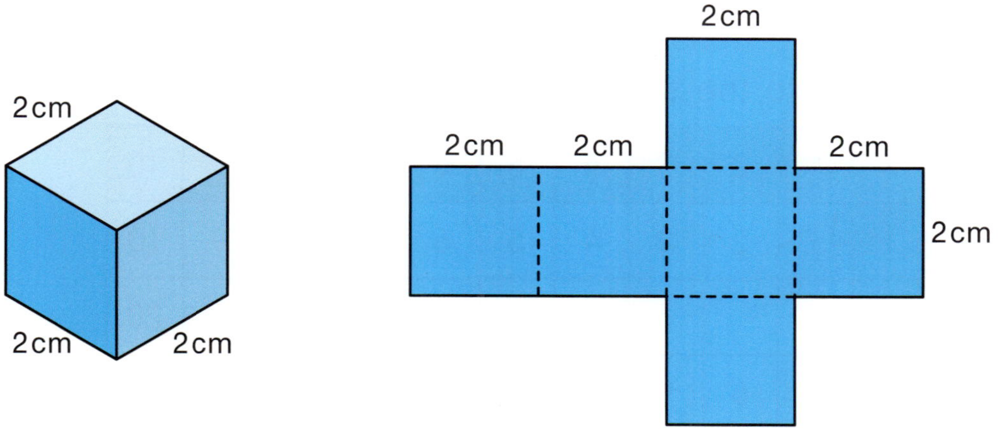

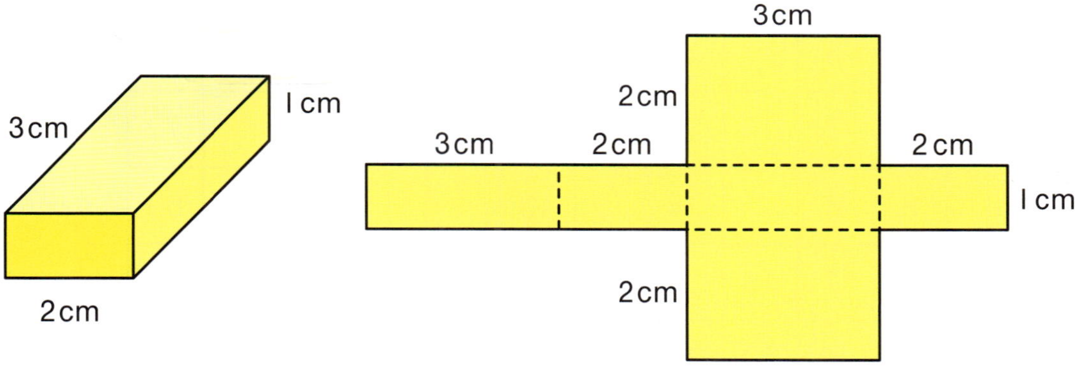

Draw the nets of the cube and cuboid above.
Cut out the shapes and fold along the dotted lines.

Draw the nets of these cubes and cuboids and make the shape.

1. 2cm × 2cm × 2cm
2. 3cm × 3cm × 3cm
3. 3cm × 2cm × 2cm
4. 4cm × 3cm × 1 cm
5. 4cm × 2cm × 2cm
6. 4cm × 3cm × 2cm

4 Multiplication

Revision of multiplication tables

Some numbers are missing from the multiplication square below. Copy and complete the square.

×	1	2	3	4	5	6	7	8	9	10
1	1	2	3	4	5	6	7	8	9	10
2	2		6	8	10					20
3	3	6	9				21			30
4	4			16		24				40
5	5	10								50
6	6		18	24				48		60
7	7	14	21			42				70
8	8		24		40					80
9	9	18			45					90
10	10	20	30	40	50	60	70	80	90	100

Test your multiplication facts. Copy and complete.

1. 8 × 7 = ☐ **2.** 7 × ☐ = 28 **3.** ☐ × 9 = 54

4. 9 × ☐ = 36 **5.** ☐ × 6 = 42 **6.** 9 × 8 = ☐

7. 4 × ☐ = 36 **8.** ☐ × 5 = 35 **9.** 3 × 6 = ☐

10. 5 × ☐ = 40 **11.** 3 × 5 = ☐ **12.** 5 × ☐ = 30

13. ☐ × 6 = 36 **14.** 9 × ☐ = 45 **15.** 7 × 9 = ☐

Reviewing multiplication of two-digit numbers

Copy and complete these calculations.

1. 54 × 2
2. 83 × 3
3. 72 × 4
4. 61 × 5
5. 47 × 2
6. 56 × 3
7. 65 × 4
8. 38 × 5
9. 36 × 6
10. 48 × 7
11. 54 × 8
12. 45 × 9

Now check your answers using a calculator.

Work out the missing numbers in these calculations.

13. □4 × □ = 68
14. 2□ × 3 = □9
15. 3□ × □ = 96
16. 21 × □ = 84
17. □6 × 6 = 15□
18. 4□ × 8 = 3□4
19. 35 × □ = 2□5
20. □4 × □ = 512
21. 5□ × 7 = 4□6
22. □4 × 6 = 20□
23. □6 × □ = 288
24. 4□ × 5 = 2□0

Now check your answers using a calculator.

Multiplication of three-digit numbers

Look at the multiplication calculations below.

	8 + 1 H	← 15̸ 12 + 3 T	← 36̸ ones
	2	3	9
×			4
	9	5	6

15̸ 36̸
2 3 9
× 4
9 5 6

9 × 4 = 36
3 × 4 = 12
2 × 4 = 8

	Th	9 + 1 H	← 13̸ 12 + 1 T	← 18̸ ones
		3	4	6
×				3
	1	0	3	8

10 13̸ 18̸
3 4 6
× 3
1 0 3 8

6 × 3 = 18
4 × 3 = 12
3 × 3 = 9

When we multiply three-digit numbers by a single-digit number we carry over tens or hundreds just as we do when we multiply two-digit numbers.

Copy and complete these calculations.

1. 213 × 4

2. 324 × 3

3. 113 × 5

4. 214 × 4

5. 145 × 3

6. 258 × 2

7. 135 × 4

8. 124 × 5

9. 214 × 3

10. 342 × 6

11. 235 × 7

12. 295 × 6

13. 325 × 4

14. 209 × 6

15. 427 × 3

16. 519 × 5

Now check your answers using a calculator.

Multiplication of four-digit numbers

1456 × 4

	Th	H	T	ones
	4 + 1	← 1~~8~~ 16 + 2	← 2~~2~~ 20 + 2	← 2~~4~~
	1	4	5	6
×				4
	5	8	2	4

Multiply ones
$6 \times 4 = 24$
Multiply tens
$5 \times 4 = 20$
Multiply hundreds
$4 \times 4 = 16$
Multiply thousands
$1 \times 4 = 4$

We can write out the working like this.

```
 5 18 22 24
   1 4 5 6
 ×       4
 ---------
   5 8 2 4
```

$6 \times 4 = 24$
$5 \times 4 = 20$
$20 + 2 = 22$
$4 \times 4 = 16$
$16 + 2 = 18$
$1 \times 4 = 4$
$4 + 1 = 5$

Copy and complete these calculations.

1. 4653 × 2

2. 3248 × 3

3. 2418 × 4

4. 1374 × 5

5. 1246 × 8

6. 1078 × 9

7. 1248 × 7

8. 1590 × 6

9. 1435 × 5

10. 2348 × 4

11. 3214 × 3

12. 1985 × 4

Now check your answers using a calculator.

Work out the missing numbers in these calculations.

13. 1□4□ × 4 = 53□0

14. 2□□6 × 3 = 730□

15. 1□63 × 5 = 73□□

16. 2□1□ × 4 = 92□4

Now check your answers using a calculator.

3 | 7308

Word problems

Work out the answer to these word problems. Show all your working.

1. A school receives 345 school meals daily. How many meals does the school receive during a school week?
2. A worker earns $425 every week. How much will the worker earn in 8 weeks?
3. Each row in a football stand has seats for 125 people. How many people can be seated in a section of the stand which has 8 rows?
4. Soft drinks are sold in cartons of six. How many drinks will one get from 115 cartons?
5. A box of apples contains 144. How many apples are there in 5 such boxes?
6. The newspaper boy delivers 168 newspapers daily to people in his district. How many newspapers does he deliver in 1 week?
7. An oil drum holds 225 litres. How many litres will 8 drums hold?
8. A bag of pet food costs $179. How much will 6 bags cost?

Rectangular and square numbers

You will need: a peg board or a checkers board.

Use pegs or counters to make rectangles and squares.

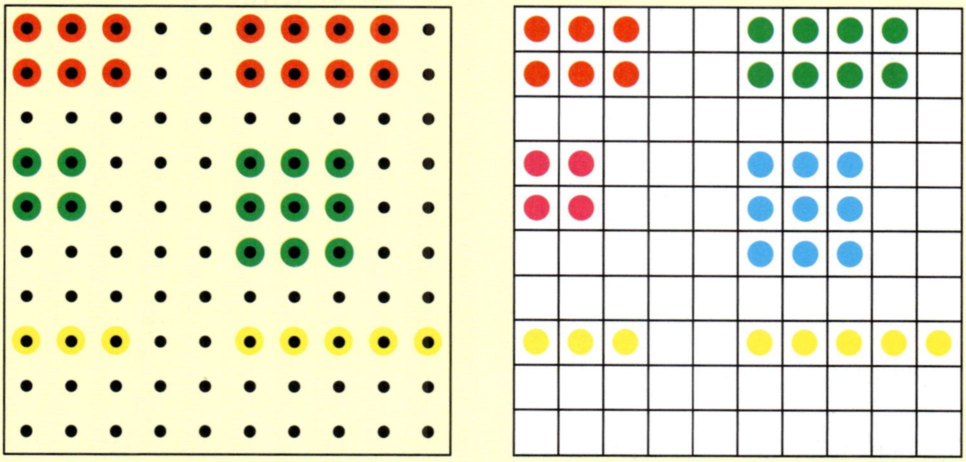

The number of pegs or counters that make rectangles, like 6 or 8, are called **rectangular** numbers.
The number of pegs or counters that make squares, like 4 or 9, are called **square** numbers.
Some numbers do not make either rectangles or squares, like 3 or 5.
These make single lines only: they can be called **line** numbers.

Use a 100 square board to make as many rectangular numbers, square numbers and line numbers as you can.

Products and factors

We can make several arrays with rectangular numbers.

1 row of 12
12 × 1 = 12
12 is the product of 12 and 1.
12 and 1 are factors of 12.

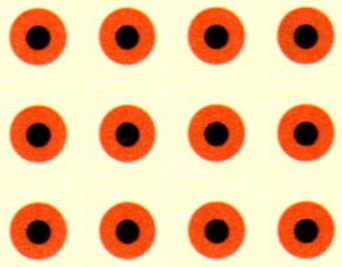

3 rows of 4
4 × 3 = 12
4 columns of 3
3 × 4 = 12
12 is the product of 3 and 4.
3 and 4 are factors of 12.

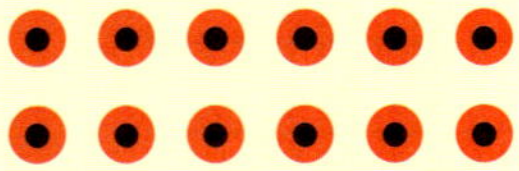

2 rows of 6
6 × 2 = 12
6 columns of 2
2 × 6 = 12
12 is the product of 2 and 6.
2 and 6 are factors of 12.

1, 2, 3, 4, 6 and 12 are all factors of 12.

Find the different sets of factors of 16 and 18 by making several rectangular arrays of these numbers.

Look at the multiplication square below.

The number 6 is the product of 1 and 6 and 2 and 3.
The factors of 6 are 1, 2, 3 and 6.

×	1	2	3	4	5	6	7	8	9	10
1	1	2	3	4	5	6	7	8	9	10
2	2	4	6	8	10	12	14	16	18	20
3	3	6	9	12	15	18	21	24	27	30
4	4	8	12	16	20	24	28	32	36	40
5	5	10	15	20	25	30	35	40	45	50
6	6	12	18	24	30	36	42	48	54	60
7	7	14	21	28	35	42	49	56	63	70
8	8	16	24	32	40	48	56	64	72	80
9	9	18	27	36	45	54	63	72	81	90
10	10	20	30	40	50	60	70	80	90	100

Copy the multiplication square above.

You will need: squared paper.

Use the multiplication square to write the different pairs of factors for each of the following numbers:

1. 8 **2.** 10 **3.** 14 **4.** 15
5. 18 **6.** 20 **7.** 21 **8.** 24
9. 30 **10.** 36 **11.** 40 **12.** 48
13. 56 **14.** 64 **15.** 72 **16.** 80

Odd and even numbers, prime numbers

Prime numbers have only 2 factors – the number itself and number 1.
All **even** numbers have 2 as a factor.
All numbers that are not even are **odd** numbers.

Copy the 1–100 square below.
Colour all the even numbers red.
Colour all the odd numbers blue.
Draw a ring around all the prime numbers.

1	2	3	4	5	6	7	8	9	10
11	12	13	14	15	16	17	18	19	20
21	22	23	24	25	26	27	28	29	30
31	32	33	34	35	36	37	38	39	40
41	42	43	44	45	46	47	48	49	50
51	52	53	54	55	56	57	58	59	60
61	62	63	64	65	66	67	68	69	70
71	72	73	74	75	76	77	78	79	80
81	82	83	84	85	86	87	88	89	90
91	92	93	94	95	96	97	98	99	100

What can you say about the units digit of all even numbers?
What can you say about the units digit of all odd numbers?

Multiples

$1 \times 2 = 2$ $2 \times 2 = 4$ $3 \times 2 = 6$ $4 \times 2 = 8$

2, 4, 6 and 8 are all products of the 2-times table.
2, 4, 6 and 8 are all **multiples** of 2.

The multiplication square below shows all the multiples up to 100, for times tables up to 10×10.

The multiples are shown down as well as across. This multiplication square shows in green the multiples of 2 up to 10×2.

1	2	3	4	5	6	7	8	9	10
2	4	6	8	10	12	14	16	18	20
3	6	9	12	15	18	21	24	27	30
4	8	12	16	20	24	28	32	36	40
5	10	15	20	25	30	35	40	45	50
6	12	18	24	30	36	42	48	54	60
7	14	21	28	35	42	49	56	63	70
8	16	24	32	40	48	56	64	72	80
9	18	27	36	45	54	63	72	81	90
10	20	30	40	50	60	70	80	90	100

1. Write down all the multiples for each of the numbers 2 to 10. Make a table like this:

Number	Multiples
2	2, 4, 6 …
3	3, 6, 9 …
4	

From the table you have made, write down the multiples that are common to each set of numbers below.

2. 2 and 3
3. 3 and 5
4. 3 and 4
5. 2 and 5
6. 2 and 6
7. 3 and 6
8. 2, 3 and 4
9. 2, 3 and 5
10. 2, 3 and 6
11. 3, 4 and 5
12. 3, 4 and 6
13. 4, 5 and 6
14. 2, 4 and 5
15. 2, 4 and 6
16. 2, 5 and 6

Working with brackets

The perimeter of a rectangle is given as (length + breadth) × 2.
The brackets tell us that we must **first** add the length and breadth and **then** multiply the result by 2 to get the perimeter.

We do the same thing in number problems when we have brackets; we must work the **parts in the brackets first**.

Examples:

$9 - (2 + 3)$ **but**	$(9 - 2) + 3$ and	$(4 \times 2) + 3$ **but**	$4 \times (2 + 3)$
$= 9 - 5$	$= 7 + 3$	$= 8 + 3$	$= 4 \times 5$
$= 4$	$= 10$	$= 11$	$= 20$

The answers to the problems depend on where the brackets are.

Write the answers to these calculations.

1. $15 - (7+3)$
2. $6 \times (4 + 1)$
3. $(24 \div 3) - 5$
4. $(5 - 2) \times 3$
5. $18 - (2 \times 5)$
6. $25 + (8 \div 2)$
7. $(14 + 2) - (5 + 3)$
8. $(16 - 3) - (10 - 2)$
9. $(14 + 2) - (4 + 5)$
10. $(6 \times 3) + (5 \times 2)$
11. $(8 \times 4) - (2 \times 3)$
12. $(30 \div 6) + (72 \div 8)$

Put in brackets in these calculations to make the answers correct.

13. $8 + 5 \times 2 = 26$
14. $20 - 3 + 8 = 9$
15. $6 + 2 \times 3 = 12$
16. $20 \div 4 - 2 = 10$

Multiplication tables

Copy and complete these tables

11 × 1 = 11	1 × 11 = 11	12 × 1 = 12	1 × 12 = 12
11 × 2 =	2 × 11 =	12 × 2 =	2 × 12 =
11 × 3 =	3 × 11 =	12 × 3 =	3 × 12 =
11 × 4 =	4 × 11 =	12 × 4 =	4 × 12 =
11 × 5 =	5 × 11 =	12 × 5 =	5 × 12 =
11 × 6 =	6 × 11 =	12 × 6 =	6 × 12 =
11 × 7 =	7 × 11 =	12 × 7 =	7 × 12 =
11 × 8 =	8 × 11 =	12 × 8 =	8 × 12 =
11 × 9 =	9 × 11 =	12 × 9 =	9 × 12 =
11 × 10 =	10 × 11 =	12 × 10 =	10 × 12 =

Copy and complete these calculations.

1. 25 × 11

2. 39 × 11

3. 42 × 12

4. 53 × 12

5. 134 × 11

6. 246 × 11

7. 123 × 12

8. 216 × 12

9. How many eggs in 25 dozen if there are 12 in a dozen?

10. How many bags will I need for 264 oranges if each bag holds 12?

11. How much will I pay for 11 notebooks if each cost $6.95?

12. (18 × 12) − (18 × 11) =

Multiplication by factors

Remember: the numbers we multiply together to give a product are called **factors of the product number.**

2 and 3 are factors of 6 because $2 \times 3 = 6$

$(14 \times 3) \times 2 = 42 \times 2 = 84$

and $(14 \times 2) \times 3 = 28 \times 3 = 84$

Also $14 \times (3 \times 2) = 14 \times 6 = 84$

and $14 \times (2 \times 3) = 14 \times 6 = 84$

$24 \times 10 = 240$

and 5 and 2 are factors of 10

$(24 \times 5) \times 2 = 120 \times 2 = 240$

and $(24 \times 2) \times 5 = 48 \times 5 = 240$

To multiply by 6 we can also multiply by its factors in any order.
To multiply by 10 we can also multiply by its factors in any order.
To multiply by any number we can multiply by the factors of that number.

Do these multiplications using factors.

1. 14×8	**2.** 33×12	**3.** 21×14	**4.** 18×10
5. 19×16	**6.** 24×32	**7.** 31×42	**8.** 15×36
9. 21×24	**10.** 15×14	**11.** 41×56	**12.** 30×25
13. 40×12	**14.** 19×18	**15.** 51×45	**16.** 20×27
17. 12×20	**18.** 15×30	**19.** 21×40	**20.** 18×50

Now check your answers using a calculator.

Multiplication by multiples of 10

$12 \times 20 = 12 \times 2 \times 10 = 24 \times 10 = 240$

Check your answer by using a calculator.

Write answers to the following calculations.

1. 152×10	**2.** 88×10	**3.** 164×10	**4.** 212×10
5. 219×10	**6.** 420×10	**7.** 101×10	**8.** 400×10

We can multiply by 20, 30, 40 and so on using factors.

$20 = 2 \times 10 \quad 30 = 3 \times 10 \quad 40 = 4 \times 10$

Examples: $18 \times 20 = 18 \times 2 \times 10 = 36 \times 10 = 360$

$253 \times 30 = 253 \times 3 \times 10 = 759 \times 10 = 7590$

Use factors to calculate these products.

9. 54×20	**10.** 44×30	**11.** 65×40	**12.** 23×50
13. 42×60	**14.** 38×70	**15.** 72×80	**16.** 91×90

Now check your answers using a calculator.

Answer these word problems. Show all your working.

17. How much will 20 bags of potatoes weigh if each weighs 25 kg?

18. What length of ribbon must I buy for 40 children if each child must have a piece 30 cm long?

19. How many chairs do you need for 30 rows if each row takes 42 chairs?

20. A packet of marbles contains 25. How many marbles will there be in 60 packets?

Rewriting products as sums

5 groups of 6 can be put into 3 groups of 6 and 2 groups of 6

$$6 \times 5 = (6 \times 3) + (6 \times 2)$$
$$30 = 18 + 12$$

5 groups of 6 can also be put into 4 groups of 6 and 1 group of 6

$$6 \times 5 = (6 \times 4) + (6 \times 1)$$
$$30 = 24 + 6$$

We can write 5 as the sum of two numbers. We can then multiply **each** number by 6 then add the two products together. Now write the 6 as the sum of any two numbers (example 4 + 2 or 5 + 1).
Multiply each number by 5 and add the results. What do you notice?

Look at the calculations below. Copy and fill in the boxes in the brackets, then give the answer to each of the calculations.

1. $6 \times 9 = (6 \times \square) + (6 \times 3)$
2. $24 \times 7 = (24 \times 2) + (24 \times \square)$
3. $54 \times 12 = (54 \times \square) + (54 \times 8)$
4. $23 \times 8 = (23 \times 4) + (23 \times \square)$
5. $43 \times 12 = (43 \times 10) + (43 \times \square)$
6. $96 \times 24 = (96 \times \square) + (96 \times 4)$

Now check your answers using your calculator.

Multiplying a pair of two-digit numbers

48 × 12	36 × 25
48 × 12 = (48 × 10) + (48 × 2)	36 × 25 = (36 × 20) + (36 × 5)

$$\begin{array}{rl} 48 & \\ \times\ 12 & \\ \hline 480 & = 48 \times 10 \\ 96 & = 48 \times 2 \\ \hline 576 & = 48 \times 12 \\ \hline \end{array}$$

$$\begin{array}{rl} 36 & \\ \times\ 25 & \\ \hline 720 & = 36 \times 20 \\ 180 & = 36 \times 5 \\ \hline 900 & = 36 \times 25 \\ \hline \end{array}$$

Copy and complete these calculations.

1. 18 × 13 **2.** 41 × 14 **3.** 42 × 45 **4.** 55 × 16
5. 12 × 21 **6.** 45 × 31 **7.** 21 × 41 **8.** 32 × 51
9. 42 × 25 **10.** 81 × 34 **11.** 34 × 45 **12.** 52 × 56
13. 48 × 20 **14.** 18 × 32 **15.** 80 × 25 **16.** 50 × 35
17. 26 × 18 **18.** 34 × 84 **19.** 42 × 16 **20.** 45 × 18

Now check your answers using a calculator.

21. Calculate the total number of cars that you can park in the following car parks.

Car park	Number of parking lanes	Number of cars in each lane	Total number of cars
A	24	18	
B	16	15	
C	25	24	
D	18	16	
E	20	15	

22. How many cars can the 5 car parks hold altogether?

5 Division

Some basic multiplication and division facts

$3 \times 2 = 6$ $6 \div 3 = 2$ and $6 \div 2 = 3$

You can use your multiplication tables to write statements similar to those above.

$3\overline{)6}$ with answer 2 means $6 \div 3 = 2$ and $2\overline{)6}$ with answer 3 means $6 \div 2 = 3$

Copy and complete.

1. $8 \times \square = 56$ $8\overline{)56}$ $\square$
2. $4 \times \square = 24$ $4\overline{)24}$ $\square$
3. $\square \times 5 = 45$ $5\overline{)45}$ $\square$
4. $\square \times 6 = 42$ $6\overline{)42}$ $\square$
5. $4 \times \square = 32$ $4\overline{)32}$ $\square$
6. $\square \times 3 = 21$ $3\overline{)21}$ $\square$
7. $8\overline{)48}$ $\square$
8. $6\overline{)54}$ $\square$
9. $7\overline{)28}$ $\square$
10. $9\overline{)63}$ $\square$
11. $4\overline{)28}$ $\square$
12. $9\overline{)45}$ $\square$
13. $3\overline{)27}$ $\square$
14. $6\overline{)36}$ $\square$
15. $5\overline{)35}$ $\square$
16. $3\overline{)24}$ $\square$
17. $8\overline{)64}$ $\square$
18. $9\overline{)36}$ $\square$

Dividing two-digit numbers

$24 \div 2$

Put out counters using red counters for tens and green for ones.

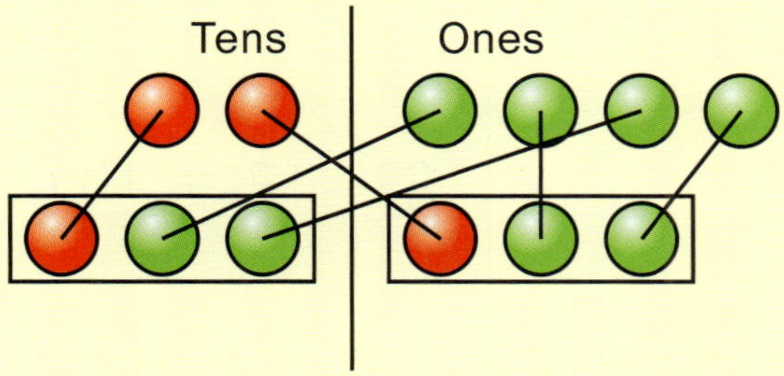

$24 \div 2 = 12$

How we write it.

$$2\overline{)2\,4}\quad \text{quotient } 1\,2$$

Divide tens
$2 \div 2 = 1$
Divide ones
$4 \div 2 = 2$

$24 \div 2 = 12$

Copy and complete these calculations.

1. $2\overline{)28}$	**2.** $2\overline{)46}$	**3.** $2\overline{)64}$	**4.** $2\overline{)82}$
5. $3\overline{)36}$	**6.** $3\overline{)63}$	**7.** $3\overline{)39}$	**8.** $3\overline{)96}$
9. $2\overline{)84}$	**10.** $3\overline{)69}$	**11.** $2\overline{)68}$	**12.** $3\overline{)99}$
13. $4\overline{)48}$	**14.** $5\overline{)55}$	**15.** $2\overline{)40}$	**16.** $5\overline{)50}$
17. $4\overline{)40}$	**18.** $2\overline{)26}$	**19.** $3\overline{)39}$	**20.** $4\overline{)44}$
21. $3\overline{)66}$	**22.** $6\overline{)60}$	**23.** $2\overline{)48}$	**24.** $6\overline{)66}$

Now check your answers using a calculator.

Division with remainders

$23 \div 2$

Put out 2 red counters and 3 green counters for 23.

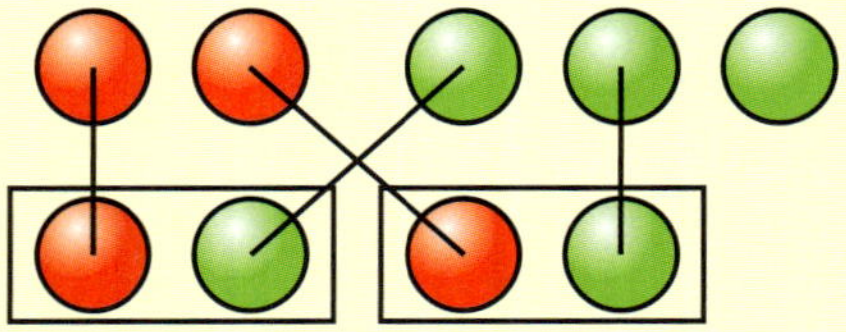

We have 1 green counter left.

$23 \div 2 = 11 \text{ r } 1$

How we write it.

```
    1 | 1
2 | 2 | 3
      | 2
        1
```

Divide tens
$2 \div 2 = 1$
Divide ones
$3 \div 2 = 1 \text{ r } 1$

$23 \div 2 = 11 \text{r} 1$

Copy and complete these calculations.

1. 2)25	**2.** 2)45	**3.** 2)67	**4.** 2)85
5. 3)34	**6.** 3)67	**7.** 3)94	**8.** 3)64
9. 4)45	**10.** 4)85	**11.** 4)49	**12.** 4)87
13. 5)56	**14.** 6)61	**15.** 7)79	**16.** 9)91
17. 5)54	**18.** 6)67	**19.** 8)89	**20.** 4)81
21. 7)78	**22.** 5)59	**23.** 6)69	**24.** 4)85
25. 3)38	**26.** 4)47	**27.** 3)62	**28.** 5)58

Regrouping in division

34 ÷ 2

	1	7
2	3	4
	2	10
	1	14
		14
		0

Divide tens 3 ÷ 2 = 1 r 1
1 ten = 10 ones
10 + 4 = 14 ones
Divide ones 14 ÷ 2 = 7

34 ÷ 2 = 17

When you have had enough practice the steps are done mentally and we write this:

$2\overline{)3\,{}^{1}4}$ with 17 written above

3 ÷ 2 = 1 r 1ten
10 + 4 = 14
14 ÷ 2 = 7

Copy and complete these calculations.

1. $2\overline{)38}$	**2.** $3\overline{)45}$	**3.** $4\overline{)56}$	**4.** $5\overline{)75}$
5. $2\overline{)54}$	**6.** $6\overline{)72}$	**7.** $7\overline{)91}$	**8.** $3\overline{)84}$
9. $8\overline{)96}$	**10.** $3\overline{)51}$	**11.** $5\overline{)85}$	**12.** $6\overline{)84}$
13. $7\overline{)84}$	**14.** $4\overline{)68}$	**15.** $6\overline{)96}$	**16.** $3\overline{)57}$
17. $2\overline{)72}$	**18.** $3\overline{)48}$	**19.** $6\overline{)78}$	**20.** $2\overline{)98}$
21. $4\overline{)64}$	**22.** $5\overline{)65}$	**23.** $3\overline{)48}$	**24.** $4\overline{)56}$
25. $2\overline{)56}$	**26.** $7\overline{)98}$	**27.** $3\overline{)54}$	**28.** $4\overline{)92}$
29. $3\overline{)72}$	**30.** $6\overline{)90}$	**31.** $4\overline{)72}$	**32.** $5\overline{)90}$

The quotient

When you divide one number by another the result is called the **quotient**.

Work out the quotient in each of the following calculations:

1. 75 ÷ 5 = ☐ **2.** 36 ÷ 3 = ☐ **3.** 64 ÷ 4 = ☐

4. 81 ÷ 3 = ☐ **5.** 72 ÷ 4 = ☐ **6.** 56 ÷ 2 = ☐

7. $3\overline{)87}$ **8.** $5\overline{)95}$ **9.** $3\overline{)39}$

10. $4\overline{)68}$ **11.** $7\overline{)84}$ **12.** $4\overline{)56}$

13. $6\overline{)85}$ **14.** $3\overline{)59}$ **15.** $8\overline{)93}$

16. $4\overline{)47}$ **17.** $5\overline{)69}$ **18.** $7\overline{)85}$

19. $4\overline{)42}$ **20.** $8\overline{)82}$ **21.** $7\overline{)73}$

22. $3\overline{)88}$ **23.** $4\overline{)53}$ **24.** $5\overline{)49}$

25. $6\overline{)33}$ **26.** $5\overline{)72}$ **27.** $7\overline{)57}$

28. $4\overline{)75}$ **29.** $8\overline{)65}$ **30.** $3\overline{)67}$

Word problems

Work out the answers to these word problems. Show all your working.

1. Forty-eight plants are to be put into 3 rows in a garden. How many plants will go into each row?

Number of plants	48	
Number of rows	3	$3\overline{)48}$
Number in each row	$= 48 \div 3$	
	$= \square$	

2. Ninety-six marbles are to be shared among some boys. Each boy will receive 8 marbles. How many boys will get marbles?

Number of marbles	96	
Number for each boy	8	$8\overline{)96}$
Number of boys	$= 96 \div 8$	
	$= \square$	

3. Eighty-four chairs are arranged in 7 rows. How many chairs are in each row?

4. Eighty cents have to be shared by 5 boys. How much will each boy get?

5. Bread is put into bags of 6 loaves each. How many bags will we need for 90 loaves?

6. How many tins go into each box if I pack 72 tins equally into 4 boxes?

7. Flowers are put out in bunches of 3. How many bunches will I get from 45 flowers?

Division of three-digit numbers – regrouping ones

984 ÷ 3

	3	2	8	Steps	
3	9	8	4	Divide hundreds	9 ÷ 3 = 3
	9	6	20	Divide tens	8 ÷ 3 = 2 r 2
	0	2	24	2 tens = 20	20 + 4 = 24
			24	Divide ones	24 ÷ 3 = 8
			0	Remainder is	0

$$\begin{array}{r} 3\ 2\ 8 \\ 3\overline{)9\ 8\ {}^{2}4} \end{array}$$

984 ÷ 3 = 328

Copy and complete these calculations. In some of your answers there will be a remainder.

1. $2\overline{)2\ 4\ 8}$
2. $3\overline{)3\ 6\ 3}$
3. $4\overline{)4\ 8\ 4}$
4. $2\overline{)6\ 4\ 0}$
5. $2\overline{)2\ 5\ 4}$
6. $3\overline{)6\ 7\ 2}$
7. $4\overline{)4\ 5\ 2}$
8. $5\overline{)5\ 6\ 5}$
9. $6\overline{)6\ 8\ 4}$
10. $7\overline{)7\ 9\ 5}$
11. $8\overline{)8\ 9\ 6}$
12. $9\overline{)9\ 1\ 8}$
13. 415 ÷ 2
14. 515 ÷ 5
15. 360 ÷ 3
16. 408 ÷ 4
17. 545 ÷ 5
18. 478 ÷ 4
19. 342 ÷ 3
20. 837 ÷ 4
21. 659 ÷ 6
22. 756 ÷ 7
23. 493 ÷ 4
24. 622 ÷ 6
25. 437 ÷ 2
26. 359 ÷ 3
27. 409 ÷ 4
28. 615 ÷ 3
29. 508 ÷ 5
30. 632 ÷ 6
31. 745 ÷ 7
32. 825 ÷ 8

Division of three-digit numbers – regrouping tens and ones

The steps are written for example (a). Copy example (b) writing in the steps.

a) 527 ÷ 3 =

	1	7	5
3	5	2	7
	3	20	10
	2	22	17
		21	15
		1	2

Steps
Divide hundreds 5 ÷ 3 = 1 r 2
2 hundreds = 20 tens
20 + 2 = 22 tens
Divide tens 22 ÷ 3 = 7 r 1
1 ten = 10 ones
10 + 7 = 17
Divide ones 17 ÷ 3 = 5 r 2

527 ÷ 3 = 175 r 2

b) 346 ÷ 4 =

	0	8	6
4	3	4	6
		30	20
		34	26
		32	24
		2	2

Doing the steps mentally

$$\begin{array}{r} 8\ 6\ \text{r}\ 2 \\ 4\overline{)\not{3}\ 4\ {}^{2}6} \end{array}$$

346 ÷ 4 = 86 r 2

Copy and complete these calculations.

1. $3\overline{)4\ 5\ 6}$ **2.** $4\overline{)5\ 2\ 8}$ **3.** $5\overline{)7\ 0\ 5}$ **4.** $6\overline{)7\ 2\ 6}$

5. $3\overline{)5\ 3\ 4}$ **6.** $4\overline{)6\ 2\ 4}$ **7.** $5\overline{)6\ 1\ 0}$ **8.** $6\overline{)8\ 1\ 6}$

9. $2\overline{)1\ 5\ 8}$ **10.** $3\overline{)2\ 3\ 4}$ **11.** $4\overline{)3\ 5\ 2}$ **12.** $5\overline{)4\ 2\ 5}$

13. $6\overline{)7\ 9\ 6}$ **14.** $7\overline{)8\ 5\ 4}$ **15.** $5\overline{)9\ 1\ 2}$ **16.** $9\overline{)9\ 2\ 7}$

17. $5\overline{)3\ 1\ 2}$ **18.** $6\overline{)4\ 1\ 8}$ **19.** $8\overline{)2\ 5\ 8}$ **20.** $7\overline{)5\ 2\ 9}$

Assessment 3

1. 519 × 5 =

2. 2419 × 4 =

Fill in the missing numbers.

3.

```
  1□3□
×    4
------
 53□2
```

4.

```
  1□4□
×    5
------
 5□25
```

5. How much will a man earn in 8 weeks if he gets $525 a week?

6. (a) (24 × 7) + (24 × 2) =

(b) 24 × 9 =

7. 24 × 18 =

8. 44 ÷ 3 =

9. Each boy was given 8 marbles out of a bag containing 96. How many boys received marbles?

10. Two hundred and forty kilograms of tomatoes are packed into 5 crates, each crate holding the same amount. How many kilograms of tomatoes will go into each crate?

How many faces, edges and vertices are in the shapes below?

11.

____ faces ____ edges ____ vertices

12.

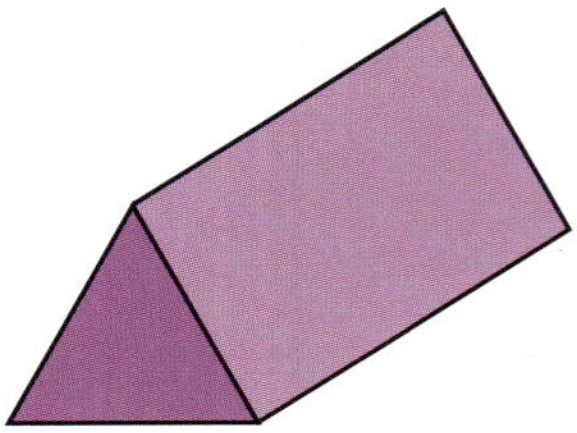

____ faces ____ edges ____ vertices

6 Geometry

Tessellations

You will need: squared paper, pens.

Use squared paper to draw these patterns. You may use whatever colours you wish. Complete these patterns.

1.

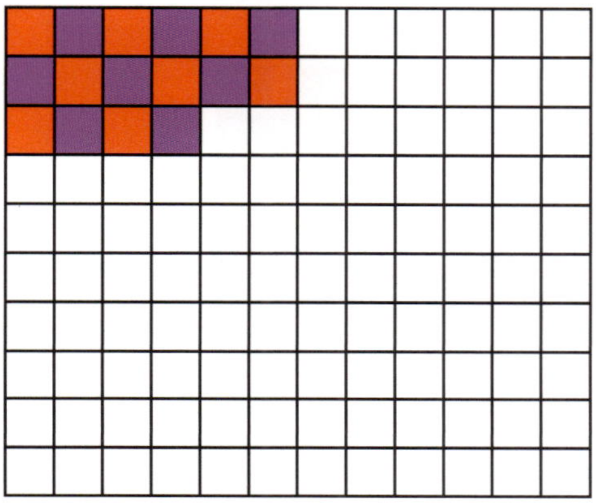

2.

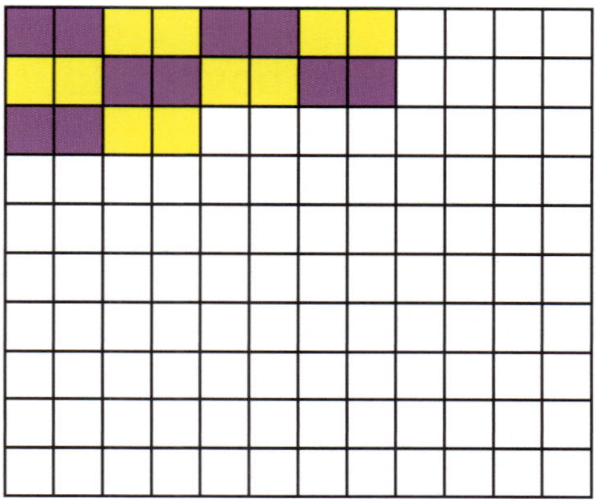

3.

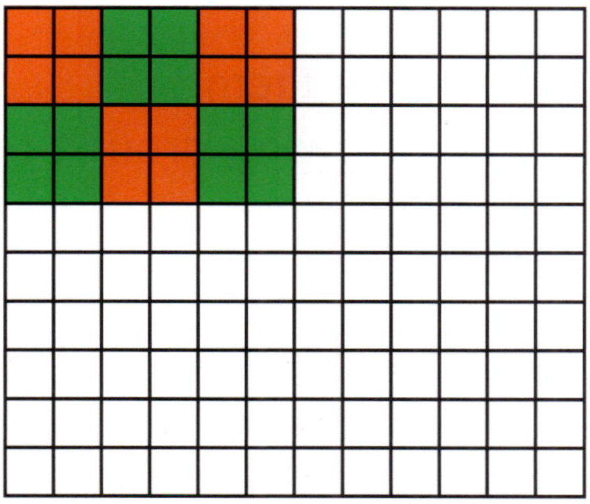

4.

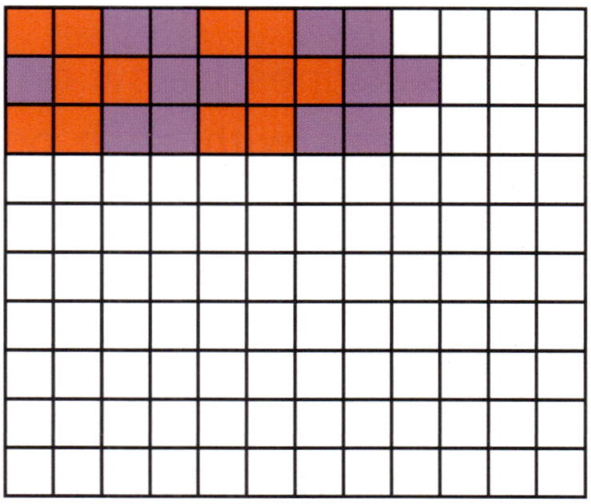

5.

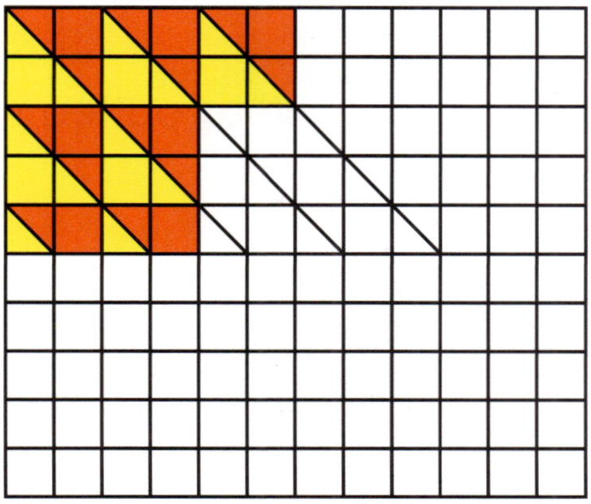

6.

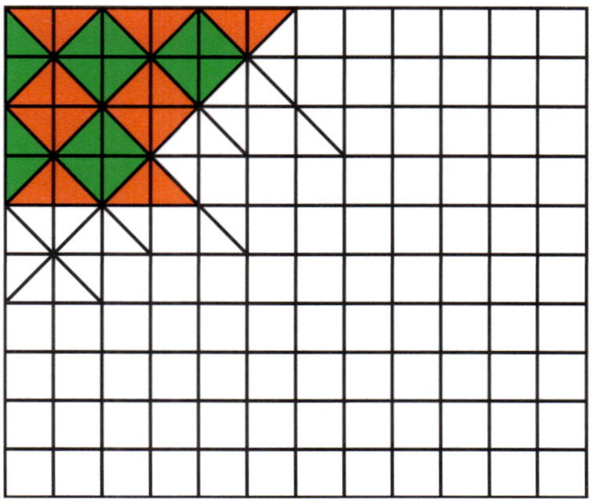

Exploring shapes that tessellate

Look at the patterns you have completed.

In some of the patterns you have coloured squares or rectangles.

In others you have coloured triangles.

In all the patterns the shapes fit together without leaving any gaps.

We say that those shapes **tessellate**.

You will need: thin card, scissors.

Trace the shapes below on to thin card and cut them out.
Make patterns with each one separately by drawing around them either after sliding or flipping the shape.
Do these shapes tessellate?

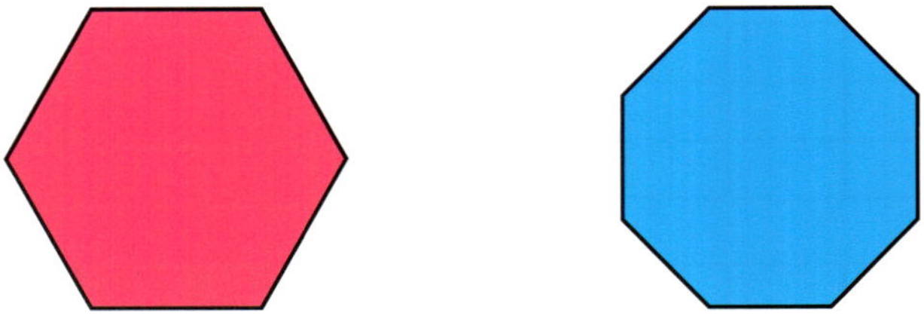

Here are some other shapes. Try making tessellating patterns with them.

Making tessellating shapes

Remember shapes which fit together without leaving gaps are said to tessellate.

Look at these patterns.

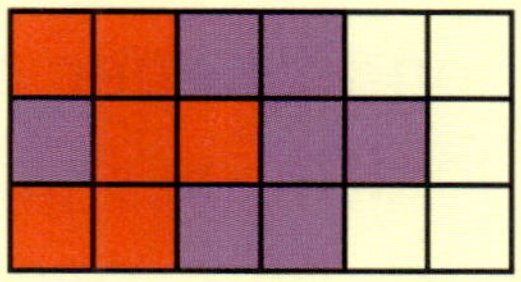

In the first pattern we have put 2 squares together.
The new shape also tessellates.

In the second pattern we have put 2 triangles together.
This new shape also tessellates.

If you join shapes which tessellate, the new shapes you make will also tessellate.

Use squares or triangles to make new shapes.
Here are some which you might make.
Use the new shapes to make tessellating patterns.

We can also make tessellating shapes by cutting off a piece of one side of a shape and adding it to the other side.

Try it!

You will need: thin card, scissors.

Symmetry

Trace the shapes below on to paper or thin card.
Cut out the shapes and fold in as many ways as possible.
Draw the lines of symmetry after opening the fold.

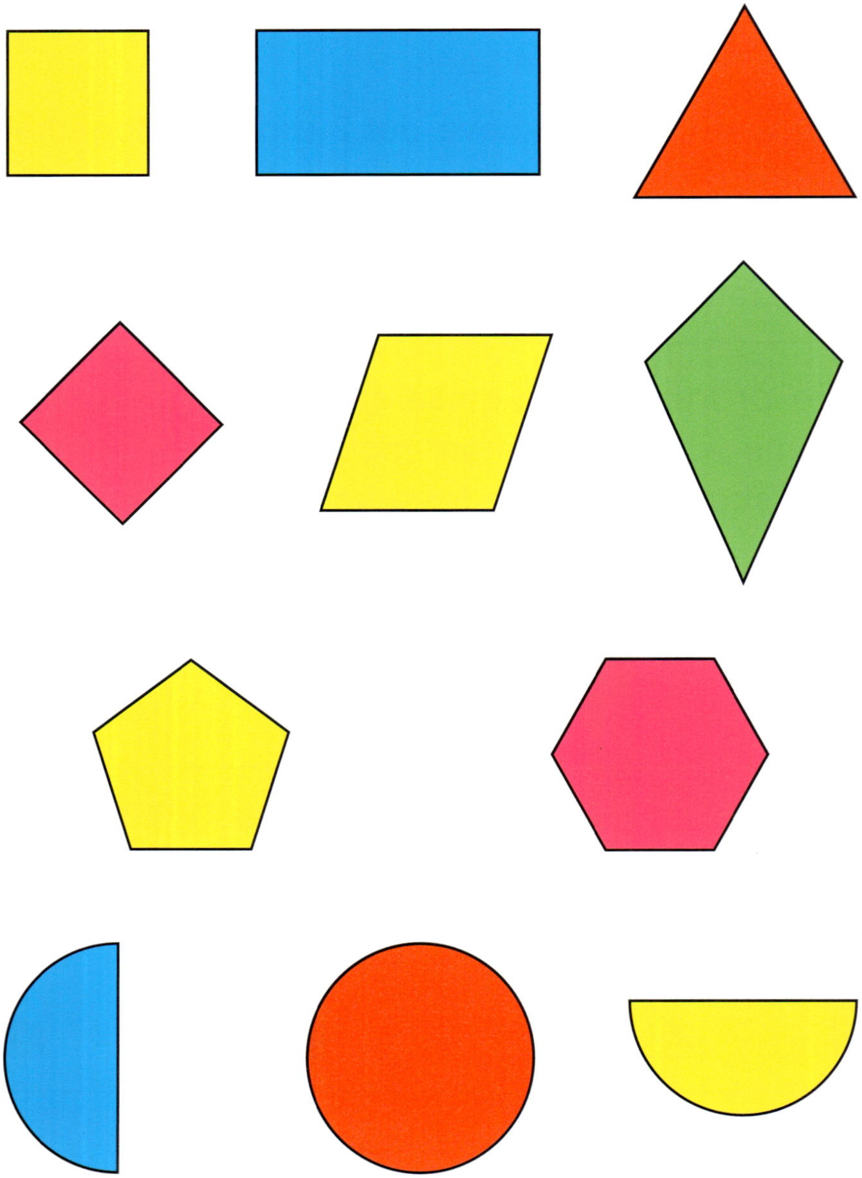

You will need: squared paper, scissors.

Use squared paper to copy these drawings.
Complete the drawings to make them symmetrical.
The line of symmetry is in red.

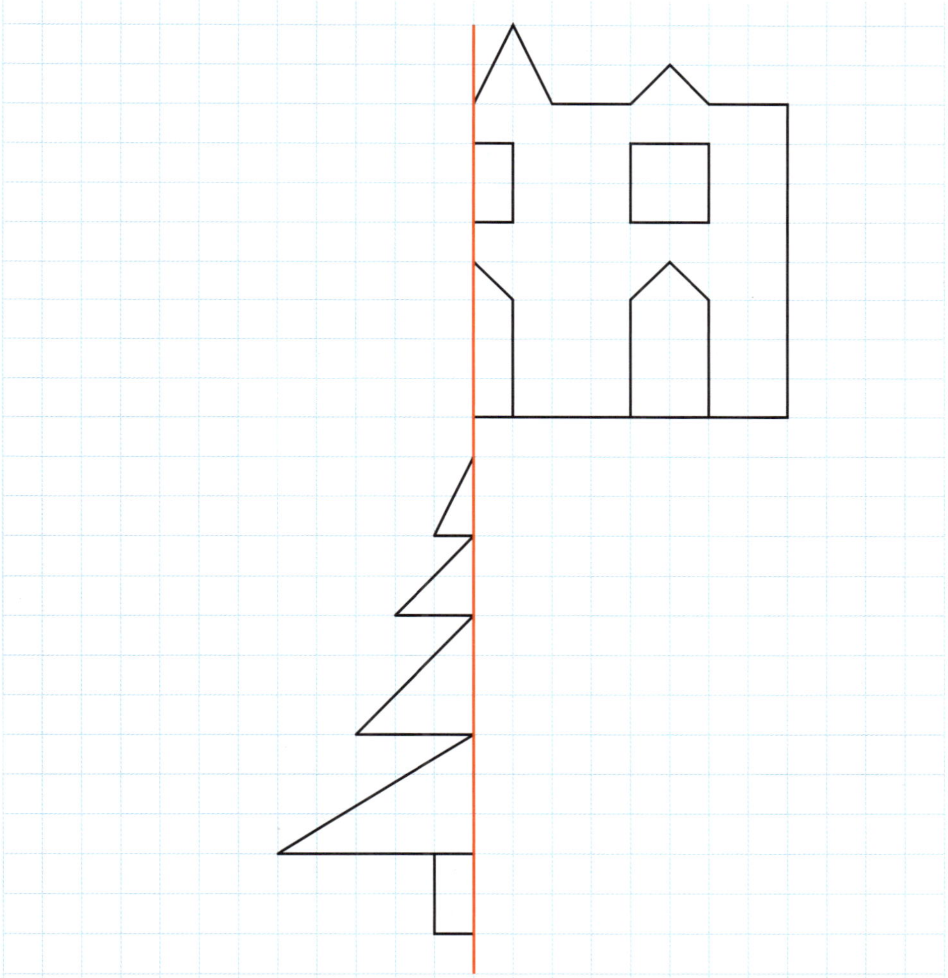

Cut sheets of paper about one quarter of the size of this page.
Fold each in four as you do when making quarters.
Cut little bits along the four edges.
Open and draw the lines of symmetry.

7 Fractions

Review of fractional parts

What fraction of each shape is shaded?

1.

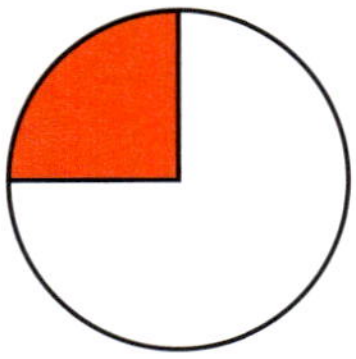

2.

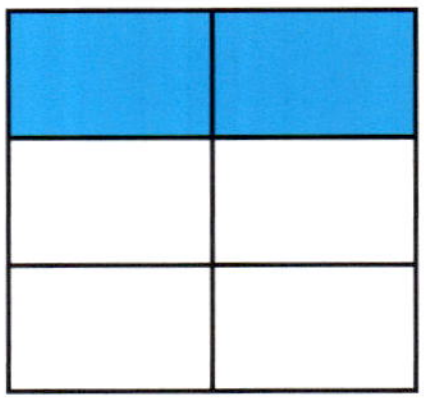

3.

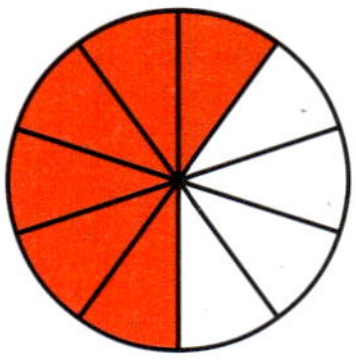

4.

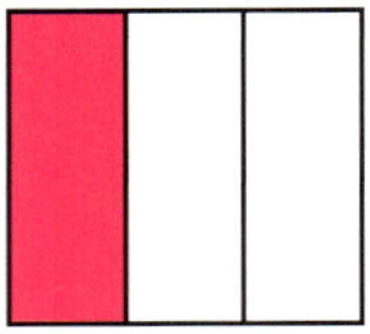

5.

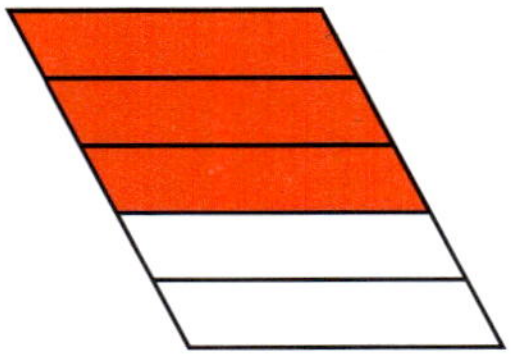

6.

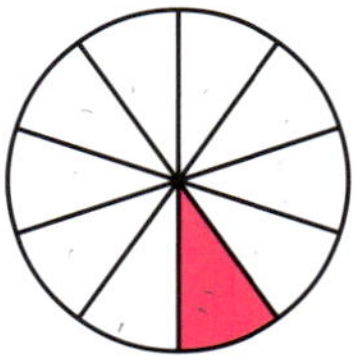

7.

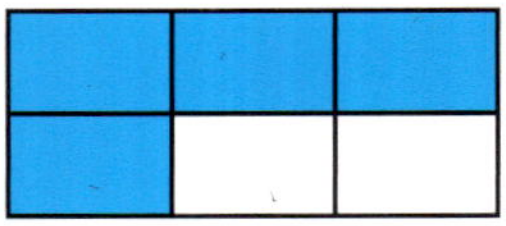

8.

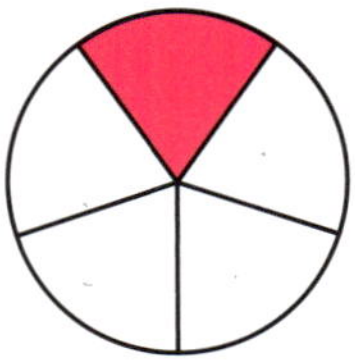

9.

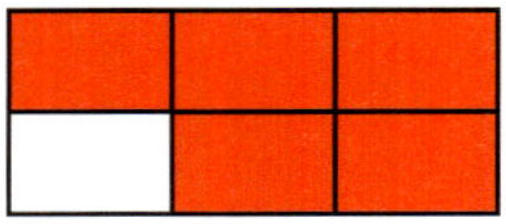

10.

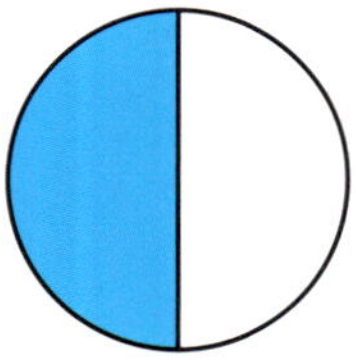

11.

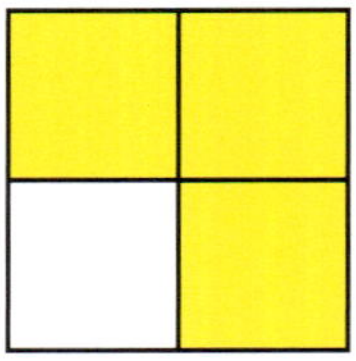

12.

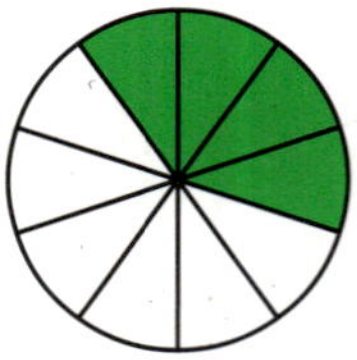

13.

14.

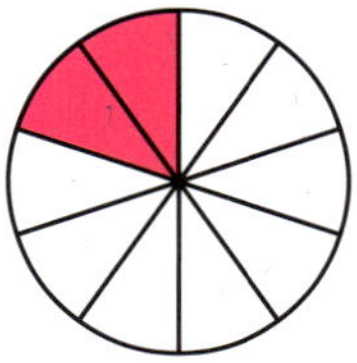

15.

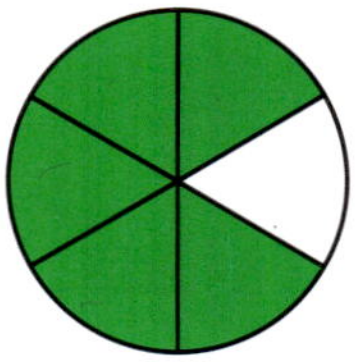

16.

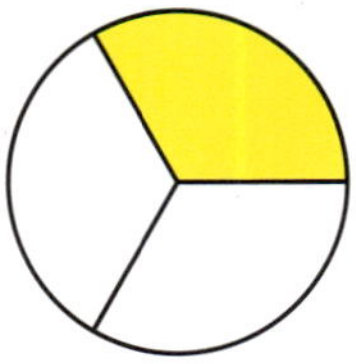

17.

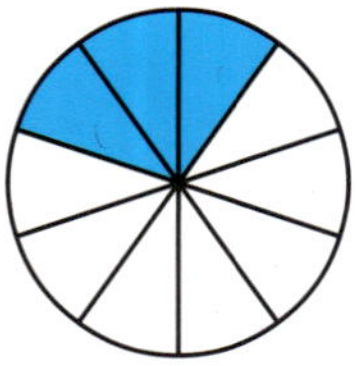

18.

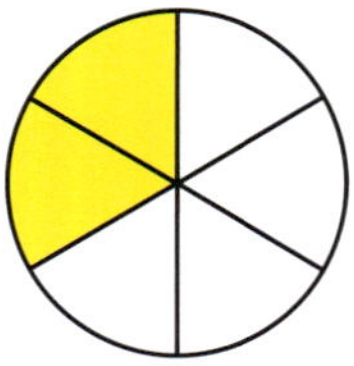

19.

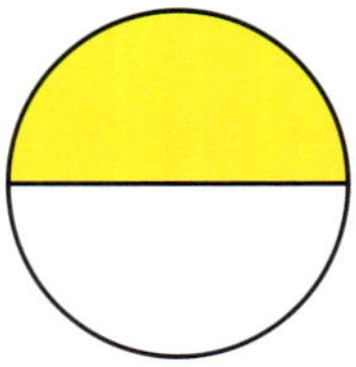

20.

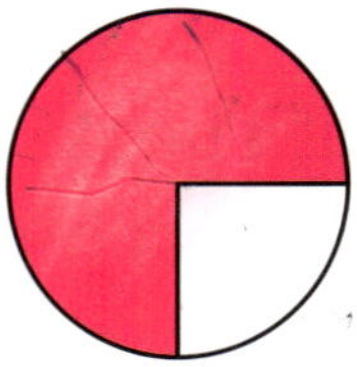

Reviewing fractions of the same value

Look at the diagrams below and complete the statements.

1.

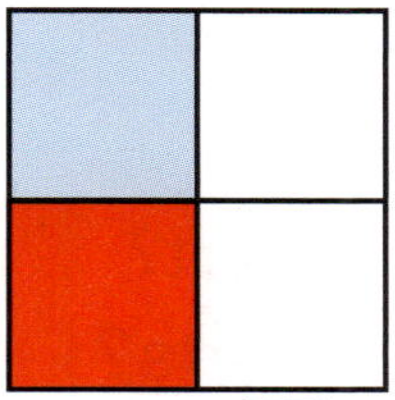

$\frac{1}{2} = \frac{\square}{4}$

2.

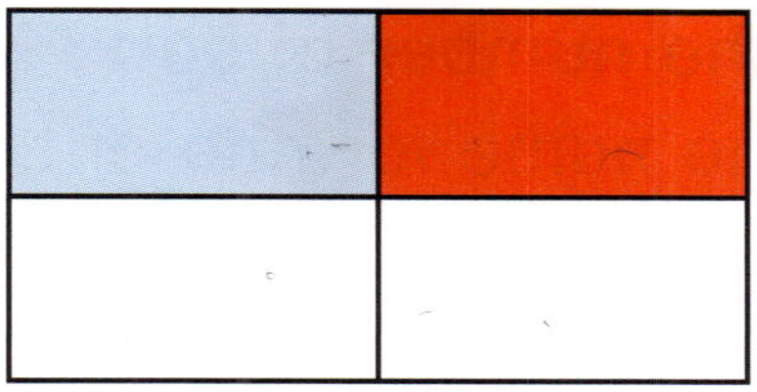

$\frac{1}{2} = \frac{\square}{4}$

3.

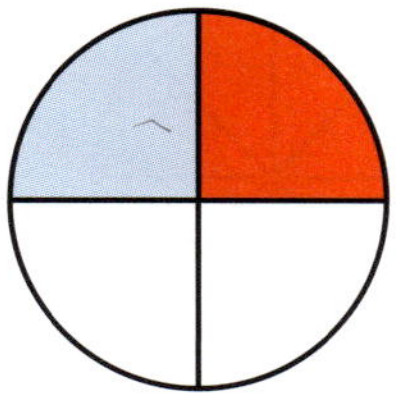

$\frac{1}{2} = \frac{2}{4}$

4.

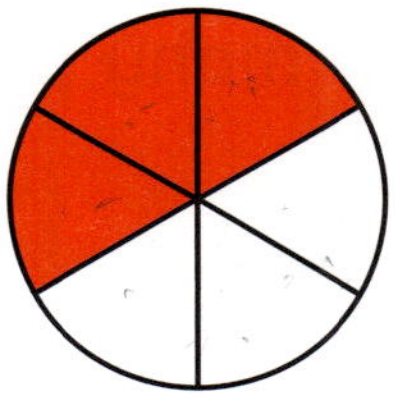

$\frac{1}{2} = \frac{\square}{6}$

5.

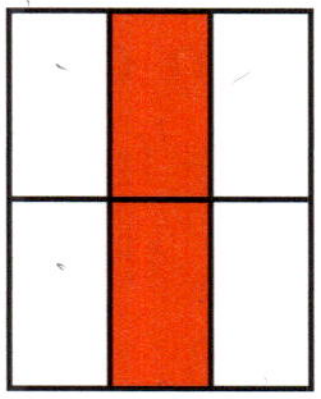

$\frac{1}{3} = \frac{2}{6}$

6.

$\frac{1}{3} = \frac{\square}{6}$

7.

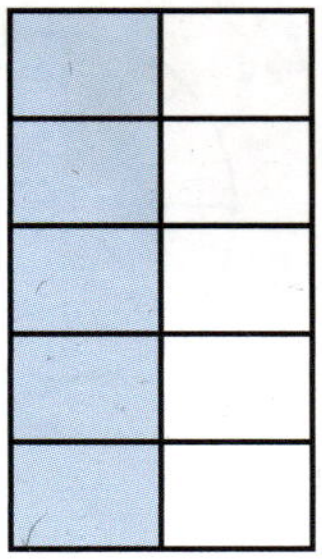

$\frac{1}{2} = \frac{5}{10}$

8.

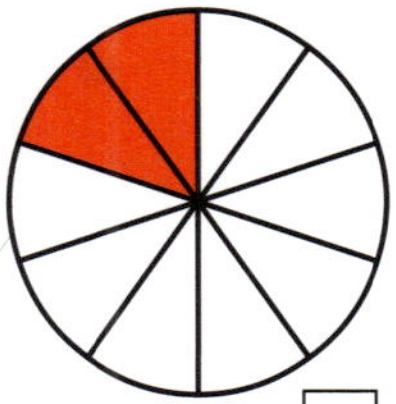

$\frac{1}{5} = \frac{\square}{10}$

9.

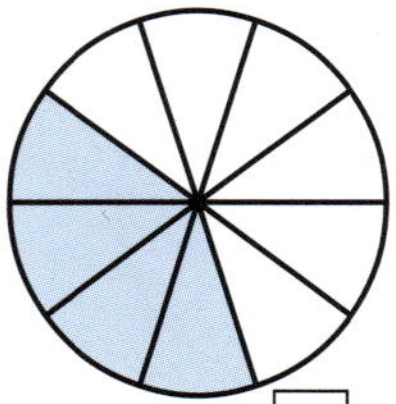

$\frac{2}{5} = \frac{\square}{10}$

10.

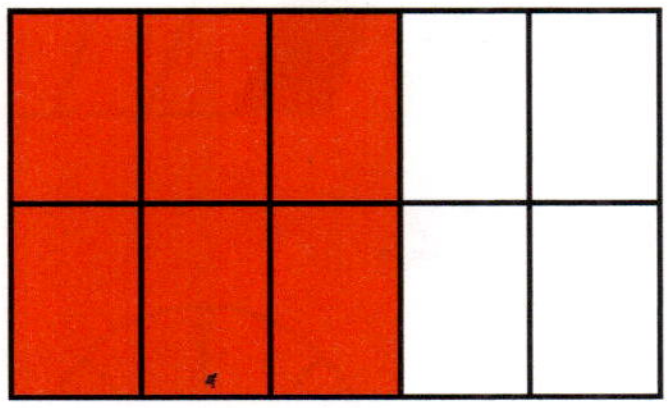

$\frac{3}{5} = \frac{\square}{10}$

11.

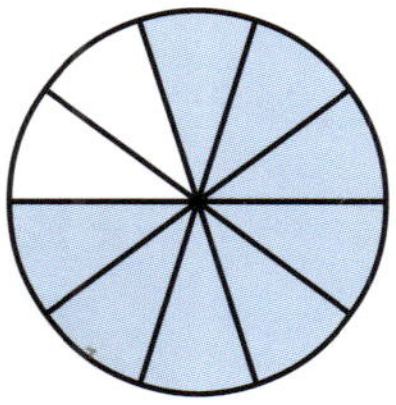

$\frac{4}{5} = \frac{\square}{10}$

12.

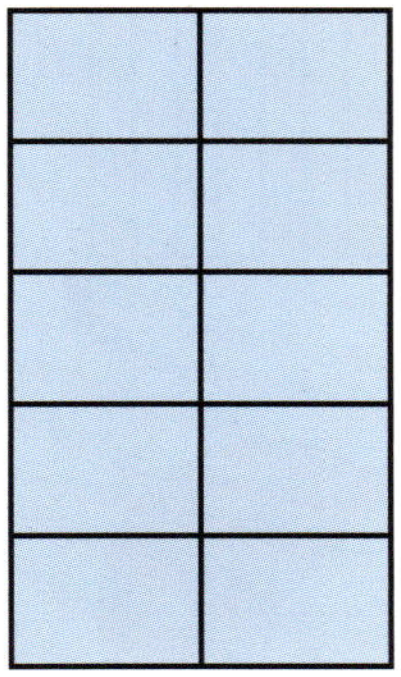

$\frac{5}{5} = \frac{\square}{10}$

Eighths

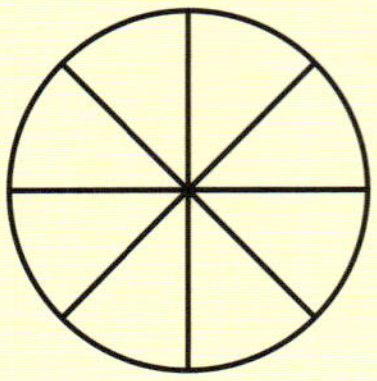

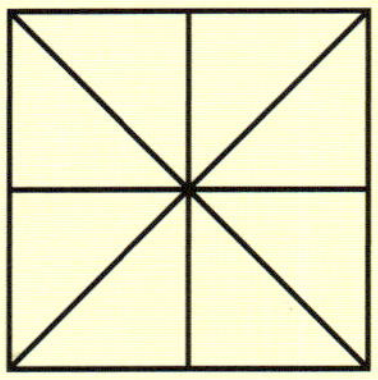

These shapes have been divided into equal parts.
Count the number of parts in each.
Write the name for one of these parts.
How do you write the fraction for one part?
How do you write the fraction for two parts?

The denominator in a fraction is the number which tells how many parts are in the whole. The numerator in a fraction tells how many parts are taken for the fraction. In the fraction $\frac{1}{8}$, the numerator is 1, the denominator is 8.

What fraction of each shape is shaded?

1. 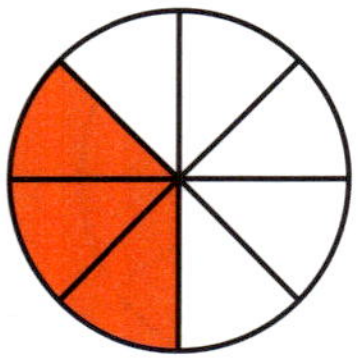

2. 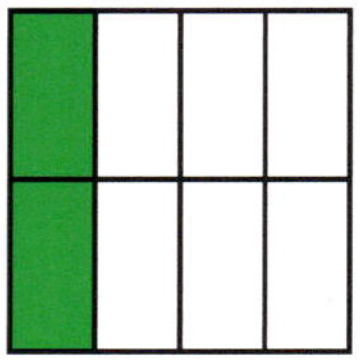

3. 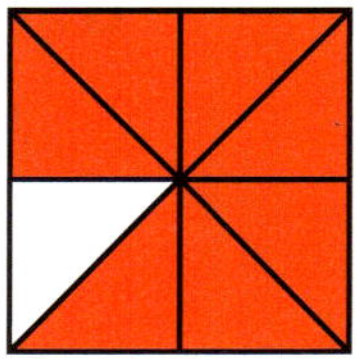

4. 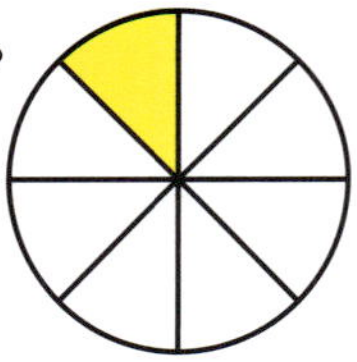

5. 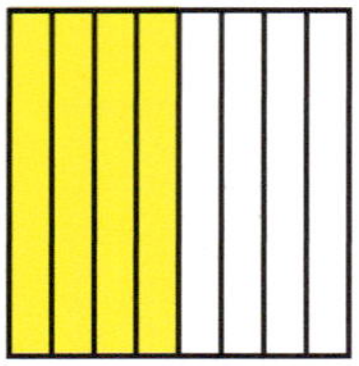

6. 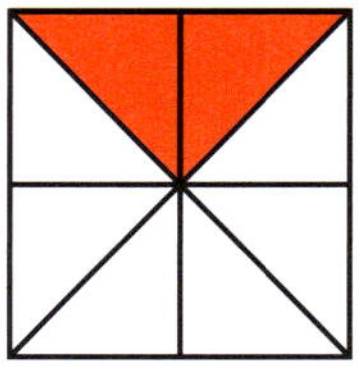

7. 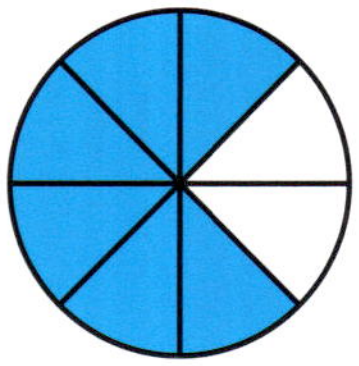

8. 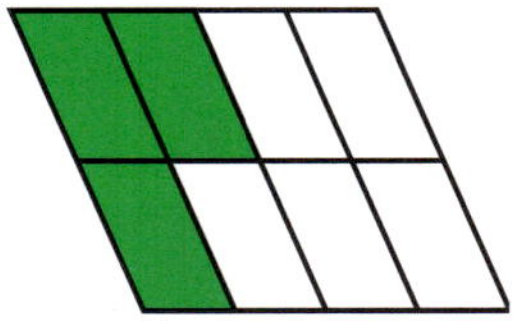

9. 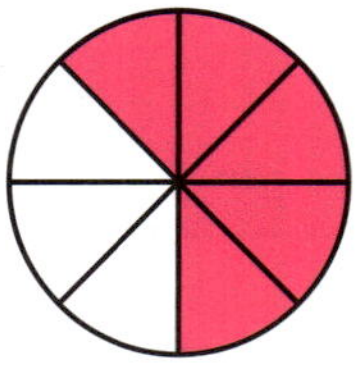

10. 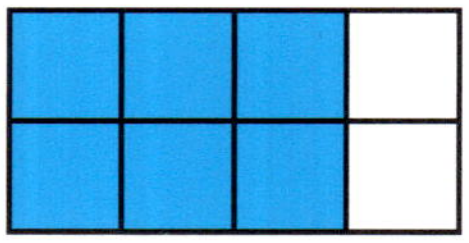

11. 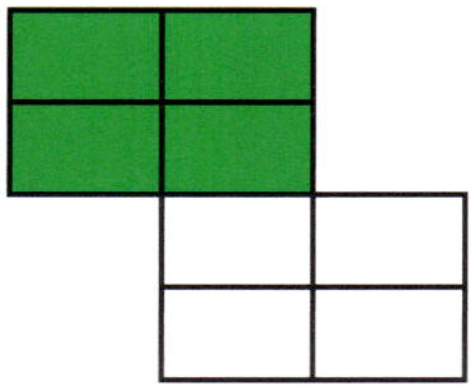

12. 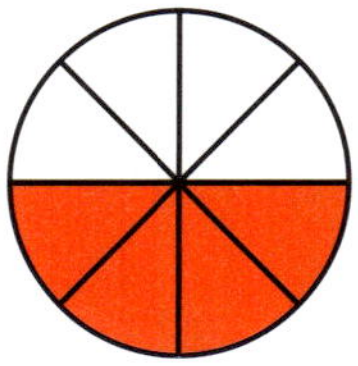

Twelfths

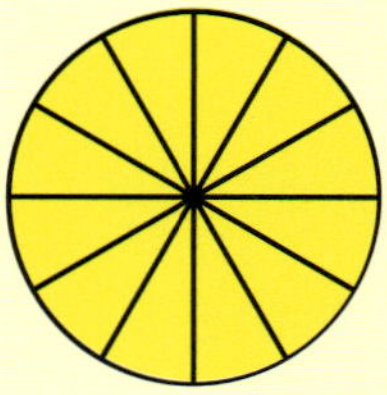

Count the number of parts into which this shape is divided.

What is each part called?

How do you write the fraction which represents each part?

Draw a strip 12 cm long and 1 cm wide.

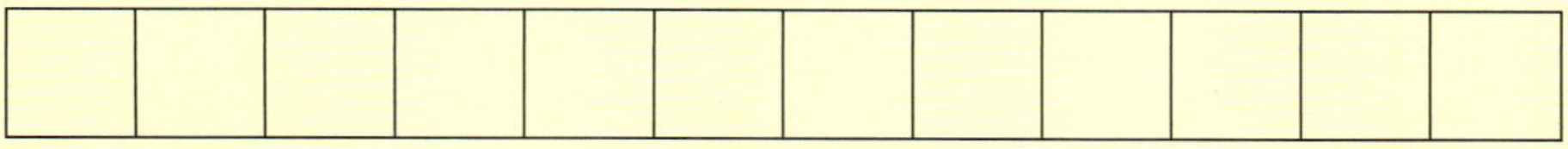

Mark off 1 cm lengths along the strip and complete the blocks.

How many blocks have you made?

What fraction of the whole does each block represent?

What fraction of each shape is shaded?

1. 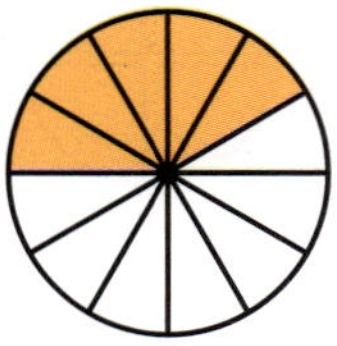
2. 
3. 
4. 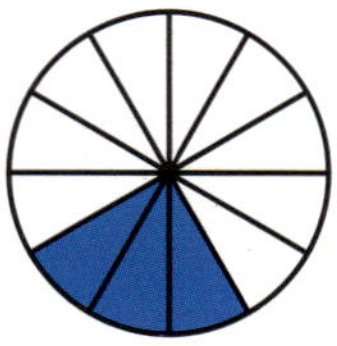
5. 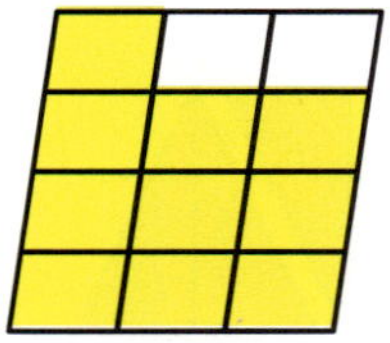
6. 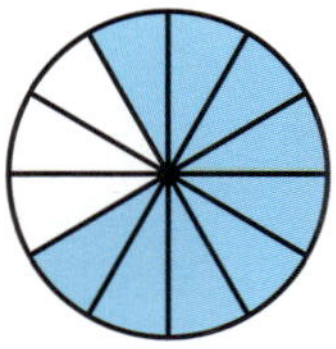
7. 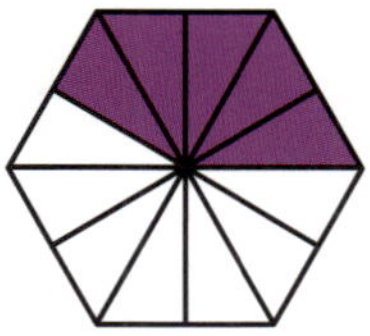
8. 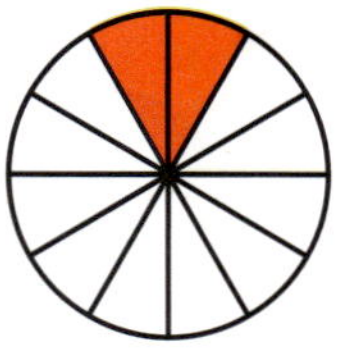
9. 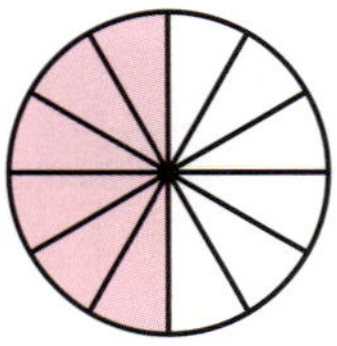
10. 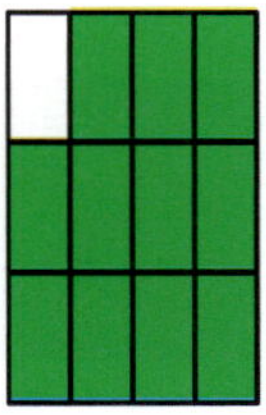
11. 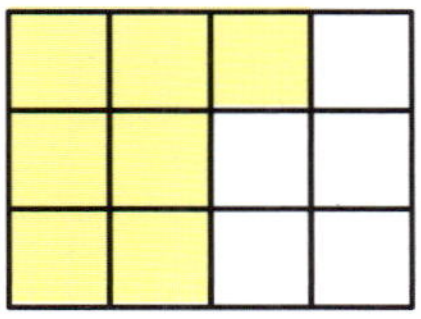
12. 

Improper fractions and mixed numbers

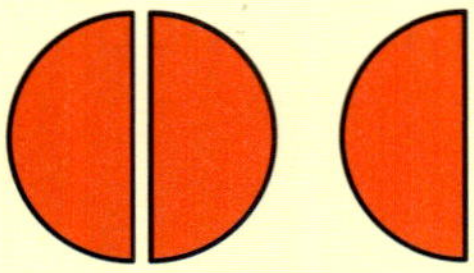

The picture on the left shows three halves.
We write three halves as $\frac{3}{2}$.
$\frac{3}{2}$ is called an **improper fraction**.

In an improper fraction the numerator is greater than the denominator.
A fraction in which the numerator is less than the denominator is called a **proper fraction**.

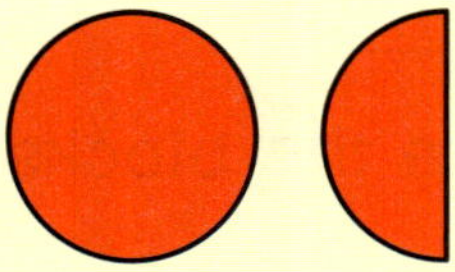

The three halves give us 1 whole and one half.
This is the number $1\frac{1}{2}$.
The number $1\frac{1}{2}$ is called a **mixed number**.

Here is another example of an improper fraction and the mixed number it gives.

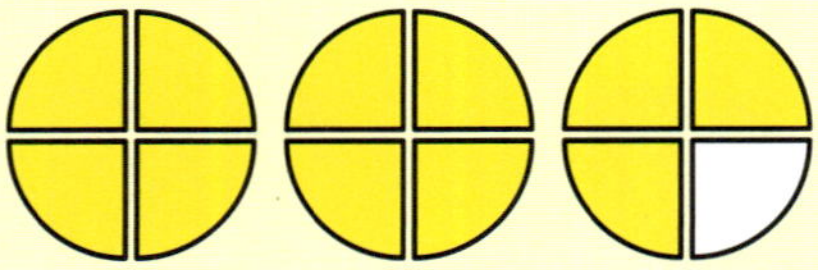

$\frac{11}{4} = 2\frac{3}{4}$

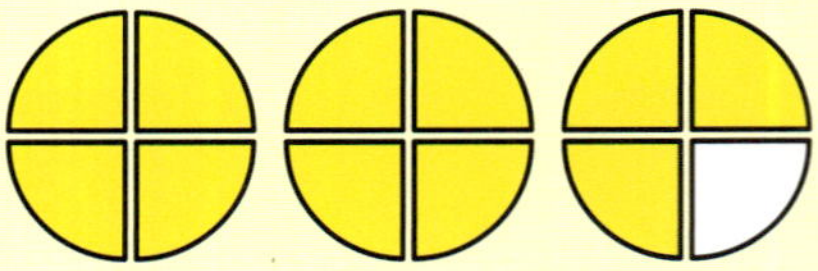

How much of these shapes is shaded? Write each answer as a mixed number and an improper fraction.

1.

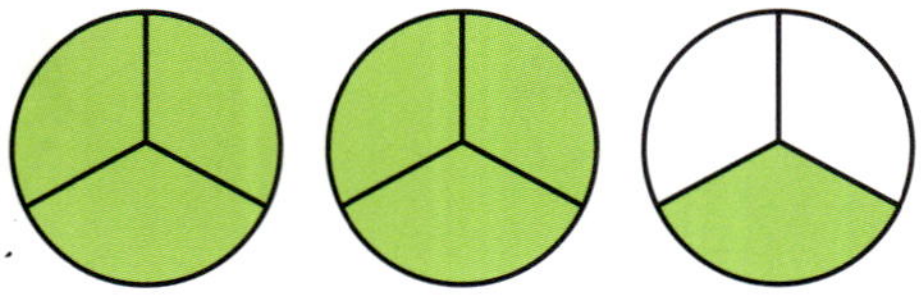

2.

3.

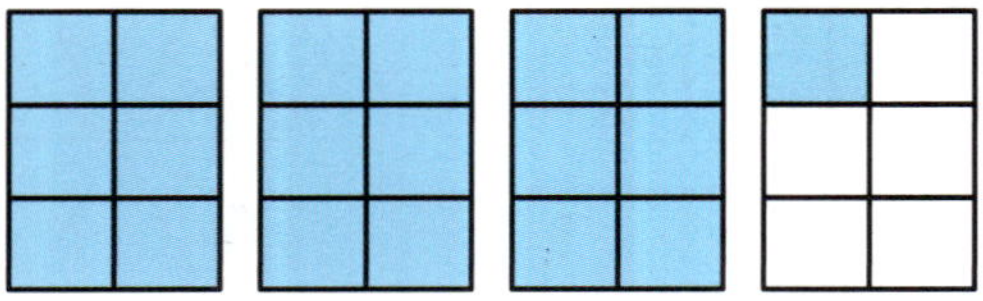

4.

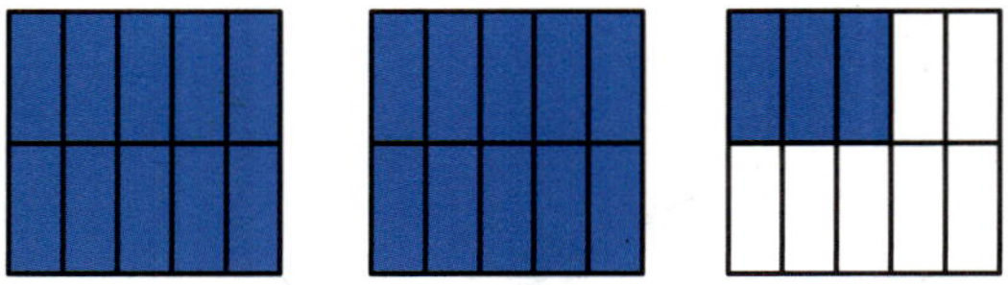

Converting improper fractions to mixed numbers

$\frac{7}{5} = \frac{5}{5} + \frac{2}{5}$ seven fifths is five fifths and two fifths

$\frac{7}{5} = 1 + \frac{2}{5}$

$= 1\frac{2}{5}$

Write mixed numbers for these improper fractions.

1. $\frac{7}{4}$	**2.** $\frac{8}{5}$	**3.** $\frac{5}{3}$	**4.** $\frac{7}{6}$	**5.** $\frac{11}{8}$
6. $\frac{8}{3}$	**7.** $\frac{11}{4}$	**8.** $\frac{13}{6}$	**9.** $\frac{19}{8}$	**10.** $\frac{13}{5}$
11. $\frac{13}{3}$	**12.** $\frac{18}{4}$	**13.** $\frac{20}{6}$	**14.** $\frac{25}{8}$	**15.** $\frac{23}{5}$

Converting mixed numbers to improper fractions

$3\frac{2}{5}$ = 3 and $\frac{2}{5}$

$3\frac{2}{5}$ is $\frac{5}{5}$ and $\frac{5}{5}$ and $\frac{5}{5}$ and $\frac{2}{5}$ or 3 wholes and $\frac{2}{5}$

$3\frac{2}{5}$ is $\frac{15}{5}$ and $\frac{2}{5}$

so $3\frac{2}{5} = \frac{17}{5}$

Write improper fractions for these mixed numbers.

1. $1\frac{5}{6}$	**2.** $1\frac{1}{3}$	**3.** $1\frac{3}{4}$	**4.** $1\frac{7}{8}$	**5.** $1\frac{3}{10}$
6. $2\frac{2}{3}$	**7.** $2\frac{1}{12}$	**8.** $1\frac{7}{10}$	**9.** $1\frac{5}{12}$	**10.** $2\frac{3}{8}$
11. $4\frac{1}{5}$	**12.** $3\frac{5}{8}$	**13.** $3\frac{1}{12}$	**14.** $2\frac{9}{10}$	**15.** $3\frac{5}{6}$
16. $2\frac{1}{3}$	**17.** $1\frac{7}{12}$	**18.** $3\frac{3}{4}$	**19.** $1\frac{3}{10}$	**20.** $2\frac{3}{4}$
21. $3\frac{1}{2}$	**22.** $4\frac{1}{4}$	**23.** $2\frac{3}{5}$	**24.** $3\frac{3}{5}$	**25.** $4\frac{1}{2}$

…problems

… out the answers to these word problems. Show all your working.

1. Four cakes were cut into quarters. Seven boys took 2 pieces each. How much was left?

2. Two large pizzas were cut into eighths and shared among a group of 13 girls. Each girl had one slice. How much was left?

3. The cricket eleven was to be given some large pies to share. Each player would receive $\frac{1}{4}$ of a pie. How many pies should be bought and how much would be left over?

4. Four children bought 6 buns and wanted to share them equally among themselves. How much would each get?

5. Three litres of water must be poured into 2 measuring cylinders, so that each cylinder has the same amount. How much water must be poured into each cylinder?

6. A chocolate bar is divided into 8 blocks. If 3 bars are shared equally among 4 boys, what fraction of a bar would each boy receive?

7. The baker needs 6 eggs for each $\frac{1}{2}$ kg of flour that he uses in a cake. How many eggs will he need if he uses 5 kg of flour?

Fractions on the number line

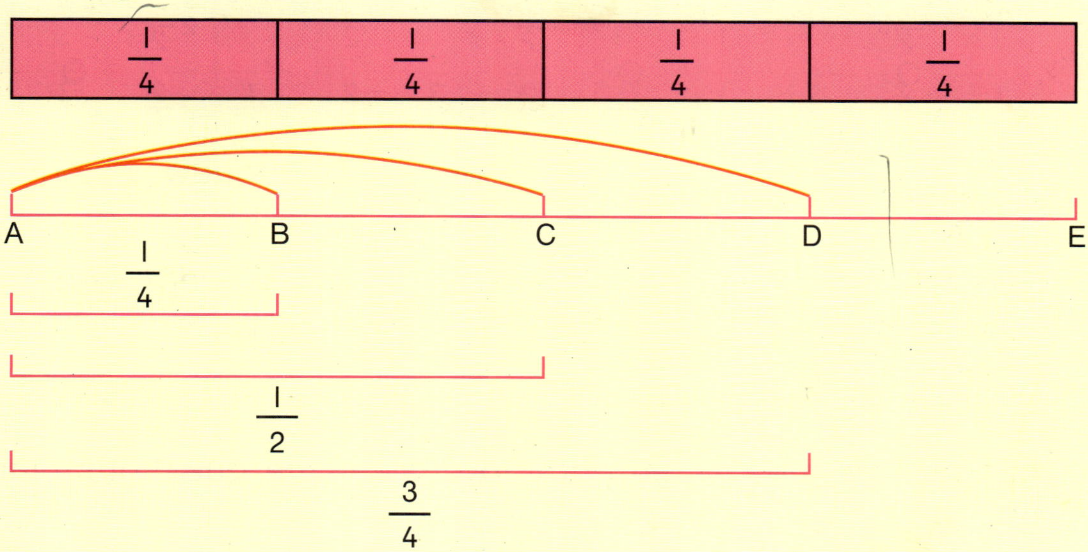

The red line is the exact length of the strip above.
To go from point A to point B on the line we must move $\frac{1}{4}$ of the length of the line.
To move from A to C we must move $\frac{1}{2}$ of the length and from A to D, $\frac{3}{4}$ of the length.

We can show $\frac{1}{4}$, $\frac{1}{2}$ and $\frac{3}{4}$ as numbers on a line.

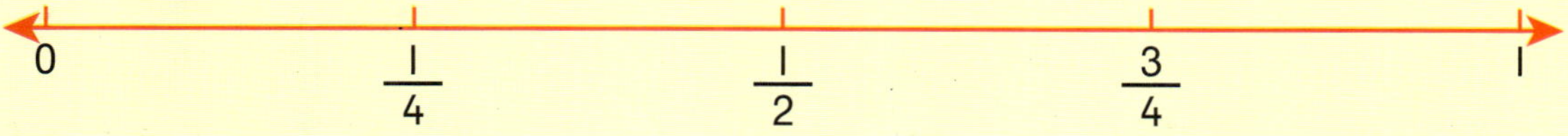

Write the numbers shown by the arrows on these lines.

1.

2.

3.

Mixed numbers on the number line

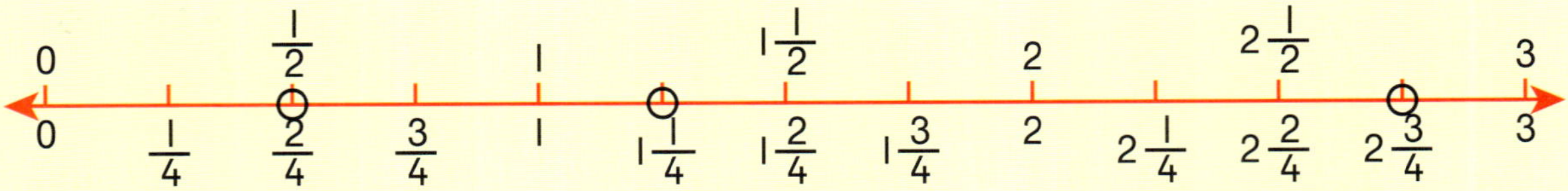

The number line can be extended beyond 1 to show mixed numbers.

The circles on the number line above show $\frac{1}{2}$, $1\frac{1}{4}$ and $2\frac{3}{4}$

You will also see from the number line above that

$1\frac{1}{4} = \frac{5}{4}$; $1\frac{1}{2} = \frac{3}{2}$; $1\frac{3}{4} = \frac{7}{4}$

Use the number lines to help you to answer the questions below.

Write the numbers shown by the arrows.

1.

2. Copy and complete:

(a) $2\frac{1}{2} = \frac{\square}{2}$ (b) $4\frac{1}{2} = \frac{\square}{2}$ (c) $5\frac{1}{2} = \frac{\square}{2}$

Write the numbers shown by the circles on the number lines below and complete the statements.

3.

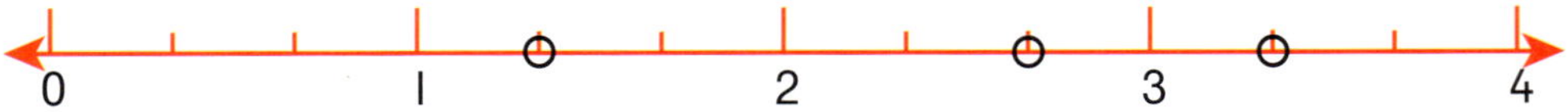

4. (a) $1\frac{2}{3} = \frac{\square}{3}$ (b) $2\frac{1}{3} = \frac{\square}{3}$ (c) $3\frac{2}{3} = \frac{\square}{3}$

5.

6. (a) $2\frac{3}{4} = \frac{\square}{4}$ (b) $3\frac{1}{4} = \frac{\square}{4}$ (c) $5\frac{1}{4} = \frac{\square}{4}$

7.

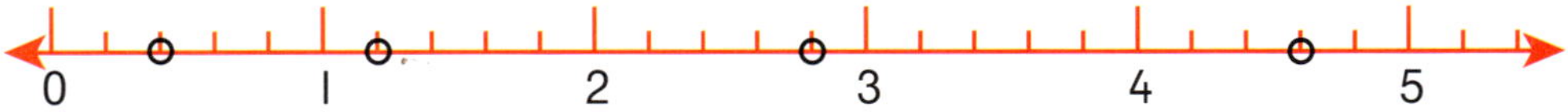

8. (a) $1\frac{3}{5} = \frac{\square}{5}$ (b) $2\frac{4}{5} = \frac{\square}{5}$ (c) $3\frac{2}{5} = \frac{\square}{5}$

Assessment 4

How much of these shapes is shaded? Write your answer as a mixed number and an improper fraction.

1. 

2. 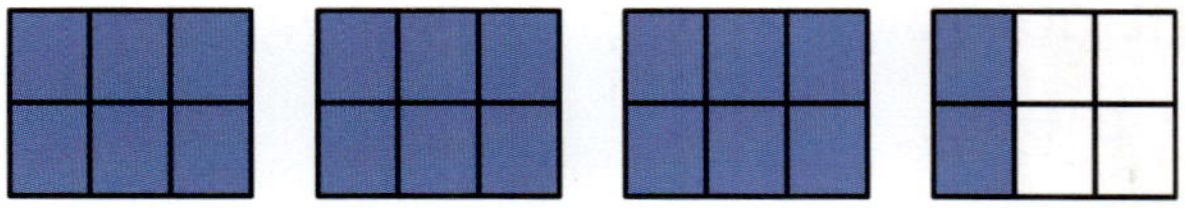

Write these mixed numbers as improper fractions.

3. $2\frac{1}{4}$ **4.** $3\frac{1}{3}$ **5.** $1\frac{3}{8}$ **6.** $1\frac{3}{5}$

Write these improper fractions as mixed numbers.

7. $1\frac{5}{4}$ **8.** $\frac{9}{2}$ **9.** $1\frac{7}{3}$ **10.** $2\frac{6}{5}$

What numbers are ringed on the number lines below?

11. 

12. 

13. 

14. Three pizzas were cut in quarters. Ten girls received one slice each. How much of a pizza was left?

8 Addition and subtraction of fractions

Thirds, sixths and twelfths

You will need: squared paper.

Glue a sheet of squared paper on to a piece of thin cardboard.
Draw three strips each having 12 squares,
Mark off one in twelfths, one in sixths, and the last in thirds.
Colour the strips in different colours.
Your strips should look like these.

Cut out all three strips.
Cut the sixths strip into its six parts and the thirds strip into three parts.
Match the pieces with the twelfths strip to find fractions which have the same value.

Copy and complete the statements below.

1. $\frac{1}{3} = \frac{\square}{6}$ **2.** $\frac{2}{3} = \frac{\square}{6}$ **3.** $\frac{1}{6} = \frac{\square}{12}$

4. $\frac{1}{3} = \frac{\square}{12}$ **5.** $\frac{2}{3} = \frac{\square}{12}$ **6.** $\frac{1}{2} = \frac{\square}{6}$

7. $\frac{1}{2} = \frac{\square}{12}$

We can use our strips to help us add some fractions.

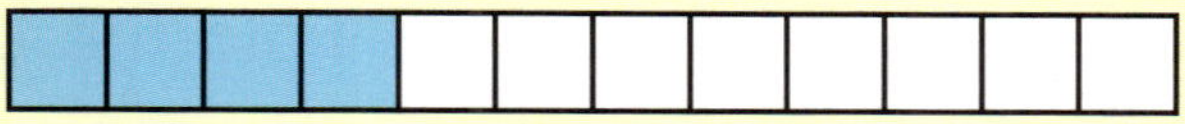

$\frac{1}{12} + \frac{3}{12} = \frac{4}{12}$

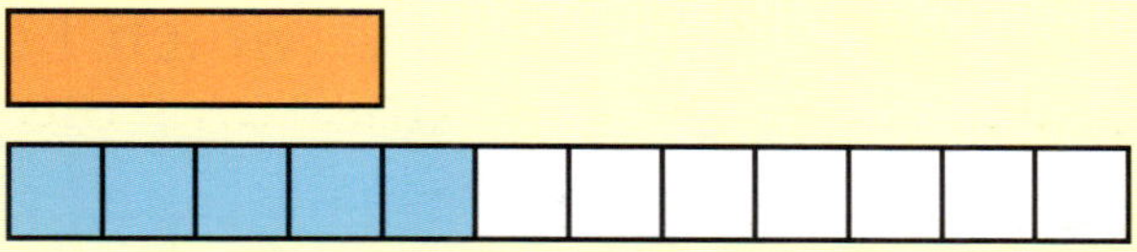

$\frac{1}{3} + \frac{1}{12} = \frac{5}{12}$

Copy and complete. Use your fraction strips to help you.

8. $\frac{1}{3} + \frac{2}{12}$ **9.** $\frac{2}{3} + \frac{1}{12}$ **10.** $\frac{1}{3} + \frac{5}{12}$ **11.** $\frac{2}{3} + \frac{1}{12}$

12. $\frac{2}{3} + \frac{3}{12}$ **13.** $\frac{2}{3} + \frac{2}{12}$ **14.** $\frac{5}{12} + \frac{3}{6}$ **15.** $\frac{1}{3} + \frac{1}{6}$

Thirds and ninths

Make a ninths strip just as you did for the other strips.

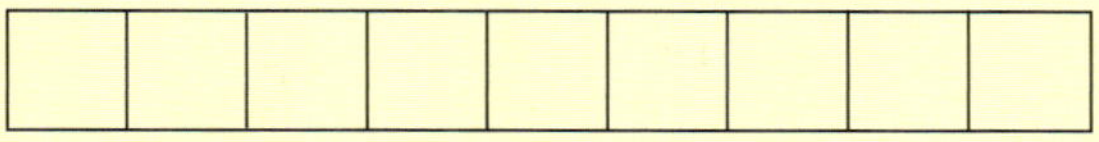

Match the thirds strip with this ninths strip to find fractions of the same value.

$\frac{1}{3} = \frac{\square}{9}$ $\frac{2}{3} = \frac{\square}{9}$

Copy and complete. Use your fraction strips to help you.

1. $\frac{1}{3} + \frac{1}{9}$ **2.** $\frac{1}{3} + \frac{2}{9}$ **3.** $\frac{1}{3} + \frac{3}{9}$ **4.** $\frac{1}{3} + \frac{4}{9}$

5. $\frac{1}{3} + \frac{5}{9}$ **6.** $\frac{2}{3} + \frac{1}{9}$ **7.** $\frac{2}{3} + \frac{2}{9}$ **8.** $\frac{2}{3} + \frac{3}{9}$

Halves, quarters and eighths

Cut out 3 circles like the ones below. Fold the circles to get the cutting lines. Cut one into halves, the second into quarters and the third into eighths. Fit the shapes together again. Match the cutouts to find the fractions which have the same value as those given below.

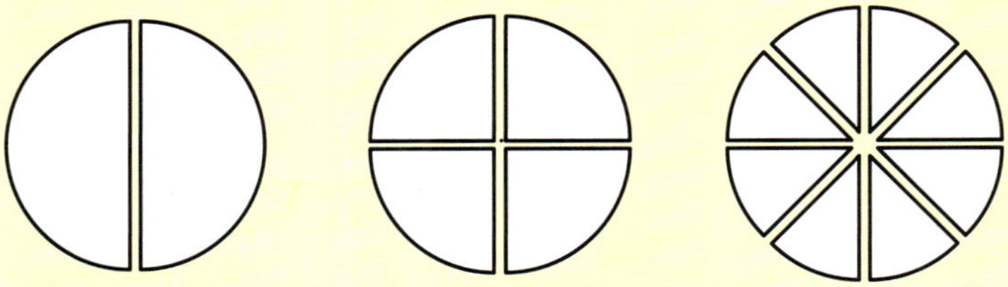

Copy and complete the statements below.

1. $\frac{1}{2} = \frac{\square}{4}$ **2.** $\frac{1}{2} = \frac{\square}{8}$ **3.** $\frac{1}{4} = \frac{\square}{8}$ **4.** $\frac{3}{4} = \frac{\square}{8}$

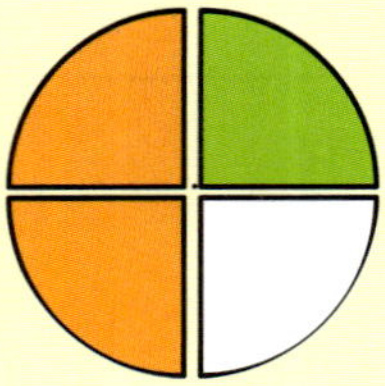

This diagram shows $\frac{1}{2} + \frac{1}{4} = \frac{3}{4}$

Use your cutouts to solve these problems. Copy and complete.

5. $\frac{1}{8} + \frac{1}{8}$ **6.** $\frac{1}{4} + \frac{1}{8}$ **7.** $\frac{1}{8} + \frac{3}{8}$ **8.** $\frac{1}{4} + \frac{1}{4}$

9. $\frac{1}{4} + \frac{3}{8}$ **10.** $\frac{1}{2} + \frac{3}{8}$ **11.** $\frac{1}{8} + \frac{5}{8}$ **12.** $\frac{1}{8} + \frac{1}{2}$

13. $\frac{1}{4} + \frac{5}{8}$ **14.** $\frac{1}{8} + \frac{5}{8}$ **15.** $\frac{1}{8} + \frac{3}{4}$ **16.** $\frac{1}{2} + \frac{1}{2}$

17. What is $\frac{1}{4} + \frac{1}{4} + \frac{1}{4} + \frac{1}{4}$?

18. What is $\frac{1}{8} + \frac{1}{8} + \frac{1}{8} + \frac{1}{8} + \frac{1}{8} + \frac{1}{8} + \frac{1}{8} + \frac{1}{8}$?

Equivalent fractions

Fractions which have the same value are called **equivalent fractions**.

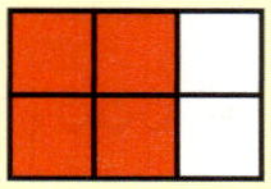

$\frac{2}{3} = \frac{4}{6}$

Complete these statements of equivalent fractions.

1. $\frac{2}{3} = \frac{\square}{6}$

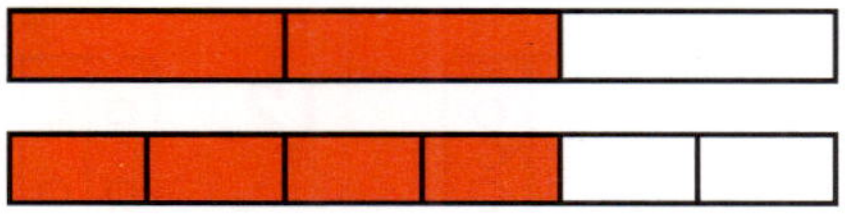

2. $\frac{3}{4} = \frac{\square}{8}$

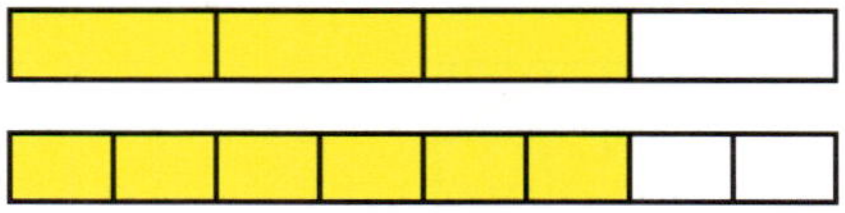

3. $\frac{5}{6} = \frac{\square}{12}$

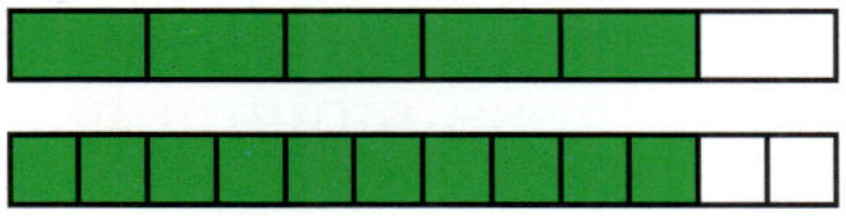

4. $\frac{3}{4} = \frac{\square}{12}$

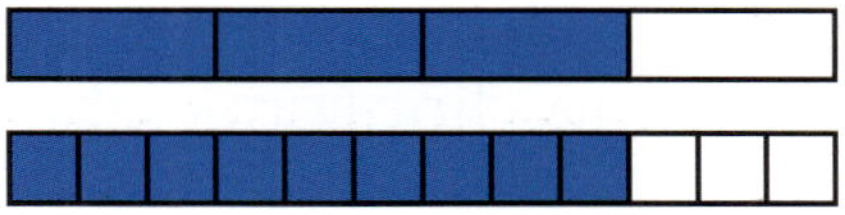

5. $\frac{1}{4} = \frac{\square}{8} = \frac{}{12}$

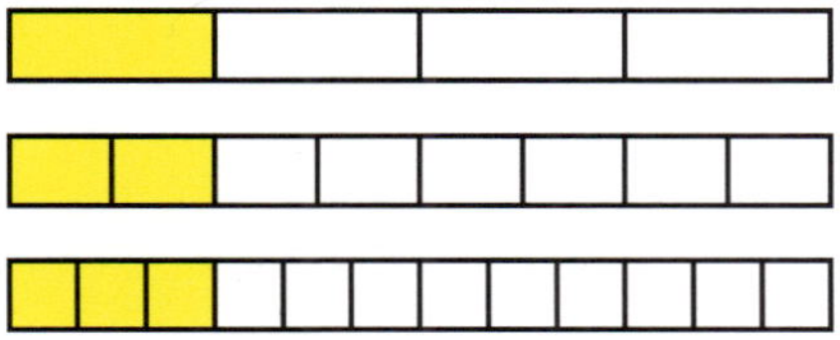

6. $\frac{1}{2} = \frac{\square}{6} = \frac{}{10}$

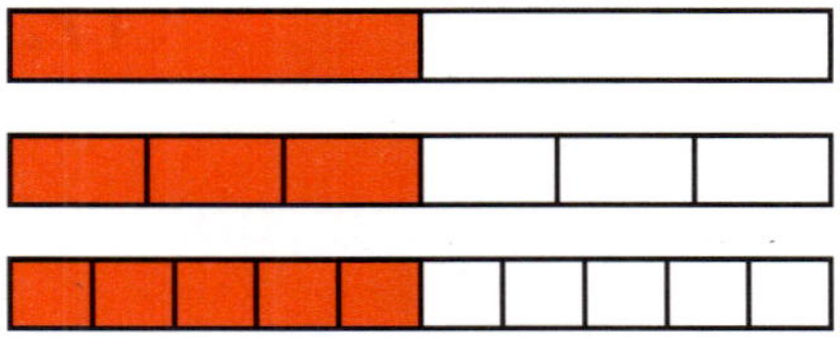

7. $\frac{1}{3} = \frac{\square}{12}$

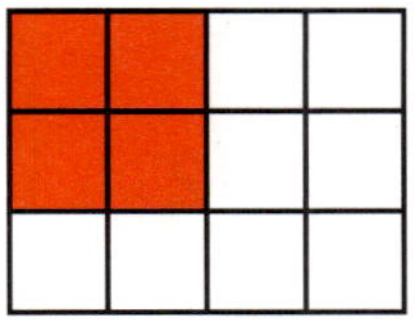

8. $\frac{1}{4} = \frac{\square}{12}$

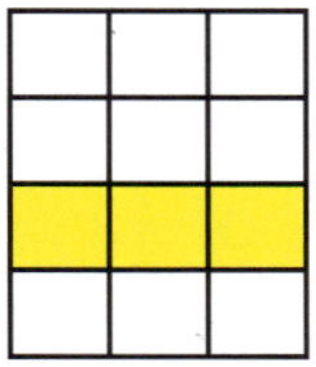

9. $\frac{1}{3} = \frac{\square}{9}$

Sets and equivalent fractions

Copy and complete the statement under each diagram.

1. 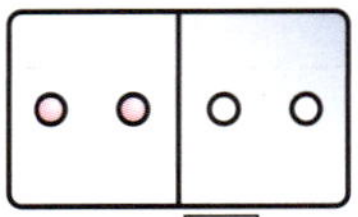

$\frac{1}{2} = \frac{\square}{4}$

2. 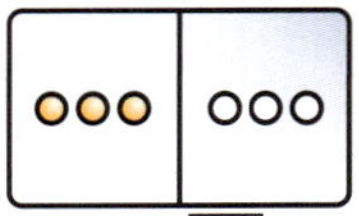

$\frac{1}{2} = \frac{\square}{6}$

3. 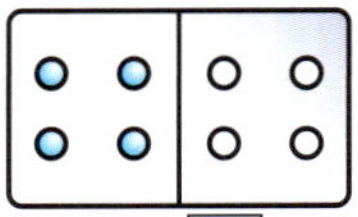

$\frac{1}{2} = \frac{\square}{8}$

4. 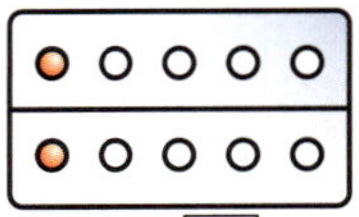

$\frac{1}{2} = \frac{\square}{10}$

5. 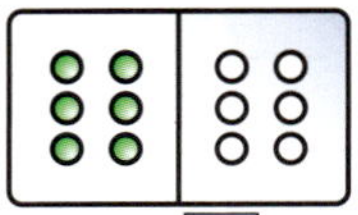

$\frac{1}{2} = \frac{\square}{12}$

6. 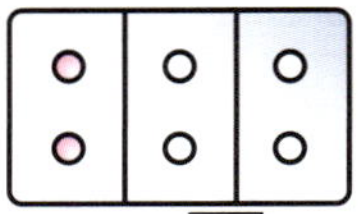

$\frac{1}{3} = \frac{\square}{6}$

7. 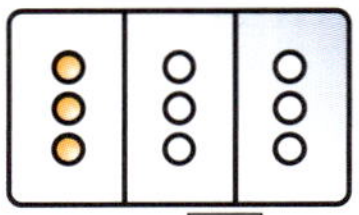

$\frac{1}{3} = \frac{\square}{9}$

8. 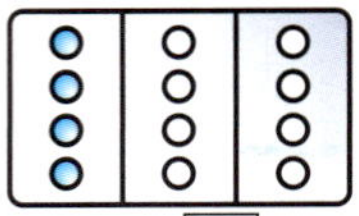

$\frac{1}{3} = \frac{\square}{12}$

9. 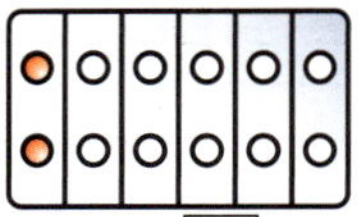

$\frac{1}{6} = \frac{\square}{12}$

10. 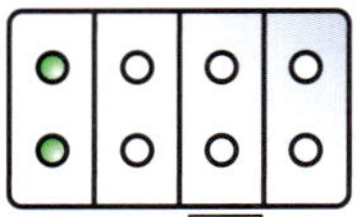

$\frac{1}{4} = \frac{\square}{8}$

11. 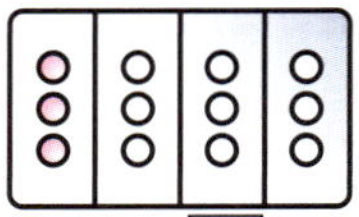

$\frac{1}{4} = \frac{\square}{12}$

12. 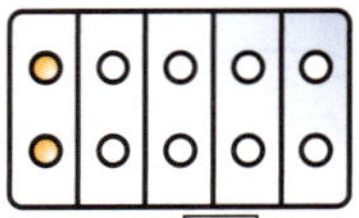

$\frac{1}{5} = \frac{\square}{10}$

Look at the diagrams above and complete these statements.

13. $\frac{2}{3} = \frac{\square}{6}$

14. $\frac{3}{4} = \frac{\square}{8}$

15. $\frac{2}{3} = \frac{\square}{9}$

16. $\frac{2}{3} = \frac{\square}{12}$

17. $\frac{5}{6} = \frac{\square}{12}$

Use the diagrams above to help you write answers to the following:

18. $\frac{1}{2}$ of 4

19. $\frac{1}{2}$ of 6

20. $\frac{1}{2}$ of 8

21. $\frac{1}{2}$ of 10

22. $\frac{1}{2}$ of 12

23. $\frac{1}{3}$ of 6

24. $\frac{1}{3}$ of 9

25. $\frac{1}{3}$ of 12

26. $\frac{1}{6}$ of 12

27. $\frac{1}{4}$ of 8

28. $\frac{1}{4}$ of 12

29. $\frac{1}{5}$ of 10

30. $\frac{2}{6}$ of 6

31. $\frac{3}{4}$ of 8

32. $\frac{5}{6}$ of 12

This fraction chart shows equivalent fractions.

For example $\frac{1}{2} = \frac{2}{4} = \frac{4}{8}$ ...

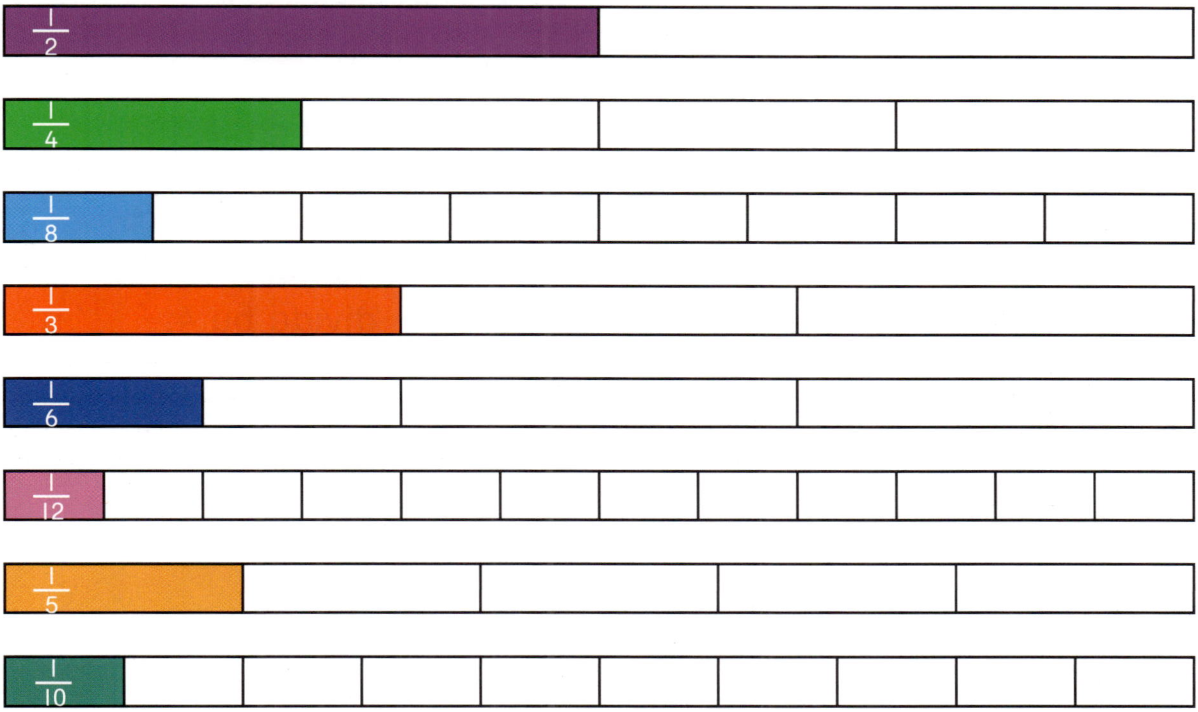

Use the fraction chart above to complete this table.

Fraction	Equivalent fractions	Fraction	Equivalent fractions
$\frac{1}{2}$	$\frac{2}{4}$ $\frac{4}{8}$ $\frac{3}{6}$ $\frac{6}{12}$ $\frac{5}{10}$	$\frac{5}{6}$	
$\frac{1}{4}$		$\frac{1}{5}$	
$\frac{3}{4}$		$\frac{2}{5}$	
$\frac{1}{3}$		$\frac{3}{5}$	
$\frac{2}{3}$		$\frac{4}{5}$	
$\frac{1}{6}$			

Fractional parts and division

16 is 2 sets of ☐	18 is 3 sets of ☐	20 is 4 sets of ☐
$16 \div 2 =$ ☐	$18 \div 3 =$ ☐	$20 \div 4 =$ ☐
$\frac{1}{2}$ of 16 = ☐	$\frac{1}{3}$ of 18 = ☐	$\frac{1}{4}$ of 20 = ☐
To find $\frac{1}{2}$ of a number we must divide by 2.	To find $\frac{1}{3}$ of a number we must divide by 3.	To find $\frac{1}{4}$ of a number we must divide by 4.

Copy and complete these statements.

1. $\frac{1}{2}$ of 36 = 36 ÷ 2 = ☐
2. $\frac{1}{3}$ of 36 = ☐ ÷ ☐ = ☐
3. $\frac{1}{4}$ of 48 = ☐ ÷ ☐ = ☐

4. $6\overline{)96}$ $\frac{1}{6}$ of 96 =
5. $5\overline{)80}$ $\frac{1}{5}$ of 80 =
6. $3\overline{)84}$ $\frac{1}{3}$ of 84 =
7. $4\overline{)80}$ $\frac{1}{4}$ of 80 =

Work out the answers to the following. Draw diagrams to help if you need to.

8. $\frac{3}{4}$ of 32
9. $\frac{2}{3}$ of 30
10. $\frac{3}{5}$ of 40
11. $\frac{2}{3}$ of 36
12. $\frac{3}{4}$ of 36
13. $\frac{2}{5}$ of 45
14. $\frac{4}{5}$ of 45
15. $\frac{2}{3}$ of 33
16. $\frac{3}{5}$ of 50
17. $\frac{2}{3}$ of 24
18. $\frac{4}{5}$ of 40
19. $\frac{3}{5}$ of 45

Word problems

Look at this problem. Complete the statements below.

Lum had 50 marbles. He gave $\frac{1}{5}$ to Bal.
How many did Lum have left?

Lum 50 marbles

Bal $\frac{1}{5}$ of 50 = ☐ marbles

Remainder = 50 − ☐

= ☐ marbles

Work out the answers to these word problems. Show all your working.

1. In a bag of 60 mangoes $\frac{1}{4}$ were spoilt. How many good mangoes were there?

2. Joan had 24 flowers. She gave away $\frac{2}{3}$ to her friends. How many did she give away?

3. I had 75 cents. I gave $\frac{1}{5}$ to Larry and $\frac{1}{3}$ to Kurt.

(a) How much did Larry get?
(b) How much did Kurt get?
(c) How much did I have left?

4. The class teacher received 40 school lunches. She gave out $\frac{5}{8}$ of this number to all the children present in the class. How many children had lunches?

5. Two thirds of a class of 36 children went on a school outing. How many children did not go?

Addition of fractions

These diagrams show addition of fractions which have the same denominators.

a) 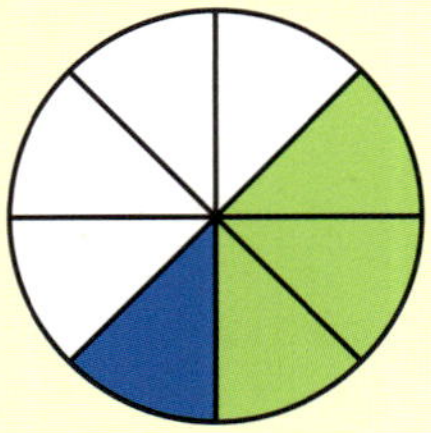

b) 

c) 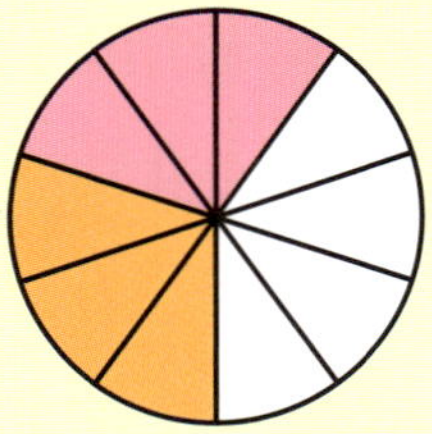

Diagram (a) shows the addition $\frac{1}{8} + \frac{3}{8}$. What is the result?

We can write $\frac{1}{8} + \frac{3}{8} = \frac{4}{8}$ or $\frac{1}{8} + \frac{3}{8} = \frac{1}{2}$

Write the addition sentences for diagrams (b) and (c).

Can you find a rule for adding fractions with the same denominators? Here is a clue.

Look at the numerators!

Copy and complete.

1. $\frac{1}{4} + \frac{1}{4}$ **2.** $\frac{1}{8} + \frac{5}{8}$ **3.** $\frac{1}{3} + \frac{1}{3}$ **4.** $\frac{1}{5} + \frac{1}{5}$

5. $\frac{1}{5} + \frac{2}{5}$ **6.** $\frac{1}{5} + \frac{3}{5}$ **7.** $\frac{1}{6} + \frac{1}{6}$ **8.** $\frac{1}{9} + \frac{2}{9}$

9. $\frac{1}{9} + \frac{4}{9}$ **10.** $\frac{1}{9} + \frac{5}{9}$ **11.** $\frac{1}{9} + \frac{7}{9}$ **12.** $\frac{1}{10} + \frac{3}{10}$

13. $\frac{1}{10} + \frac{7}{10}$ **14.** $\frac{1}{12} + \frac{5}{12}$ **15.** $\frac{1}{12} + \frac{7}{12}$ **16.** $\frac{1}{3} + \frac{2}{3}$

17. $\frac{1}{5} + \frac{4}{5}$ **18.** $\frac{1}{4} + \frac{3}{4}$ **19.** $\frac{3}{10} + \frac{7}{10}$ **20.** $\frac{5}{12} + \frac{7}{12}$

21. $\frac{3}{8} + \frac{5}{8}$ **22.** $\frac{2}{6} + \frac{3}{6}$ **23.** $\frac{3}{12} + \frac{4}{12}$ **24.** $\frac{3}{10} + \frac{5}{10}$

Addition of fractions with different denominators

Here is a problem.

Ravi ate $\frac{1}{4}$ of a pie for lunch. He wanted more of the pie for dinner. There was only $\frac{3}{8}$ left and Ravi's mother gave it to him. How much of the whole pie did Ravi eat?

The picture on the right gives us the answer.

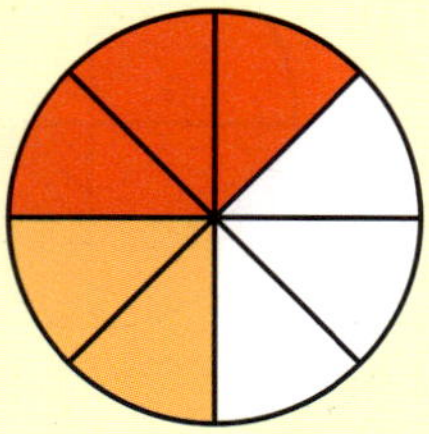

Ravi ate $\frac{1}{4} + \frac{3}{8} = \frac{5}{8}$.

The picture gives us a clue for adding fractions with different denominators.

We can add $\frac{1}{4} + \frac{3}{8}$ if we change $\frac{1}{4}$ to $\frac{2}{8}$ and then add.

Example: What is $\frac{1}{5} + \frac{3}{10}$?

Here we must add in tenths. We can see from the equivalent fractions chart on page 85 that

$$\frac{1}{5} = \frac{2}{10}$$

$$\frac{1}{5} + \frac{3}{10} = \frac{2}{10} + \frac{3}{10} = \frac{5}{10} \text{ or } \frac{1}{2}$$

Copy and complete. Use the equivalent fraction chart on page 85 to help you.

1. $\frac{1}{2} + \frac{1}{4}$ **2.** $\frac{1}{2} + \frac{1}{8}$ **3.** $\frac{1}{2} + \frac{3}{8}$ **4.** $\frac{1}{4} + \frac{1}{8}$

5. $\frac{1}{4} + \frac{3}{8}$ **6.** $\frac{1}{4} + \frac{5}{8}$ **7.** $\frac{1}{3} + \frac{1}{6}$ **8.** $\frac{2}{3} + \frac{1}{6}$

9. $\frac{1}{3} + \frac{1}{12}$ **10.** $\frac{1}{3} + \frac{5}{12}$ **11.** $\frac{1}{4} + \frac{5}{12}$ **12.** $\frac{1}{4} + \frac{7}{12}$

13. $\frac{1}{3} + \frac{7}{12}$ **14.** $\frac{1}{2} + \frac{5}{12}$ **15.** $\frac{1}{6} + \frac{1}{12}$ **16.** $\frac{1}{6} + \frac{5}{12}$

17. $\frac{1}{5} + \frac{3}{10}$ **18.** $\frac{1}{5} + \frac{7}{10}$ **19.** $\frac{2}{5} + \frac{3}{10}$ **20.** $\frac{1}{2} + \frac{3}{10}$

Subtraction of fractions

The diagrams show three subtraction problems.
The shaded part of the shape is the fraction we start with.
The part crossed out is the fraction we want to take away.

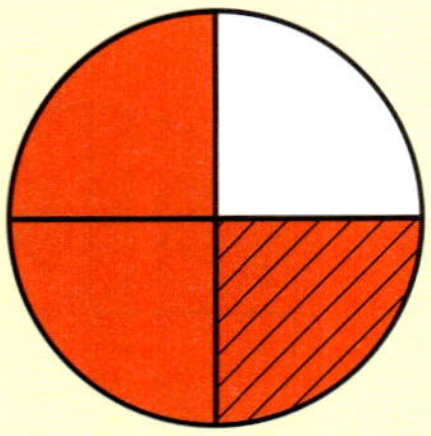

$\frac{3}{4} - \frac{1}{4} = \frac{2}{4}$ or $\frac{1}{2}$

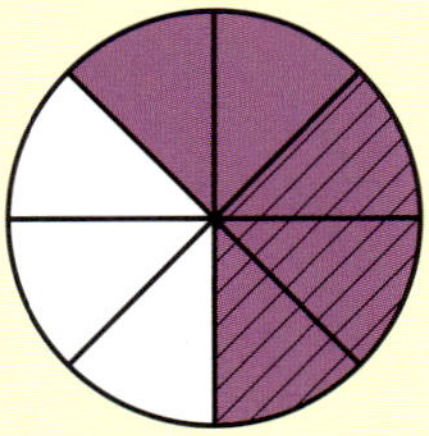

$\frac{5}{8} - \frac{3}{8} = \frac{2}{8}$ or $\frac{1}{4}$

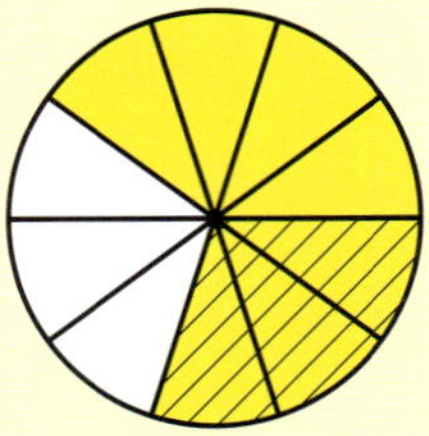

$\frac{7}{10} - \frac{3}{10} = \frac{4}{10}$ or $\frac{2}{5}$

What is the rule for subtracting fractions with the same denominator?

Copy and complete.

1. $\frac{3}{4} - \frac{1}{4}$ **2.** $\frac{7}{8} - \frac{5}{8}$ **3.** $\frac{7}{8} - \frac{3}{8}$ **4.** $\frac{7}{8} - \frac{1}{8}$

5. $\frac{5}{6} - \frac{1}{6}$ **6.** $\frac{9}{10} - \frac{7}{10}$ **7.** $\frac{9}{10} - \frac{3}{10}$ **8.** $\frac{9}{10} - \frac{1}{10}$

9. $\frac{7}{10} - \frac{3}{10}$ **10.** $\frac{7}{10} - \frac{1}{10}$ **11.** $\frac{11}{12} - \frac{7}{12}$ **12.** $\frac{11}{12} - \frac{5}{12}$

13. $1 - \frac{5}{12}$ **14.** $1 - \frac{3}{10}$ **15.** $1 - \frac{5}{6}$ **16.** $1 - \frac{2}{5}$

Copy and complete. Use the equivalent fraction chart on page 85 to help you.

17. $\frac{3}{4} - \frac{3}{8}$ **18.** $\frac{4}{5} - \frac{3}{10}$ **19.** $\frac{3}{4} - \frac{1}{12}$ **20.** $\frac{3}{5} - \frac{1}{10}$

21. $\frac{1}{2} - \frac{3}{10}$ **22.** $\frac{2}{3} - \frac{1}{6}$ **23.** $\frac{5}{6} - \frac{1}{3}$ **24.** $\frac{1}{2} - \frac{1}{6}$

25. $\frac{3}{4} - \frac{7}{12}$ **26.** $\frac{5}{6} - \frac{2}{3}$ **27.** $\frac{4}{5} - \frac{1}{10}$ **28.** $\frac{3}{4} - \frac{5}{12}$

29. $\frac{4}{5} - \frac{7}{10}$ **30.** $\frac{1}{2} - \frac{1}{12}$ **31.** $\frac{2}{3} - \frac{1}{12}$ **32.** $\frac{1}{2} - \frac{1}{10}$

Addition and subtraction of fractions with different denominators

Add $\frac{1}{2}$ and $\frac{1}{3}$

First rewrite the fractions with a common denominator $\frac{1}{2} = \frac{3}{6}$ and $\frac{1}{3} = \frac{2}{6}$ [Use the equivalent fractions chart on page 85.]

Therefore $\frac{1}{2} + \frac{1}{3} = \frac{3}{6} + \frac{2}{6}$

$= \frac{5}{6}$

Here is a tip when choosing the common denominator.
Multiples of 2 are 2, 4, 6, 8, 10, 12, and so on.
Multiples of 3 are 3, 6, 9, 12 and so on.
We choose the smallest multiple common to 2 and 3.

Copy and complete.

1. $\frac{1}{2} + \frac{2}{3}$ **2.** $\frac{1}{3} + \frac{1}{4}$ **3.** $\frac{1}{3} + \frac{3}{4}$ **4.** $\frac{2}{3} + \frac{1}{4}$

5. $\frac{2}{3} + \frac{3}{4}$ **6.** $\frac{1}{4} + \frac{1}{6}$ **7.** $\frac{1}{2} + \frac{1}{5}$ **8.** $\frac{1}{2} + \frac{2}{5}$

9. $\frac{1}{2} + \frac{3}{5}$ **10.** $\frac{1}{2} + \frac{4}{5}$ **11.** $\frac{1}{6} + \frac{1}{4}$ **12.** $\frac{1}{6} + \frac{3}{4}$

Solve $\frac{2}{3} - \frac{1}{4}$

Multiples of 3 are 3, 6, 9, 12 and so on
Multiples of 4 are 4, 8, 12, ...

Rewrite $\frac{2}{3}$ and $\frac{1}{4}$ as twelfths

$\frac{2}{3} = \frac{8}{12}$ and $\frac{1}{4} = \frac{3}{12}$

Therefore $\frac{2}{3} - \frac{1}{4} = \frac{8}{12} - \frac{3}{12}$

$= \frac{5}{12}$

Copy and complete.

13. $\frac{2}{3} - \frac{1}{2}$ **14.** $\frac{1}{2} - \frac{1}{3}$ **15.** $\frac{3}{4} - \frac{1}{3}$ **16.** $\frac{3}{4} - \frac{2}{3}$

17. $\frac{4}{5} - \frac{1}{2}$ **18.** $\frac{5}{6} - \frac{1}{4}$ **19.** $\frac{5}{6} - \frac{3}{4}$ **20.** $\frac{2}{3} - \frac{1}{6}$

9 Decimals

Tenths and decimals

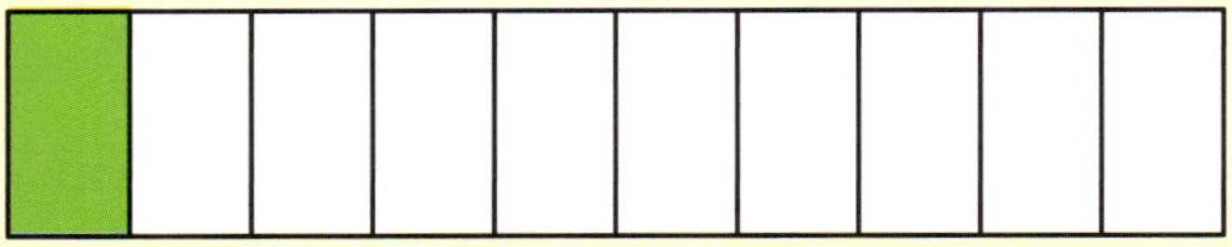

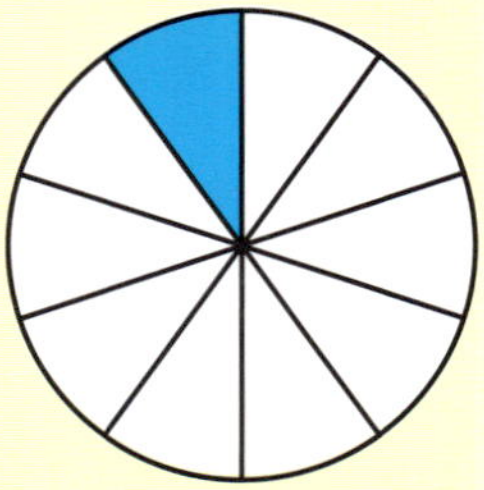

The shapes above are divided into tenths.
Each part or fraction is one tenth which is written $\frac{1}{10}$

Another way of writing $\frac{1}{10}$ is ·1 or 0·1
The fraction $\frac{2}{10}$ is written as ·2 or 0·2; $\frac{3}{10}$ as ·3 or 0·3

·1 or 0·1 and ·2 or 0·2 are called **decimal numbers**.
We read ·1 as point one and 0·2 as zero point 2

For each pair of shapes below write the proper fraction and decimal number to show what parts are shaded.

1.

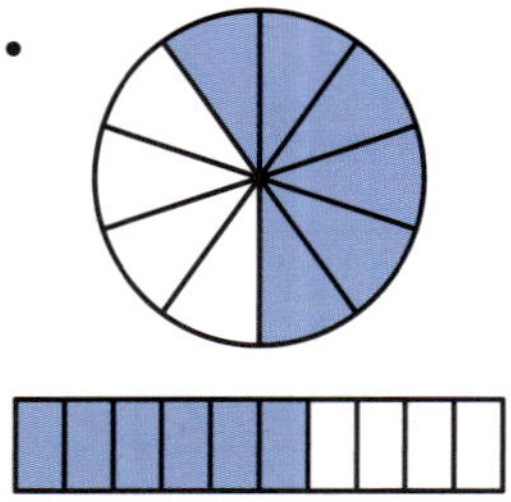

2.

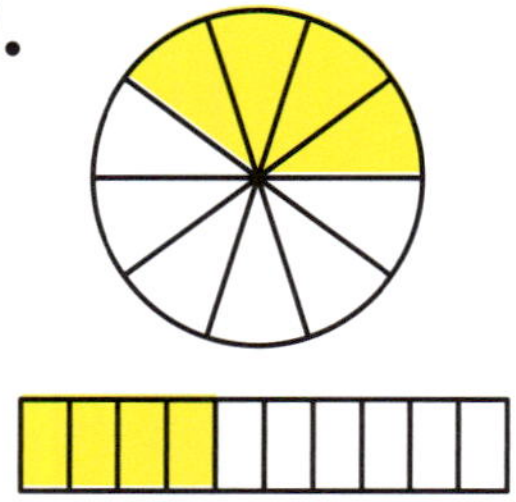

3.

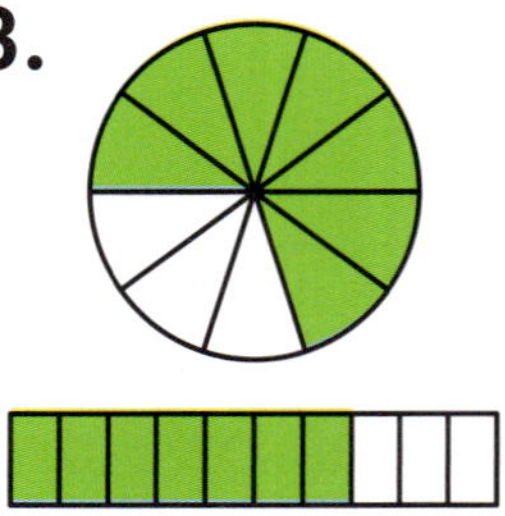

4.

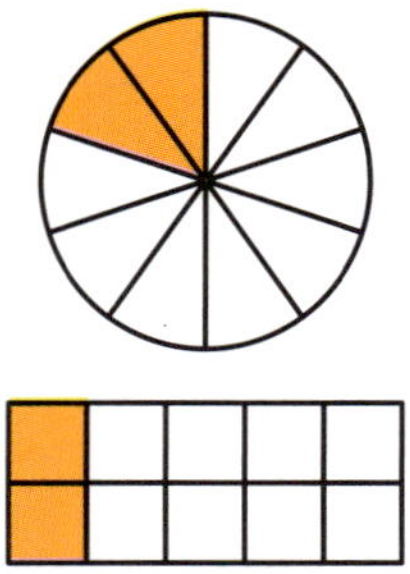

5.

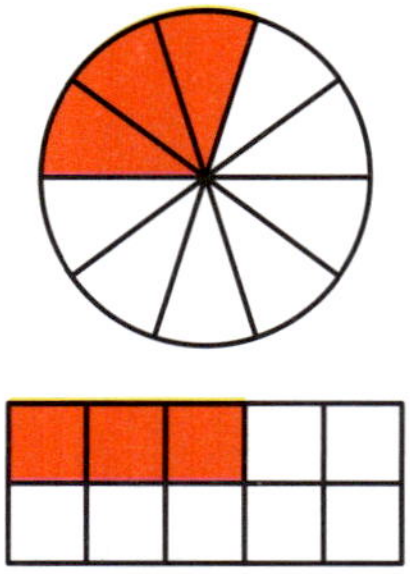

6.

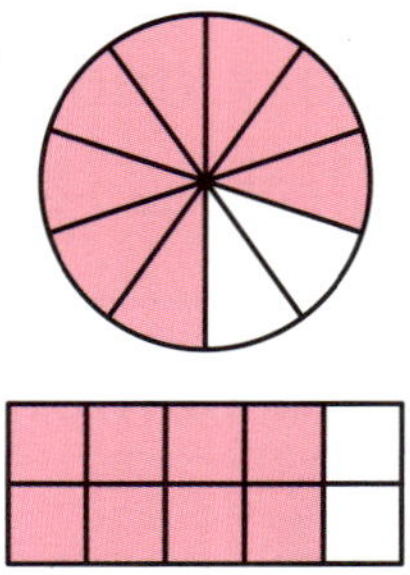

Tenths on the number line

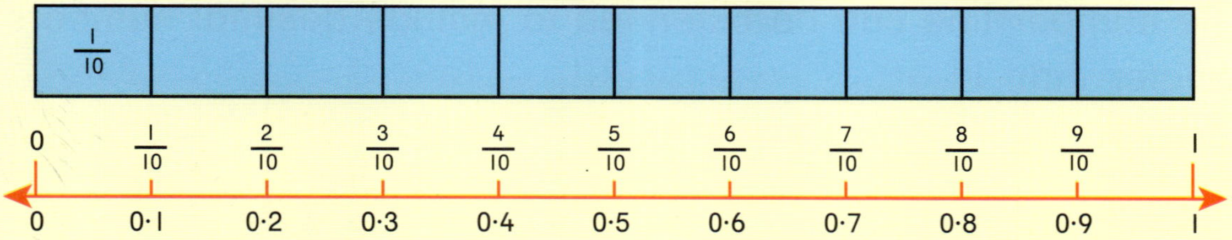

The 0 to 1 number line above is the exact length of the strip which has been divided into tenths.
We can therefore mark off this number line in tenths to match the division of the strip.

Copy and complete the problems below. Give your answers as a fraction and then re-write the problem using decimal numbers.

$\frac{1}{10} + \frac{1}{10} = \frac{2}{10}$ $\qquad$ $0{\cdot}1 + 0{\cdot}1 = 0{\cdot}2$

1. $\frac{1}{10} + \frac{8}{10}$ **2.** $\frac{2}{10} + \frac{7}{10}$ **3.** $\frac{3}{10} + \frac{5}{10}$ **4.** $\frac{2}{10} + \frac{4}{10}$

5. $\frac{3}{10} + \frac{2}{10}$ **6.** $\frac{1}{10} + \frac{6}{10}$ **7.** $\frac{5}{10} + \frac{4}{10}$ **8.** $\frac{1}{10} + \frac{7}{10}$

9. $\frac{6}{10} + \frac{3}{10}$ **10.** $\frac{2}{10} + \frac{5}{10}$ **11.** $\frac{4}{10} + \frac{4}{10}$ **12.** $\frac{5}{10} + \frac{4}{10}$

13. $\frac{3}{10} + \frac{1}{10}$ **14.** $\frac{5}{10} + \frac{1}{10}$ **15.** $\frac{2}{10} + \frac{6}{10}$ **16.** $\frac{4}{10} + \frac{1}{10}$

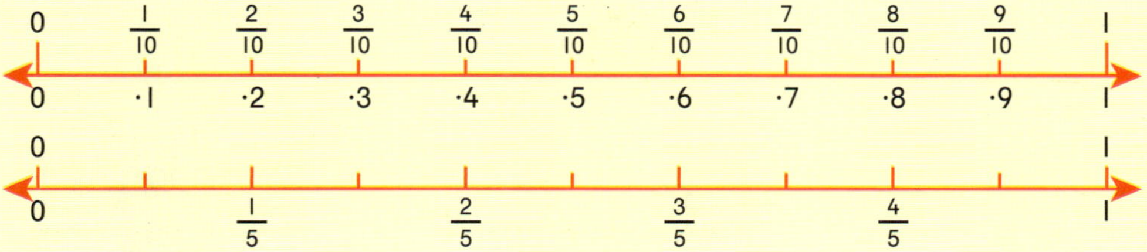

Use the number lines to help you write the decimal numbers for:

17. $\frac{2}{5}$ **18.** $\frac{3}{5}$ **19.** $\frac{4}{5}$ **20.** $\frac{1}{2}$

Example $\frac{2}{5} = 2 \div 5$
$= 0{\cdot}4$

$5\,\overline{)\,2{\cdot}0}$ = 0·4
-0
$2{\cdot}0$

Extending the number line for decimals

The number line can be extended to include decimal numbers greater than 1.

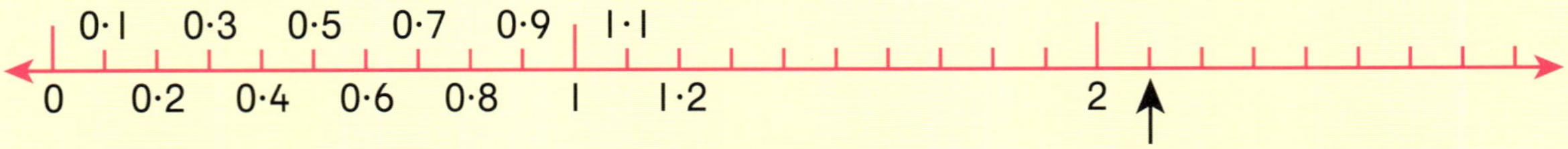

Draw a number line like the one above.
Count on from 1·1, 1·2... until you get to 2.
Write the numbers on the line as you call them out.
What number is shown by the arrow?
What numbers between 0 and 1 shown on the number line are greater than $\frac{1}{2}$?
What numbers between 1 and 2 are less than $1\frac{1}{2}$?

Write down the decimal numbers shown by the arrows.

1. 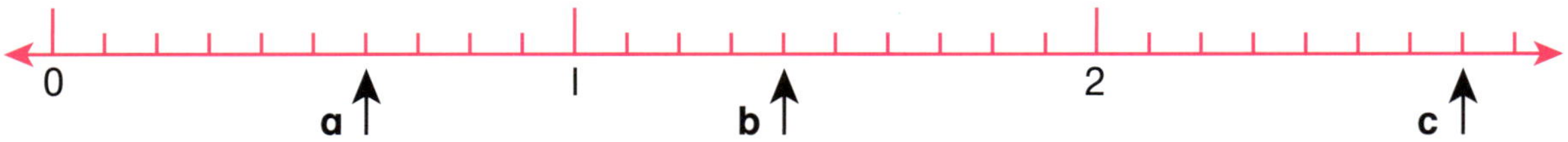

2. 

3. 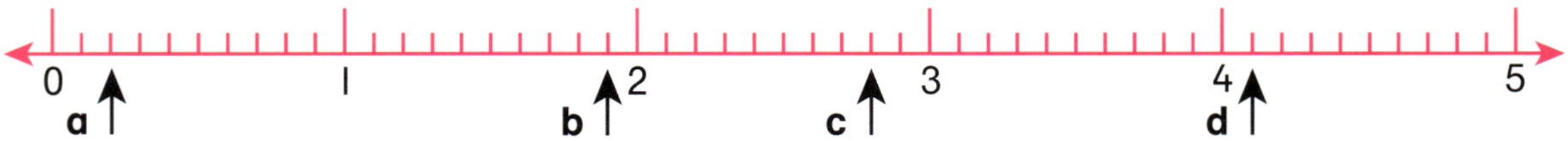

Decimal numbers with blocks and rods

A decimal number is made up of two parts: the whole number, and the decimal or fraction part.
The zero we write in 0·1 and 0·2 is used for decimal numbers that are between 0 and 1.

Make a rod of 10 blocks; this is 1 whole.
Each block is $\frac{1}{10}$ of the rod.

The picture on the right shows $1\frac{4}{10}$ or 1·4

1 ·4

This picture shows 0·5

0·5

Look at these groups of rods. What decimal numbers do they show?

1. 

2. 

3. 

4. 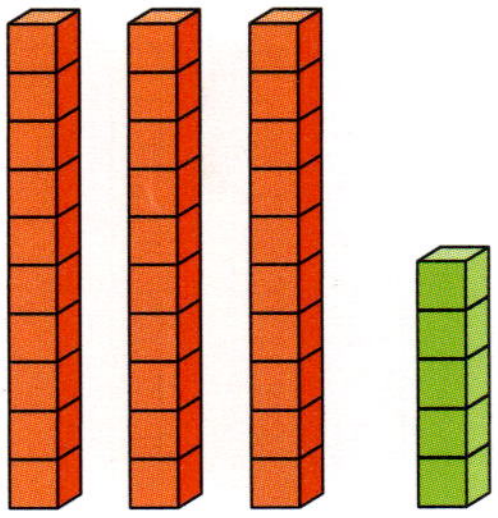

5. 

6. 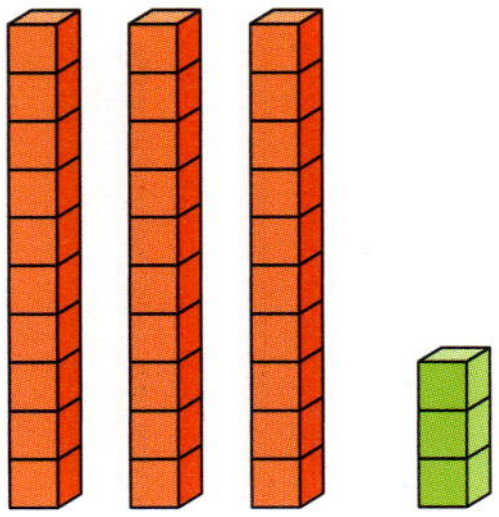

7.

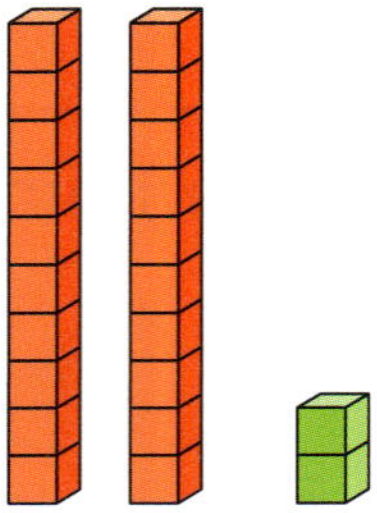

8.

9.

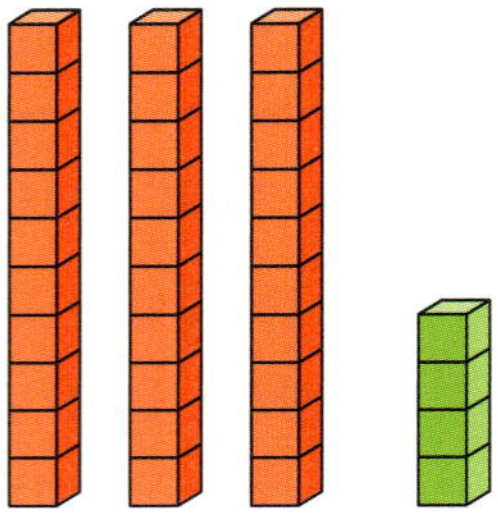

10.

11.

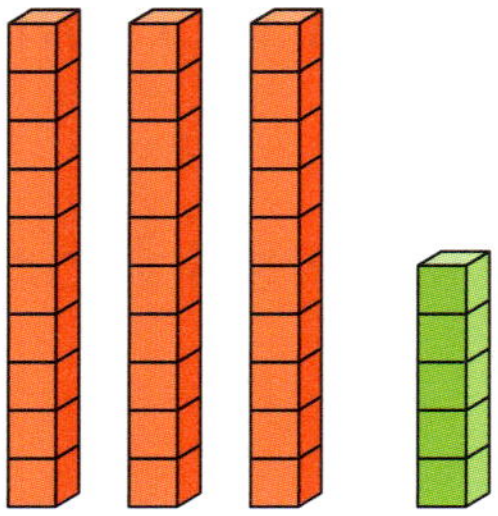

12.

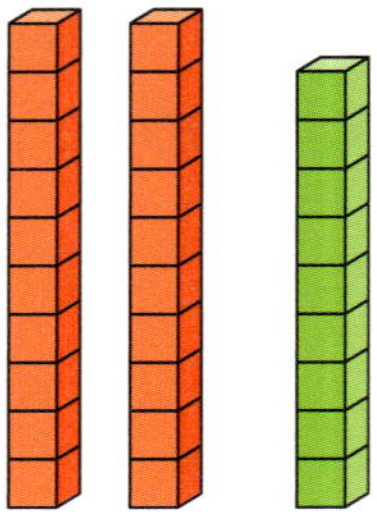

13.

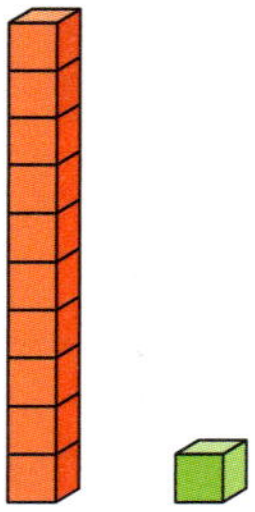

14.

15.

16.

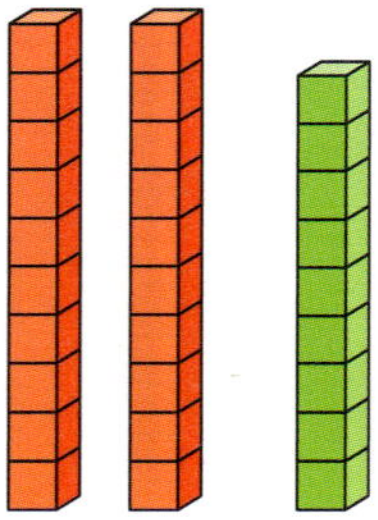

17.

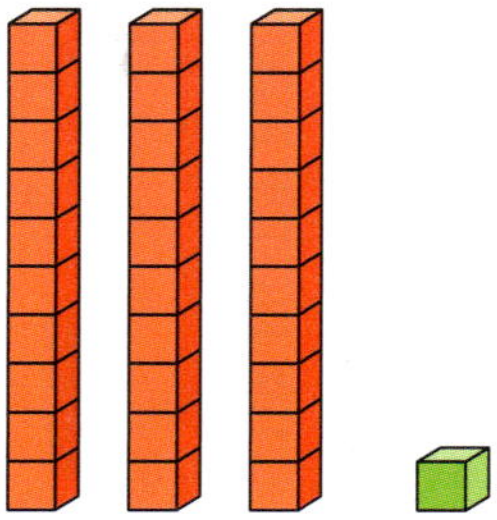

18.

19.

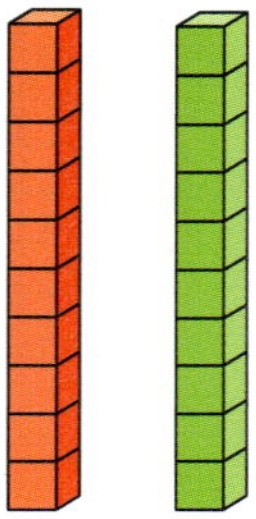

20.

21.

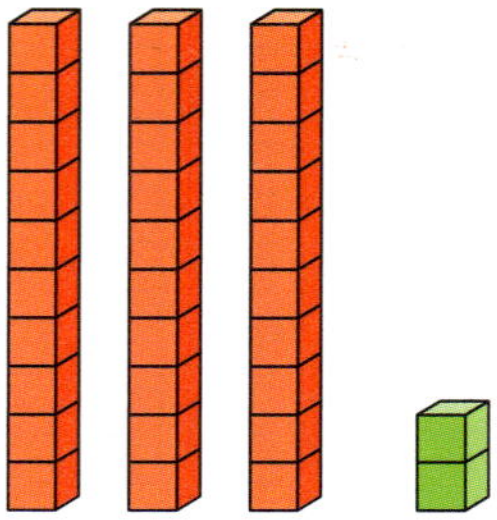

Place value in decimal numbers

Decimal numbers on the abacus.

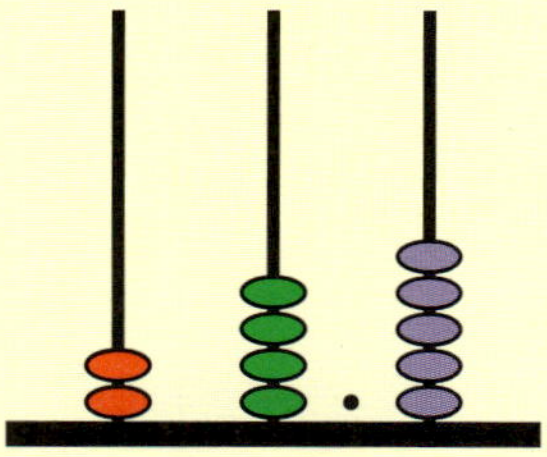

Look at this abacus. It shows decimal numbers.
The dot is the point which separates the whole number part from the decimal part.
It is called the **decimal point**.
Our number is 2 tens 4 ones 5 tenths, that is 24·5.

Write the numbers shown on the abacus pictures below.

1.

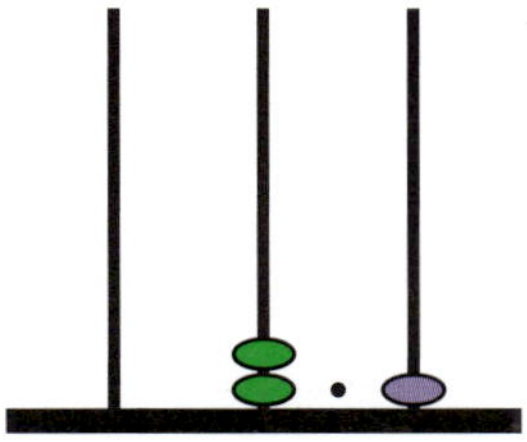

2.

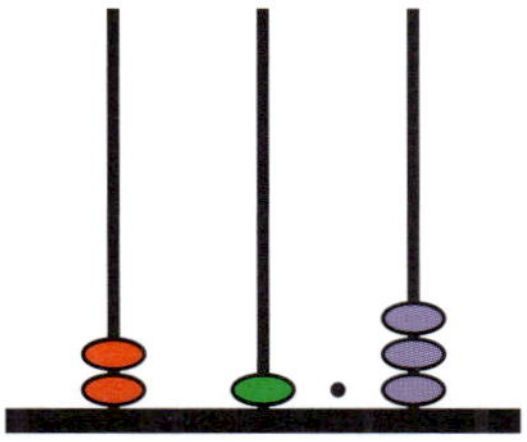

3.

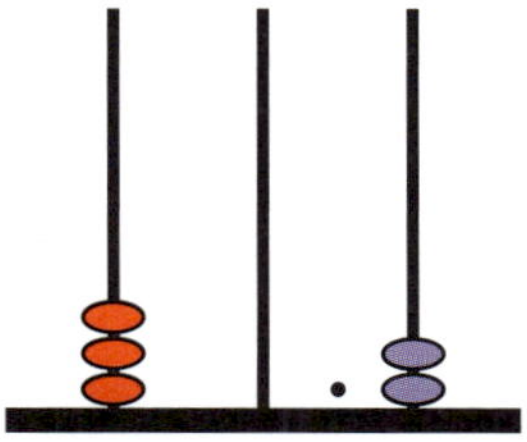

4.

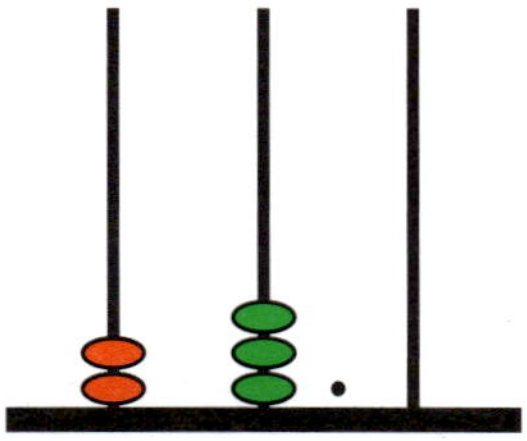

5.

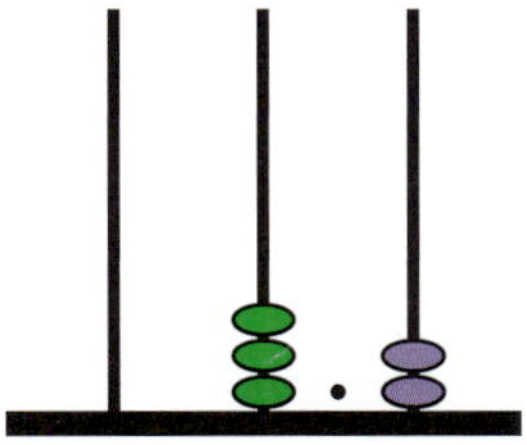

6.

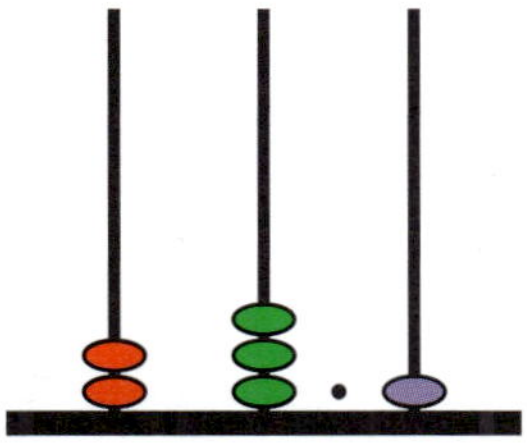

7.

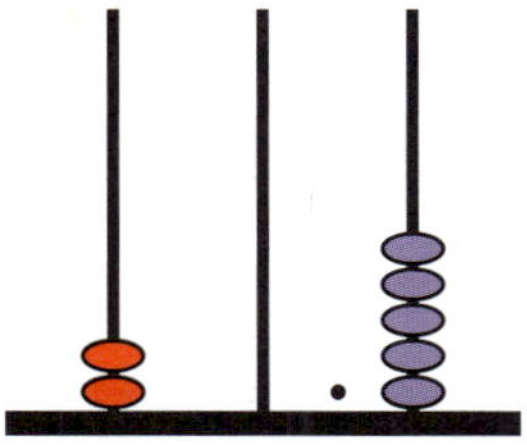

8.

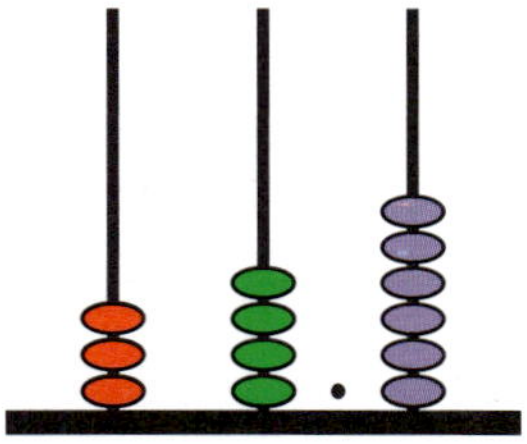

9. Copy the table below and complete it by writing in the numbers.

Hundreds	Tens	Ones	Tenths	Number
	1	1	• 1	eleven and one-tenth
		1	• 5	
	2	4	• 3	
	3	0	• 5	
1	4	2	• 1	
2	4	9	• 2	
3	1	4	• 7	

Write these numbers in words.

10. 12·3
11. 21·3
12. 23·1
13. 31·2
14. 20·5
15. 5·1
16. 10·4
17. 15·2
18. 110·2
19. 243·5
20. 309·7
21. 100·9

Write decimal numbers for the following:

22. sixteen and three-tenths
23. twelve and two-tenths
24. forty-four and five-tenths
25. sixty-two and seven-tenths
26. one hundred and four and three-tenths
27. two hundred and thirty-one and five-tenths
28. four hundred and twelve and one-tenth
29. one hundred and ten and one-tenth
30. twenty-one and six-tenths

Ordering decimal numbers

Look at the numbers 1·5, 1·8 and 2·3 shown by the blocks on the right.

In the numbers 1·5 and 1·8 both have a single ones tower but 1·8 has more tenths blocks than 1·5.

1·5 1·8 2·3

Therefore 1·8 > 1·5 or we can say 1·5 < 1·8.

If we now look at 1·8 and 2·3 the number 2·3 has 2 ones towers, 1·8 has only one.

Therefore 2·3 > 1·8 or 1·8 < 2·3.

Use the abacus models below to help you compare the numbers 23·1, 23·4 and 42·1. Put in the correct sign, < or >, between each pair of numbers:

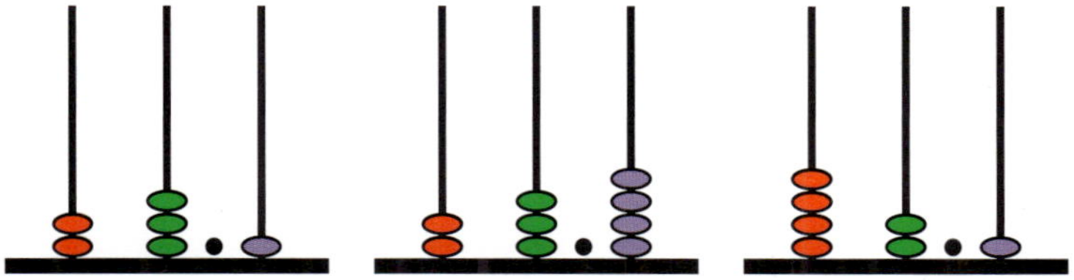

23·1 23·4 42·1

1. 23·1 ☐ 23·4 **2.** 23·1 ☐ 42·1 **3.** 23·4 ☐ 42·1

Put in the correct sign, < or >, between each pair of numbers.

4. 25·3 ☐ 25·8 **5.** 39·7 ☐ 32·1 **6.** 16·5 ☐ 15·9

7. 10·1 ☐ 11·1 **8.** 58·2 ☐ 46·7 **9.** 18·9 ☐ 19·3

We can use our number line also to compare decimal numbers.

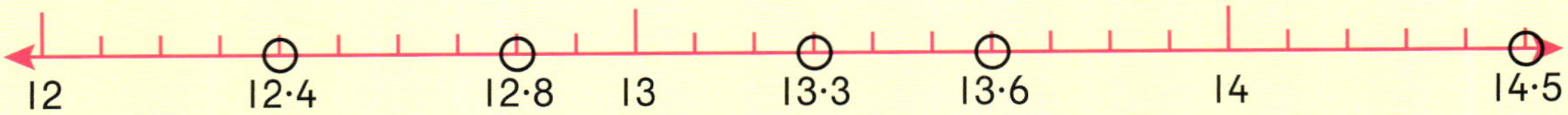

We see that 12·4 < 12·8 and 13·3 > 12·8 and 13·6 < 14·5

Put in the correct sign, < or >, between each pair of numbers shown by the letters below.

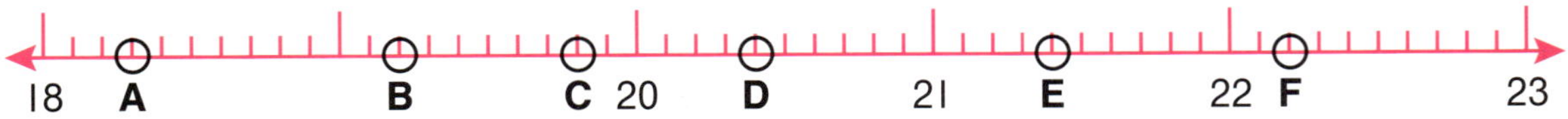

7. A ☐ B **8.** C ☐ A **9.** B ☐ C

10. F ☐ E **11.** D ☐ F **12.** D ☐ B

Draw abacuses to show the numbers in questions 7 to 12.

Approximation to the nearest whole number

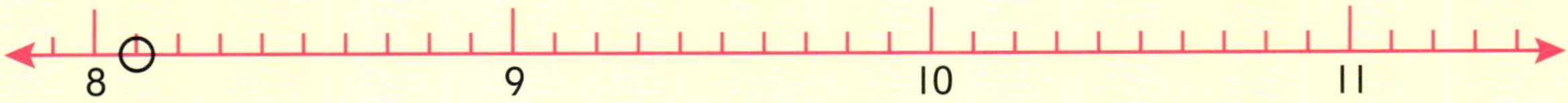

The nearest whole number to 8·1 is the number 8.

We say or write: <u>To the nearest whole number 8·1 is approximately equal to 8.</u>

If the decimal part of the number is ·5 we must round up to the next whole number.

Write these decimal numbers to their nearest whole number.

1. 7·9 **2.** 8·4 **3.** 9·1 **4.** 9·6 **5.** 10·5

Assessment 5

Write equivalent fractions for the following:

1. $\frac{2}{5} = \frac{\square}{10}$ **2.** $\frac{1}{2} = \frac{\square}{8}$ **3.** $\frac{5}{6} = \frac{\square}{12}$

What is:

4. $\frac{1}{3}$ of 24 **5.** $\frac{2}{5}$ of 20 **6.** $\frac{1}{8}$ of 72

7. One quarter of a class of 24 girls wore white socks. How many girls did not wear white socks?

8. $\frac{1}{10} + \frac{5}{10}$ **9.** $\frac{5}{12} + \frac{1}{12}$ **10.** $\frac{1}{3} + \frac{1}{12}$

11. $\frac{1}{5} + \frac{1}{10}$ **12.** $\frac{5}{12} - \frac{1}{12}$ **13.** $\frac{1}{3} - \frac{1}{4}$

Write these fractions as decimal numbers.

14. $\frac{3}{10}$ **15.** $\frac{7}{10}$ **16.** $2\frac{3}{10}$

Write decimal numbers for:

17. twenty-seven and three-tenths

18. one hundred and ten and one-tenth

Write these decimal numbers in words.

19. 12·5 **20.** 215·3

Put in the correct sign, < or >, between each pair of numbers:

21. 12·1 ☐ 11·2 **22.** 10·3 ☐ 13·0

Write these decimal numbers to the nearest whole number:

23. 15·5 **24.** 10·1

10 Money

Buying and getting change

Here are pictures of some dollar notes. Your teacher will show you notes used in your country.

How much change will you get from a \$20 note if you spend \$8.42?

One way we can work out this is by counting on from \$8.42 to \$20.

\$8.42 →(8c) \$8.50 →(50c) \$9.00 →(\$11.00) \$20.00

Change = \$11.00 + 50c + 8c = \$11.58

How much change from a \$100 note if you spend \$25.75?

\$25.75 →(5c) \$25.80 →(20c) \$26.00 →(\$4.00) \$30.00 →(\$70.00) \$100

Change = \$70.00 + \$4.00 + 20c + 5c = \$74.25

1. Copy and complete this table. Show all your workings.

Spend	Note given	Change received
\$9.36	\$20.00	
\$11.84	\$20.00	
\$6.51	\$20.00	
\$28.18	\$100.00	
\$39.73	\$100.00	

You can also calculate change by subtraction.
Try this method to find change from a $10 note, a $20 note or a $100 note.

Spend $2.56
Change from $10.00

	$	c
		9 10
$10.00	9 .	~~1~~ ~~0~~ ~~0~~
− 2.56	2 .	5 6
	7 .	4 4

Spend $8.73
Change from $20.00

	$	c
		9 10
$20.00	1 9 .	~~1~~ ~~0~~ ~~0~~
− 8.73	8 .	7 3
	1 1 .	2 7

Spend $37.81
Change from $100.00

	$	c
		9 10
$100.00	9 9 .	~~1~~ ~~0~~ ~~0~~
− 37.81	3 7 .	8 1
	6 2 .	1 9

2. Copy and complete this table. Show all your workings.

Spend	Note given	Change
(a) A book for $29.95	$100.00	
(b) A hamburger for $6.75	$20.00	
(c) 1 chicken and chips $14.75 1 potato salad $4.55 1 ice cream $2.25	$100.00	
(d) 1 bag of flour $5.95 1 kg of potatoes $3.49 1 tin of chocolate $16.70	$100.00	
(e) 2 notebooks at $6.35 each	$20.00	
(f) 3 tins of biscuits at $22.75 each	$100.00	
(g) 2 large pizzas at $39.95 each	$100.00	

Multiplying dollars and cents

Find the cost of 5 notebooks if 1 costs $6.35

Cost of 5 notebooks = $6.35 × 5 = ☐

	Dollars	cents
(multiply dollars)	6	35
6 × 5 = 30	×	5
	30	175
	31	75

$31.75

5 × 5 = 25 (multiply cents)
3 × 5 = 15
15 × 2 = 17 (changing to dollars)
30 + 1 = 31

Hundreds	tens	ones
Dollars	10c	1c
6	3	5
×		5
31	7	5

$31.75

5 × 5 = 25
3 × 5 = 15
15 × 2 = 17
6 × 5 = 30
30 + 1 = 31

$$\begin{array}{r} \$6.35 \\ \times \quad 5 \\ \hline \$31.75 \end{array}$$
(carried: 1, 2)

Multiplying dollars and cents is just like multiplying ordinary numbers.
We must remember the decimal point and the dollar sign.
The 5 notebooks cost $31.75.

Copy and complete.

1. $1.84 × 3 = ____

2. $9.45 × 6 = ____

3. $7.82 × 7 = ____

4. $4.90 × 5 = ____

5. $3.05 × 8 = ____

6. $2.01 × 3 = ____

7. $6.18 × 4 = ____

8. $10.05 × 6 = ____

Bills

When you go to the supermarket you receive a bill from the cashier for the things you have bought.
Here is what some bills look like.

DATE 04.07.05	TUE
4× @ 3.45	
GEN GROC	$13.80
GEN GROC	$4.99
O/RATED	$2.99
GEN GROC	$15.50
GEN GROC	$5.50
GEN GROC	$5.85
GEN GROC	$5.85
COLD CUTS	$3.79
COLD CUTS	$8.99
COLD CUTS	$9.65
COLD CUTS	$5.75
GEN GROC	$6.50
GEN GROC	$0.99
TOTAL	$84.65
CASH	$100.00
CHANGE	$15.35

CCS	
Mid-Centre CHAGUANAS	
TAX-INV VAT 103160	
JULY 13 2005	
7×	.22
COPICENTRE	1.54
STAT & SUPP	.54
SUBTOTAL	2.39
SUBTOTAL	2.08
V.A.T	.31
SUBTOTAL	2.39
CASH	3.00
CHANGE	.61
	8Q
777A0019	8.45R
671-7636	

06.29.05
2× 1.65
2× *3.30
4× 4.40
2* 17.60
3× 124.05
2* 42.15
2*8.75
2* 16.60
2*8.65
2*1.30
2*2.00
2*8.20
2*2.45
2*2.50
*11.250 ST
*112.50 CA

Your bill shows how much each item cost, as well as the number of items bought.

How much will you pay for these?

1. 2 packets of flour at $5.95 per packet
2. 2 packets of rice at $7.49 per packet
3. 3 tins of milk at $5.49 per tin
4. 4 cartons of juice at $6.15 per carton
5. 6 tins of sardines at $2.99 per tin
6. What is the total cost?
7. Find the change from a $100 note.

More bills

Sometimes you get a bill with the names of the items written on the bill as well as the quantity and the cost.

1. The table below shows some items bought in a clothing store. Copy and complete this table. (Unit cost means the cost of one.)

Quantity	Item	Unit cost	Total
3	shirts	$29.50	
6 pairs	socks	$5.95	
2 pairs	trousers	$44.50	
1 pair	shoes	$99.00	

What is the total bill for all the items bought in the clothing store?

2. Here is a table for items bought in a hardware store. Copy and complete this table.

Quantity	Item	Unit cost	Total
5 lengths	PVC pipe	$16.50	
2	taps	$21.00	
4 lengths	steel	$365.00	
6 sheets	plyboard	$48.00	

What is the total bill for the items bought at the hardware store?

Word problems – regular price/cash price

Look at the TV set in this picture.
How much more is the regular price than the cash price?
How much do you save if you pay the cash price?
What discount do you get if you pay cash for this set?

Regular Price: $2250
CASH: $1985

Look at these pictures and use them to answer the word problems below. Show all your working.

Regular Price: $6195
CASH: $5495

Regular Price: $255
CASH: $225

Regular Price: $199
CASH: $175

Regular Price: $4495
CASH: $3995

Regular Price: $2095
CASH: $1855

1. What is the difference between the regular price and cash price of the cooker?
2. How much do you save on the refrigerator when you pay cash?
3. What discount do you get when you pay cash price for the TV?
4. How much do you save on both the fan and iron if you pay cash for them?
5. How much will you pay if you buy both the TV and the fan for cash?

Word problems – rates involving time

Work out the answers to these word problems. Show all your working.

1. A market vendor pays $125 per month to rent a stall in the market. How much money does the vendor pay in a year?
2. A second market vendor prefers to pay weekly and is charged $30 per week. How much more does this vendor pay than the vendor who pays $125 per month?
3. To rent a car for a day, a rental firm charges $120. If the car is rented for a week, the rate per day is $100. How much money do you save if you rent the car for one week??
4. The same car rental firm will charge you $2500 if you rent the car for a month. How much money would you save if you rent the car for 1 month instead of renting it for 4 weeks?
5. How much does a man earn in a 5 day work week if he works 8 hours a day and his wages are $10 per hour?
6. A house helper works 5 half days per week in 5 different homes. She is paid $8 an hour and she works 4 hours in each of the homes. How much money does she earn in a week?
7. The telephone company charges 23 cents for each local call. How much will a customer have to pay for 123 local calls?
8. A telephone call to Canada costs $2.00 per minute if the call is made during the day but $1.70 if made at night. How much will a caller save if she calls during the night and speaks for 12 minutes?

Word problems – profit and loss/better buys

Work out the answers to these word problems. Show all your working.

1. Material for curtains was sold at one store at $19.99 per metre. The same material was bought at another store at $17.49 per metre. How much did the buyer save when she bought 20 metres?

2. A high grade motor oil was sold at $65 for a 5 litre bottle. If the oil was bought in litre bottles the price was $14.50 per litre. How much do you save when you buy a 5 litre bottle instead of 5 separate litre bottles?

3. Soft drinks are sold to the shopkeeper at $48.00 per case of 24 bottles. The shopkeeper sells to his customers at $2.75 per bottle. How much profit does the shopkeeper make on a case of soft drinks?

4. A 10 kg bag of flour costs $39.95. The 2 kg pack costs $8.97. How much do you save when you buy the 10 kg bag?

5. Tomatoes are bought by the supermarket at $500 per 100 kg and sold at $5.49 per kg. How much profit does the supermarket make on 400 kg of tomatoes?

6. A market vendor bought 100 kg of ripe bananas at $2.00 per kg, and sold them at $3.00 per kg. How much profit did she make if she sold only 90 kg because 10 kg were spoilt?

Assessment 6

1. How much change will you get from $10.00 if you spend $6.36?
2. A bag of flour costs $7.95, a kg of potatoes $3.99, and a tub of margarine $5.55. How much would I pay if I bought all 3 items?
3. Larry gave his brother $3.75 from his allowance of $20.00. How much did Larry have left?
4. If you buy 6 notebooks at $4.95 each, how much would they cost?
5. How much will you pay altogether for:
   2 bags of flour at $6.95 each
   1 bag of rice at $7.75
   4 tins of milk at $4.25 per tin
   2 bottles of oil at $5.15 a bottle
   3 tins of corned beef at $7.25 per tin.
6. A store gives $750 discount on a refrigerator which has a price tag of $7299. How much will you pay for the refrigerator?
7. A market trader bought 600 oranges. She paid $20 for every 100. She sold all the oranges for a total of $180. How much profit did she make?
8. Make a bill for: 2 shirts at $39.95 each, 3 ties at $8.95 each and 4 pairs of socks at $5.25 a pair.
9. A wholesale dealer sells avocadoes at $300 per 100 avocadoes. A market vendor bought 60 and sold 54; the rest were spoilt. She sold them at $4 each. How much profit did she make?

11 Linear measurement

Metres and centimetres

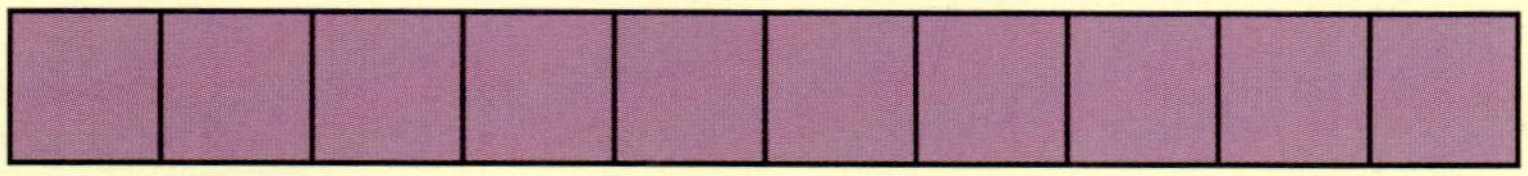

What is the length of this strip? Measure it.

How many strips of this length placed end to end will measure 1 metre?

How many centimetres are there in $\frac{1}{2}$ m?

How many in $\frac{1}{4}$ m? How many in $\frac{1}{10}$ m?

This is Salick.

How tall is he?

He is more than 1 m tall.

He is about 115 cm or 1 m 15 cm tall.

115 cm = 100 cm + 15 cm = 1 m 15 cm

1.15 m also means 1 m 15 cm.

1. Measure your height and write it in the following 3 ways:

☐ cm   ☐ m ☐ cm   ☐ m

Do the same for the length of:

2. the blackboard

☐ cm   ☐ m ☐ cm   ☐ m

3. your desk

☐ cm   ☐ m ☐ cm   ☐ m

4. your bench

☐ cm   ☐ m ☐ cm   ☐ m

This car measures 3 m 5 cm.

3 m 5 cm = 300 cm + 5 cm
= 305 cm

We must always have 2 digits after the decimal point when writing metres and centimetres as metres.

3 m 5 cm = 305 cm = 3·05 m.

5. Copy and complete this table.

cm	m cm	m
119	1 19	1·19
	2 25	
		3·26
	5 38	
444		
620		

Write each of the following lengths in metres.

6. 230 cm = 2.30 m

7. 405 cm = ☐ m

8. 1 m 50 cm = 1.50 m

9. 3 m 5 cm = ☐ m

10. 4 m 9 cm = 4.09 m

11. 8 m 10 cm = ☐ m

12. 101 cm = ☐ m

13. 200 cm = ☐ m

100 cm = 1m
200 cm = 2 m

Adding lengths in centimetres and metres

A string 2 m 70 cm long is joined to another string 3 m 45 cm long. What is the combined length of both strings?

The combined length of both strings is

2 m 70 cm + 3 m 45 cm
= 6 m 15 cm

m	cm
2	70
+ 3	45
6	15

Add cm
75 + 40 = 115
115 cm = 1 m 15 cm
Add metres
1 + 2 + 3 = 6

Add 270 and 345 in the usual way. What is the answer? Check your answer using a calculator.

Now add 2·70 and 3·45 on the calculator. What is the answer?

Look carefully at questions 1 and 2 below. Each question shows the same problem presented in 3 ways: in cm, in m and cm, and in m only. Copy and complete.

1. (a)

cm
135
215
+ 460
____

(b)

m	cm
1	35
2	15
+ 4	60
____	

(c)

m
1·35
2·15
+ 4·60
____

2. (a)

cm
216
408
+ 192
____

(b)

m	cm
2	16
4	8
+ 1	92
____	

(c)

m
2·16
4·08
+ 1·92
____

Now check your answers using a calculator.

Subtracting lengths in centimetres and metres

From a piece of ribbon 2 m 25 cm long, a piece 1 m 50 cm is cut off. What length of ribbon is left?

Length of ribbon left
= 2 m 25 cm – 1 m 50 cm
= 75 cm

	m	cm
	2	25
–	1	50
	0	75

Change 1 m and add to 25 cm.
125 – 50 = 75
Subt metres
1 – 1 = 0

Subtract 150 from 225. What is the answer? Check your answer using a calculator.

Now do this on the calculator: 2·25 – 1·50 What is the answer?

Look carefully at questions 1, 2 and 3 below. Each question shows the same problem presented in three ways. Copy and complete.

1. (a) cm: 654 – 126 = ____ (b) m cm: 6 54 – 1 26 = ____ (c) m: 6·54 – 1·26 = ____

2. (a) cm: 428 – 145 = ____ (b) m cm: 4 28 – 1 45 = ____ (c) m: 4·28 – 1·45 = ____

3. (a) cm: 632 – 256 = ____ (b) m cm: 6 32 – 2 56 = ____ (c) m: 6·32 – 2·56 = ____

Now check your answers using a calculator.

Word problems

Work out the answers to these problems. Show all your working.

1. A toy car ran 15 m 10 cm along a track and stopped. It was started again and ran 12 m 25 cm. How far did it run altogether?
2. Maisie is 1 m 25 cm tall. Janet is 1 m 35 cm. How much taller is Janet?
3. Mother bought 3 m of cloth for Joan's dress. She used up 2 m 75 cm. How much cloth was left?
4. Samlal is 1 m 20 cm tall. His brother Raj is 45 cm taller. How tall is Raj?
5. The school garden has rectangular plots each measuring 4 m long and 3 m wide. How far must you walk to go around one plot?
6. The school playground is a square. Each side measures 32 m 50 cm. What distance do you run going around it?
7. Tom threw the cricket ball 50 m. Harry threw it 39 m 20 cm. How much further was Tom's throw?
8. In a 100 m race Roy fell at the three-quarter mark. How far did he run?
9. Three pieces of rope 2 m 40 cm, 3 m 15 cm and 2 m 80 cm, etc. are cut from a long piece. How long was the piece to begin with?
10. How many centimetres must I cut from a rod 5·2 m long to have 4·5 m left?

The kilometre

Distances on the highway are shown by signs like the one seen here.

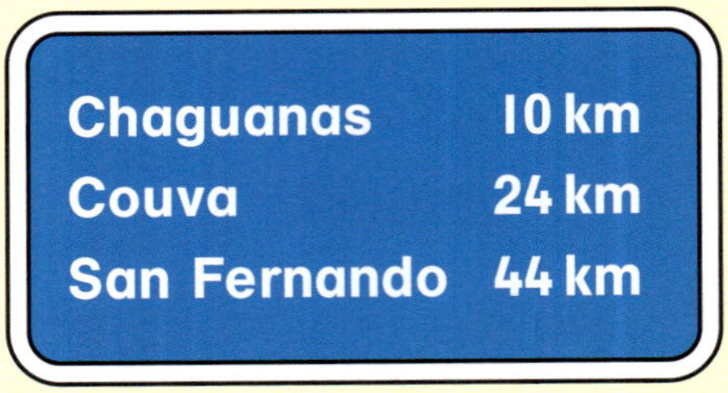

The distances are given in **kilometres** and tell how much further the motorist must travel to reach a particular place.

A kilometre is 1000 metres 1 km = 1000 m

Answer these questions.

1. How far away is this motorist from Chaguanas?

2. How far away is this motorist from Couva?

3. How far away is this motorist from San Fernando?

4. How far is it between Chaguanas and Couva?

5. How far is it between Chaguanas and San Fernando?

6. How far is it between Couva and San Fernando?

Which unit would you use to measure the following?
Use cm, m or km.

7. a belt for your trousers

8. a cricket pitch

9. the height of your desk

10. a pencil

11. a race track

12. a bread knife

13. the distance between Trinidad and Tobago

14. the length of your bed

15. the garden hose

16. the football pitch

Distances between places in Trinidad

How far away from your school do you live?

Is it more than 1 km? Or less than 1 km?

What distance can you think of that might be about 1 km?

If you travelled from San Fernando, or Chaguanas, or Arima to Port of Spain do you know how many kilometres you would have travelled?

Here is a table which gives approximate distances in kilometres between districts in Trinidad.

APPROXIMATE DISTANCES IN KILOMETRES BETWEEN DISTRICTS

Arima	13	60	16	68	45	85	19	21	64	66	60	26	108	58	63	42	90	87	82	129	72	15	31	39
Blanchisseuse	52	98	55	106	84	124	58	60	103	105	98	64	146	97	101	80	129	126	121	167	111	53	71	
Chaguanas	18	90	19	52	29	55	19	52	34	50	40	24	77	27	72	40	71	117	92	98	42	35		
Cumuto	27	60	16	68	45	85	34	21	64	64	60	40	108	63	63	56	90	87	82	129	72			
Debe	60	129	56	31	34	13	61	85	8	43	16	66	48	15	66	82	37	156	85	69				
Fullarton	116	185	113	87	90	58	117	142	64	100	72	122	31	71	122	138	98	212	142					
Guayaguayar	95	108	90	55	63	98	101	61	80	12	69	108	121	84	19	124	92	135						
Matelot	100	27	100	135	129	169	106	74	148	122	143	113	192	145	116	129	113							
Moruga	89	145	74	37	87	40	90	188	42	50	31	95	77	48	72	111								
Mt. Pleasant	29	101	56	92	69	95	23	63	74	90	80	16	117	68	105									
Mayaro	76	89	71	35	43	79	82	42	61	23	50	89	101	64										
Pointe-a-Pierre	45	117	47	32	26	27	47	79	6	42	18	52	50											
Point Fortin	95	164	92	66	69	37	97	121	43	79	52	101												
Port of Spain	13	85	40	76	53	79	6	47	58	74	101													
Princes Town	58	116	43	15	21	29	60	72	11	27														
Rio Claro	68	95	50	13	21	56	69	48	39															
San Fernando	52	121	48	26	26	21	53	77																
Sangre Grande	34	47	29	61	58	98	40																	
San Juan	6	79	34	71	48	74																		
Siparia	72	142	69	43	47																			
Tabaquite	47	101	29	23																				
Tableland	69	108	52																					
Talparo	29	72																						
Toco	72																							
Tunapuna																								

The distance between Port of Spain and Debe is 66km.

Use the table on page 117 to find the distance between:

1. Port of Spain and Arima
2. San Fernando and Port of Spain
3. Chaguanas and Arima
4. Toco and Port of Spain
5. Mayaro and Rio Claro
6. Chaguanas and Mayaro
7. Tunapuna and Sangre Grande
8. Princes Town and San Fernando
9. Toco and Princes Town
10. Here are 2 routes to get from Chaguanas to Mayaro:

    (a) Chaguanas to Rio Claro to Mayaro
    (b) Chaguanas to Sangre Grande to Mayaro

    Which is the shorter route and by how many kilometres?
11. Cyclists in a road race from Port of Spain passed through Sangre Grande, Mayaro, Rio Claro, Princes Town and San Fernando before returning to Port of Spain. How many kilometres did the cyclists travel?

Perimeter

The total distance around any shape is its **perimeter**.

Measure the sides of each of these shapes and calculate the perimeter.

1.

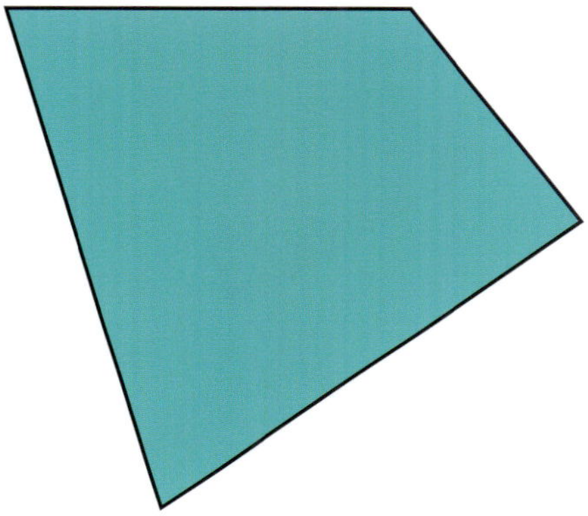

2.

3.

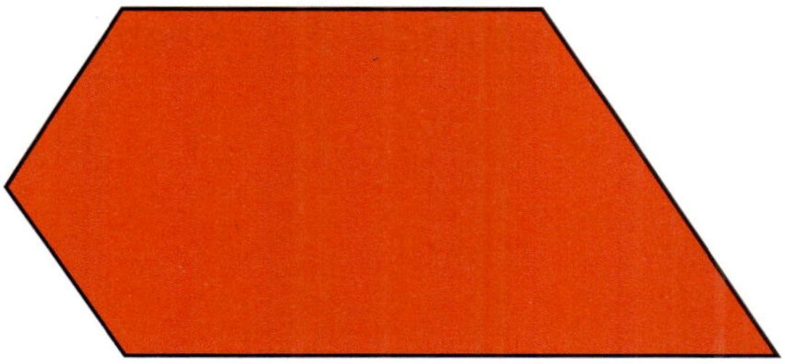

4.

5.

6.

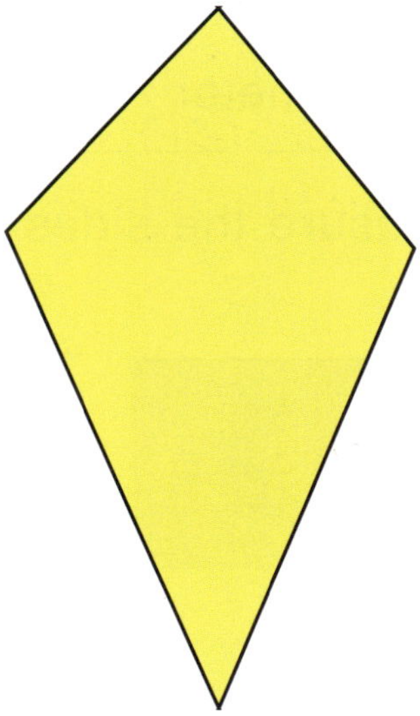

Measure the sides of these 2 shapes and calculate their perimeters.

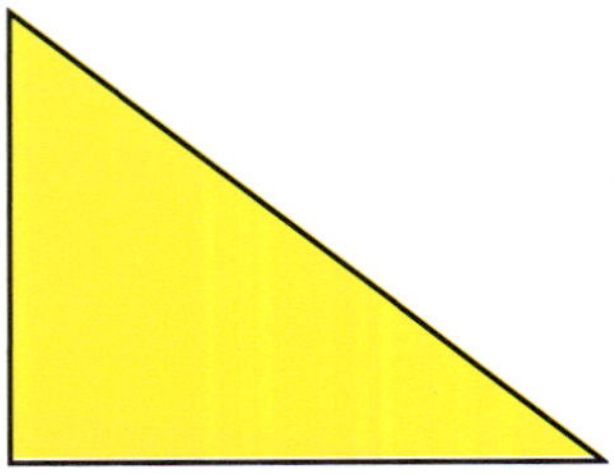

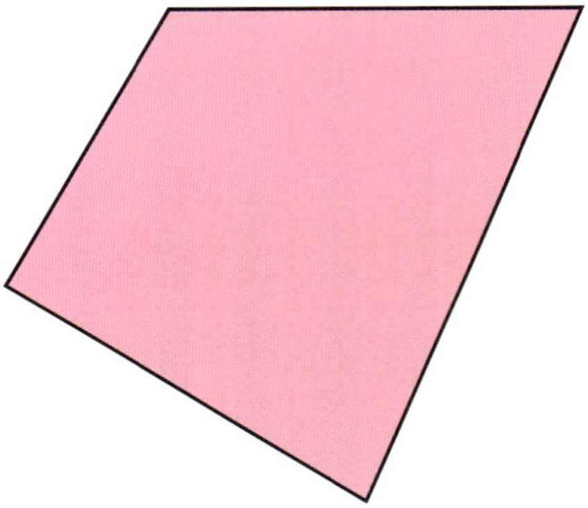

Now draw 2 squares that have the same perimeter as the 2 shapes above.

Perimeter of rectangles

1. Copy the table.

	Rectangle 1	Rectangle 2	Rectangle 3
Length			
Width			
Length + width			
One half of perimeter			
Whole perimeter			

Now measure the sides of the 3 rectangles below and complete the table.

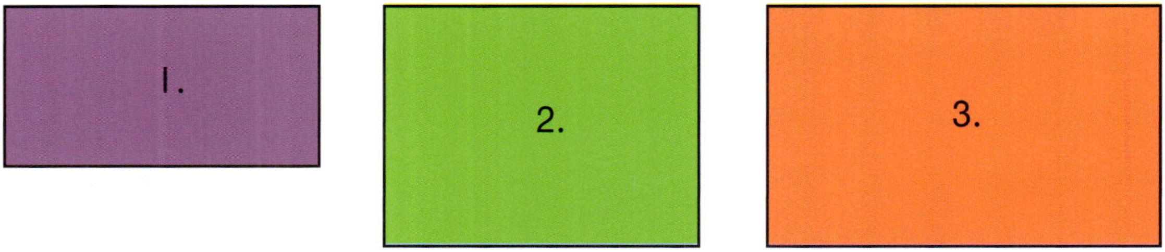

From the previous page which you completed you can see that **the perimeter of a rectangle is the (length + width) × 2**

2. Measure the length and width of these rectangles. Calculate the perimeter of each.

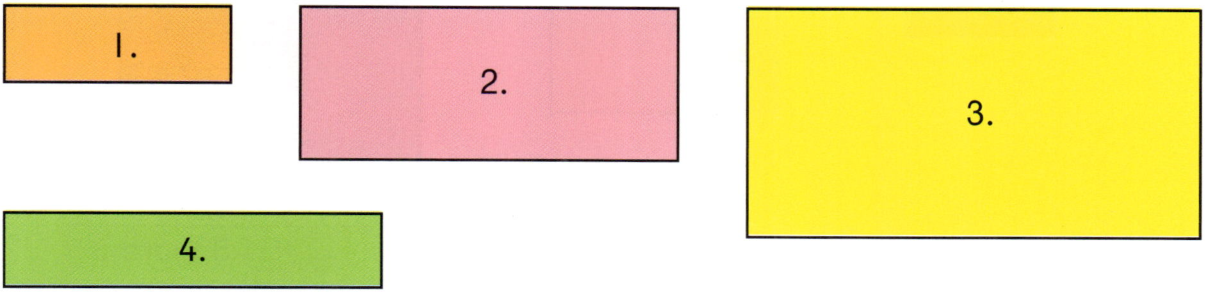

3. Copy and complete this table.

Length	Width	Length + width	Perimeter
12 cm	6 cm		
15 cm	5 cm		
10 m	4 m		
25 m	10 m		
2 m 5 cm	1 m 25 cm		
3 m 10 cm	1 m 15 cm		

Work out the answers to these word problems. Show all your working.

4. Find the perimeter of a square plot of land 1·25 m along each side.

5. A classroom measures 6·50 m by 8·50 m. What is its perimeter?

6. A rectangular garden measures 9·50 m by 6·00 m. What is the distance around it?

Perimeter of squares

Measure the sides of the squares.

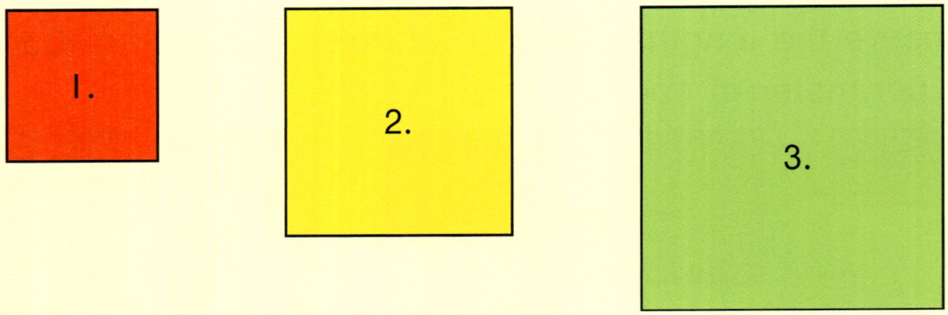

	Square 1	Square 2	Square 3
Length of side	2 cm	3 cm	4 cm
Perimeter	2 + 2 + 2 + 2 4 × 2 cm	3 + 3 + 3 + 3 4 × 3 cm	4 + 4 + 4 + 4 4 × 4 cm

In every case the perimeter of the square is 4 times the length of a side of the square.

Find the perimeter of the squares whose sides are:

1. 5 cm

2. 15 cm

3. 5 m

4. 15 m

5. 4 m 20 cm

6. 6 m 15 cm

7. 3·20 m

8. 3·25 m

9. 4·50 m

10. Which plot has greater perimeter: a square plot whose side measures 6 m or a rectangular one that is 8 m long and 4 m wide?

12 Area and volume

Area of rectangles

What is the area of this square?
Remember that its area is measured in **square centimetres**. Square centimetres is written as **cm^2**.

1.

2.

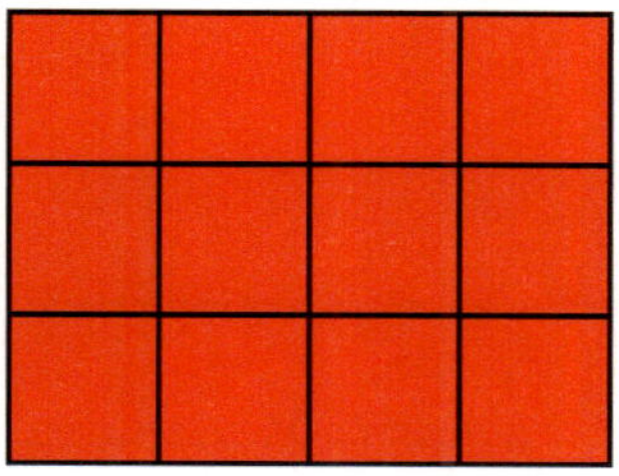

3.

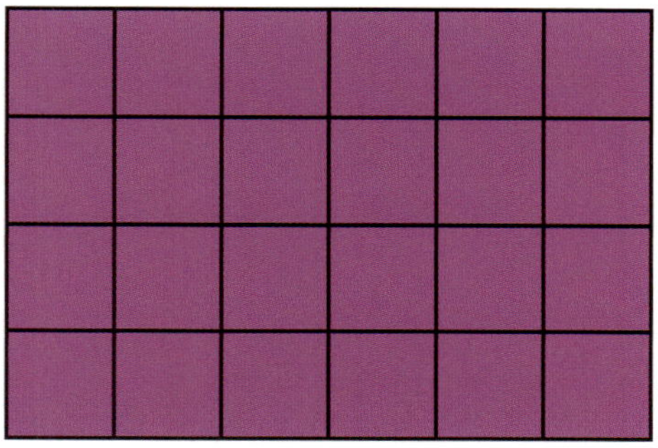

Copy and complete this table using the 3 rectangles above.

	Rectangle 1	Rectangle 2	Rectangle 3
Number of cm^2 blocks in each row	3	4	6
Number of rows	2	3	4
Total number of cm^2 blocks Area by counting	□ × □ = □ ______ cm^2	□ × □ = □ ______ cm^2	□ × □ = □ ______ cm^2
Length Width	3 cm 2 cm	4 cm 3 cm	6 cm 4 cm
Product of length and width	______ cm^2	______ cm^2	______ cm^2

Remember: Area = length × breadth

Draw rectangles 1–6.

Write the length, width and area of these rectangles.

Check the area of each rectangle by counting cm^2 blocks.

1.

2.

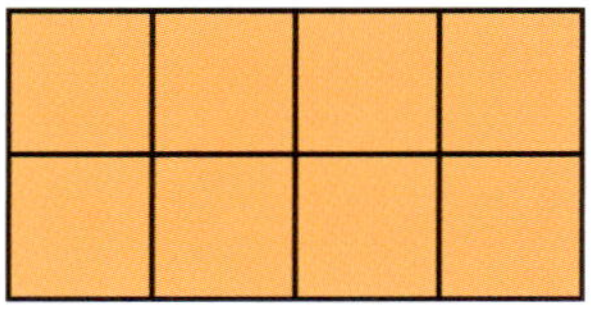

3.

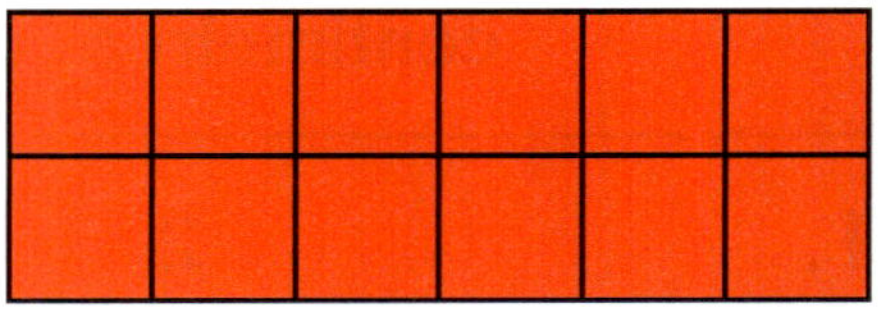

4.

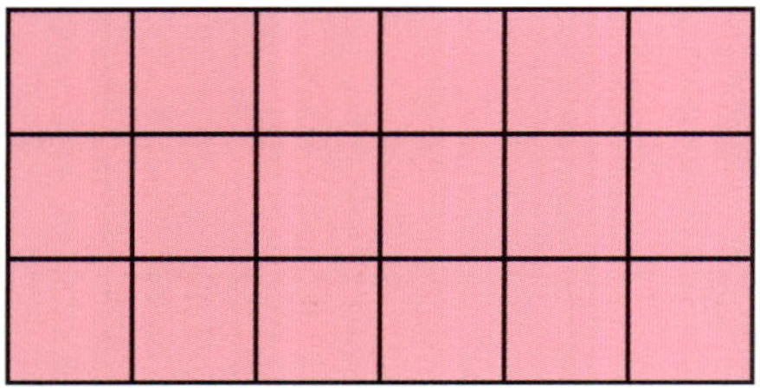

5.

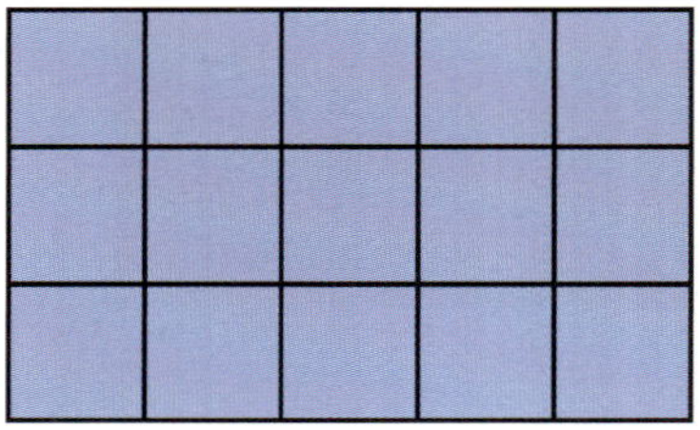

6.

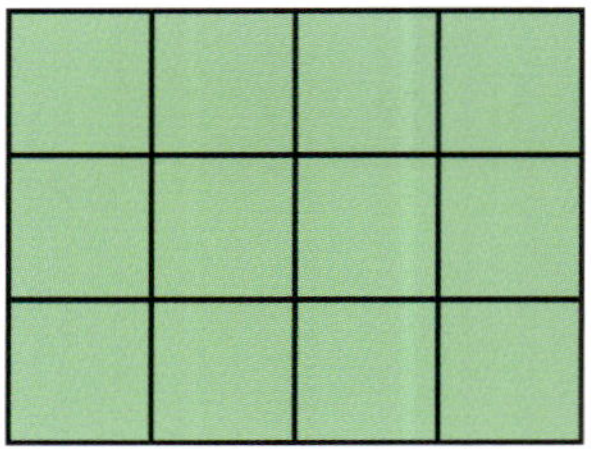

Measure the length and width of each rectangle and calculate its area.

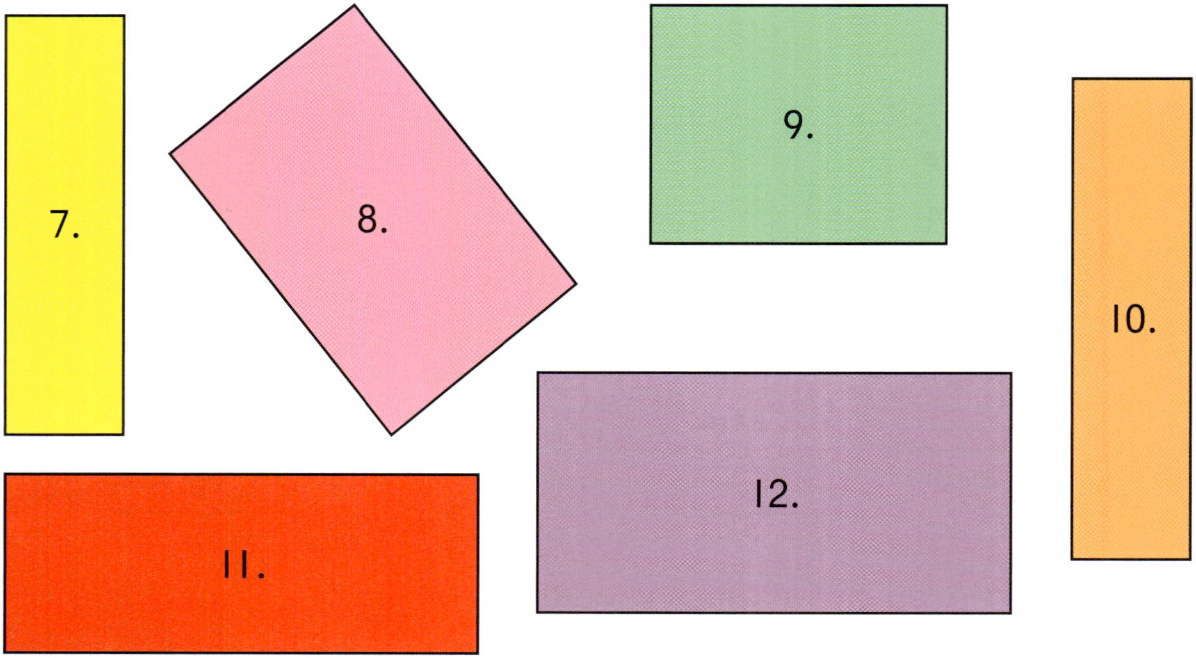

Drawing rectangular areas

Measure the length and width of each of these rectangles.
Calculate the area. Check by counting square cm blocks.

A

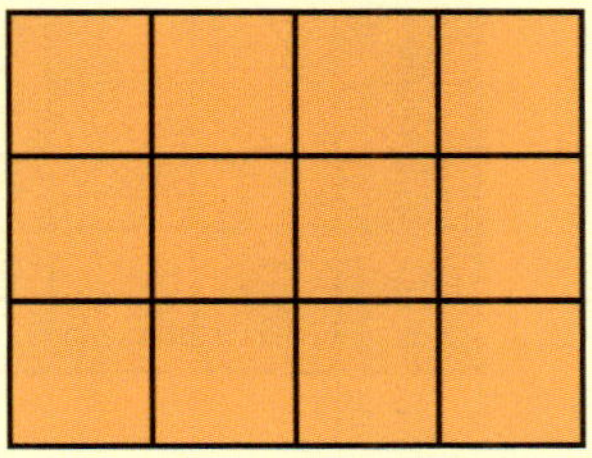

B

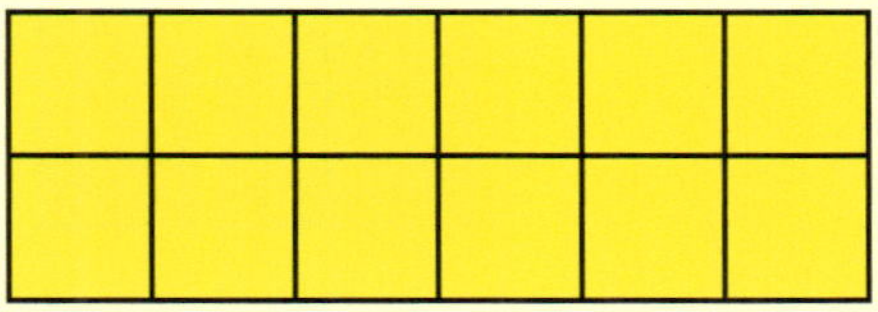

C

We can draw different rectangles of the same area by using suitable lengths and widths.

Look at the measurements of the rectangles above.

A	Length 4 cm	Width 3 cm	Area $4 \times 3 = 12$ cm^2
B	Length 6 cm	Width 2 cm	Area $6 \times 2 = 12$ cm^2
C	Length 12 cm	Width 1 cm	Area $12 \times 1 = 12$ cm^2

The numbers which we multiply in every case are a pair of factors of the number which gives the area.

1. Complete the different pairs of factors for the numbers below. Draw the rectangles with the areas shown.

Numbers	Pairs of factors				Rectangles
6	1, 6	3, 2			6 cm^2
8					8 cm^2
20					20 cm^2
24					24 cm^2

Area of squares

1. 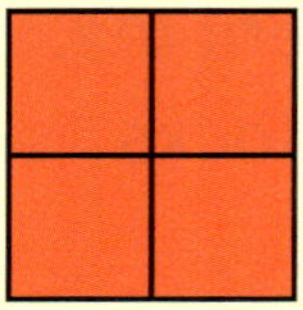

2. 

3. 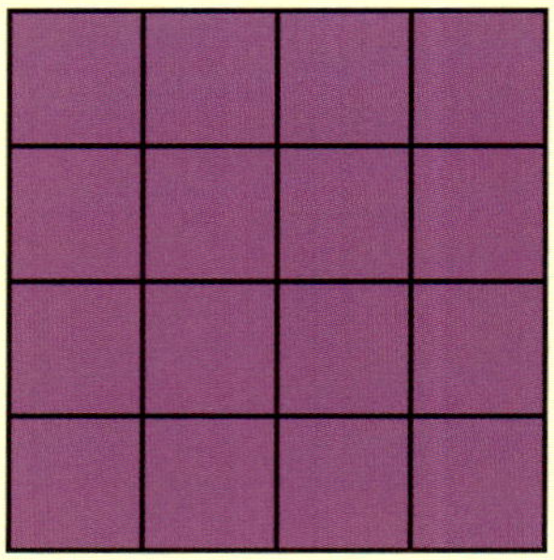

Check this table.

	Square 1	Square 2	Square 3
Length of side	2 cm	3 cm	4 cm
Sq cm blocks in row	2	3	4
Number of rows	2	3	4
Total sq cm blocks	$2 \times 2 = 4$	$3 \times 3 = 9$	$4 \times 4 = 16$
Area by counting	4 cm^2	9 cm^2	16 cm^2

The area of any square is the product we get when we multiply the number measuring the length of a side by itself.

Measure the sides of these squares and calculate their areas. Check by counting square centimetre blocks.

1. 

2. 

3. 

Remember:
When we paint a wall, or a door, or any object, we are covering a surface; we paint an **area**.
When we tile or carpet a floor we cover a surface; we tile or carpet an area.
When length and width are in metres, area is in square metres, written m^2.

4. Find the areas of these shapes.

(a) A square with sides each measuring 10 cm.

(b) A rectangle 12 cm long and 8 cm wide.

(c) A rectangular plot measuring 4 m by 2 m.

(d) A square field with sides of 8 m.

(e) The floor in a classroom 10 m long and 6 m wide.

(f) The top of a desk 2 m long and 1 m wide.

(g) The size of an envelope 15 cm by 9 cm.

(h) Carpet covering a floor 4 m × 4 m.

5. A floor tile is 1 metre square. How many tiles will I need for a floor 4 m by 3 m?

6. How much carpet must I buy for a floor 4 m long and 5 m wide?

7. Lenny's father painted the outside of his fence which measured 15 m long and 2 m high. What was the area he painted? How much paint did he use if 1 litre of paint covered 10 m^2?

Volume

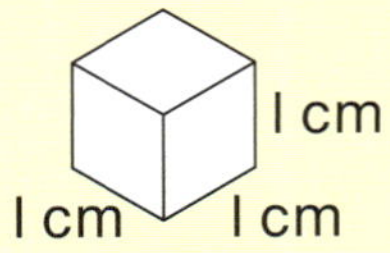

This cube measures 1 cm along all its edges. Find a centimetre cube and measure the edges. It is called a centimetre cube because its **volume** is 1 cubic centimetre (1 cm^3). The volume is the amount of space the cube occupies.

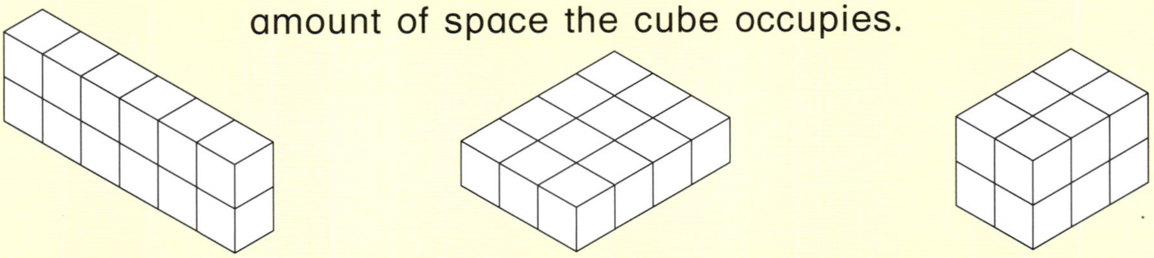

The cuboids above are made up of centimetre cubes.
Count the number of cubes in each. How many are there?
These cuboids all have the same volume.
The volume of each is 12 centimetre cubes or 12 cm^3.
Each cuboid occupies 12 cm^3 of space.

Use centimetre cubes to build these shapes. Count the number of cubes and write the volume of each in cm^3.

1. 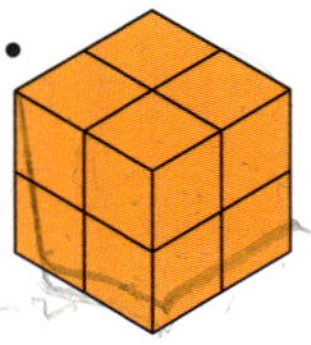

2. 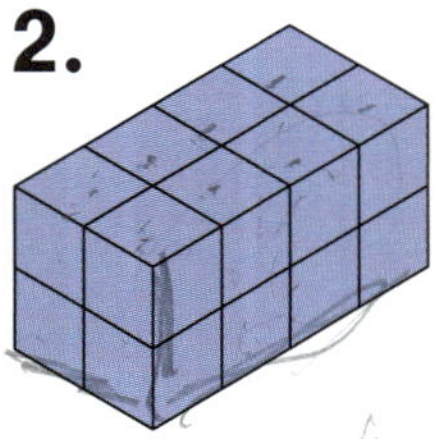

3. 

4. 

5. How many cubes are in this cuboid?

6. How many other cuboids can you make with this number of cubes?

7. How many cuboids can you make from a set of 18 cubes?

Volume of rectangular solids

Look at these shapes. Each has several layers.

Shape 1

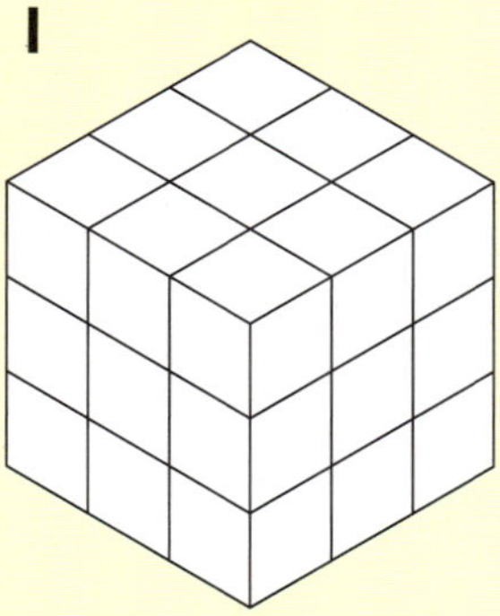

Shape 2

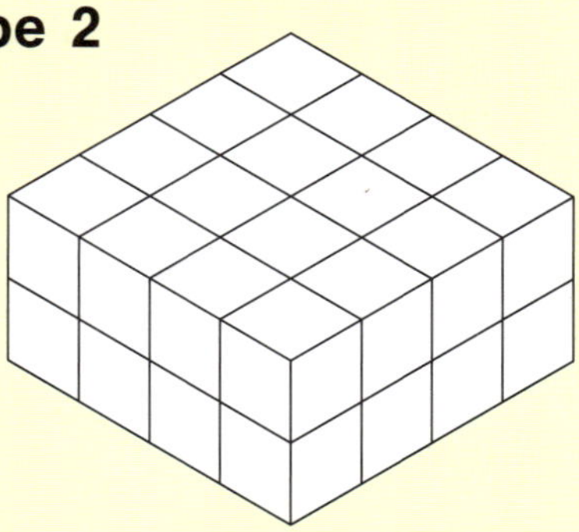

	Number of cubes in a layer	Number of layers	Volume
Shape 1	9	3	$27\,cm^3$
Shape 2	16	2	$32\,cm^3$

If each layer has the same number of cubes, the volume is (number of cubes in each layer) × (number of layers)

Make a table like the one above for these blocks and calculate the volume of each.

1. 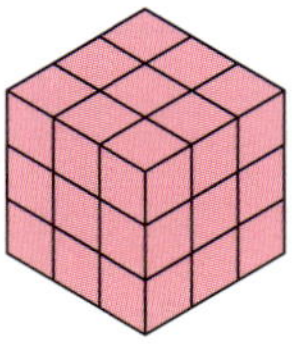

2. 

3. 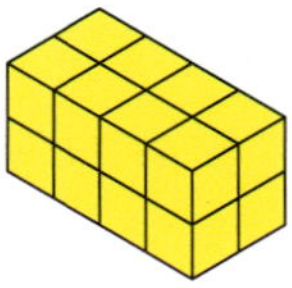

4. 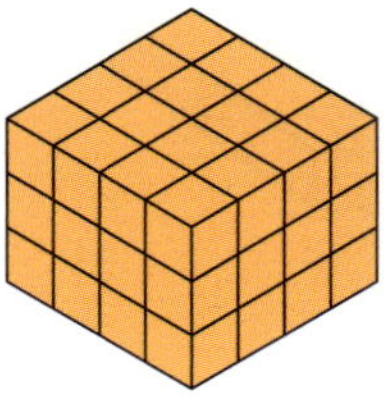

5. 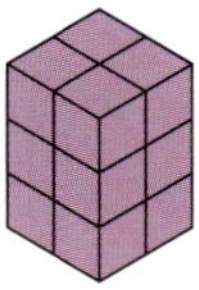

6. 

7. 

8. 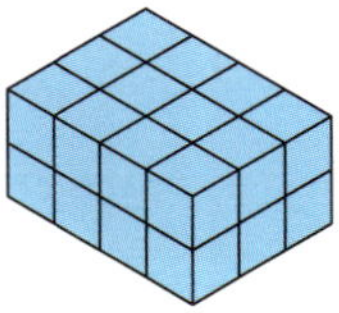

9. 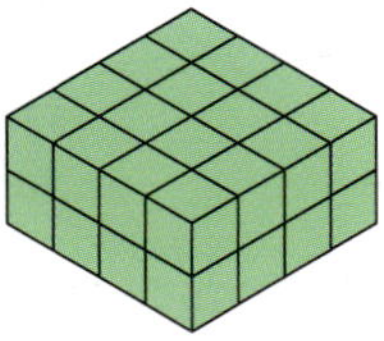

Volume of boxes

Here is a cuboid, and here is a matching box.

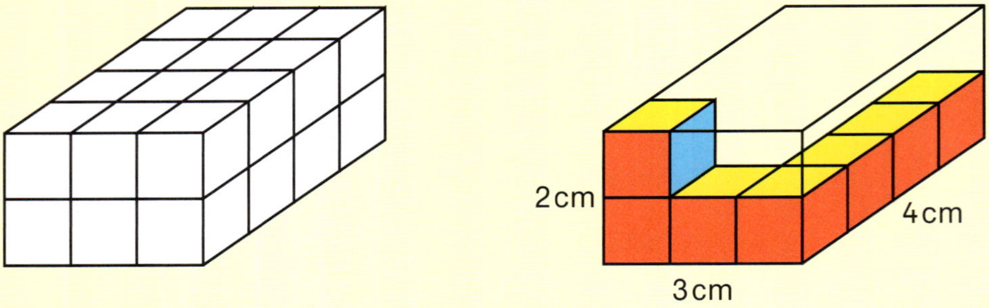

How many cubes will fit along the long side, short side and height of the box?

Long side		Short side		Height		Volume
Length	Number of cubes	Length	Number of cubes	Length	Number of cubes	
4 cm	4	3 cm	3	2 cm	2	

Number of cubes in layers = 4 × 3 = 12 Number of layers 2 24 cm^3

The box holds 24 centimetre cubes. We say its volume is 24 cm^3. The space which the block occupies (24 cm^3) is the same as the space in the box.

Calculate the volumes of these boxes.

1.
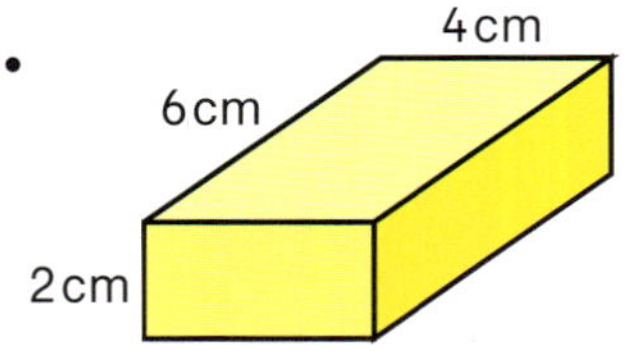

2.
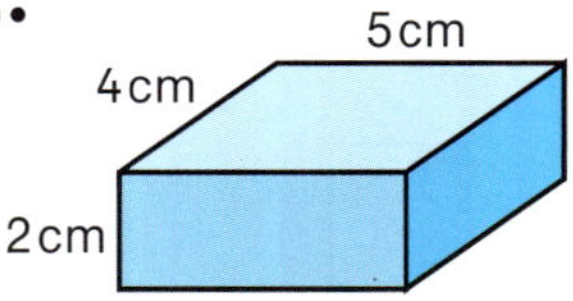

3.
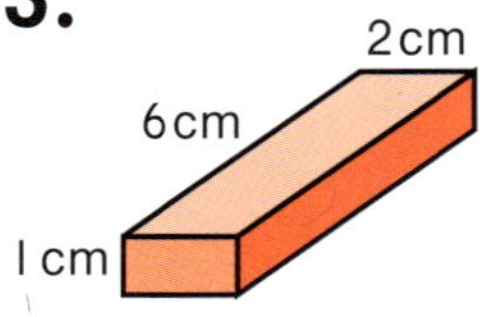

4.
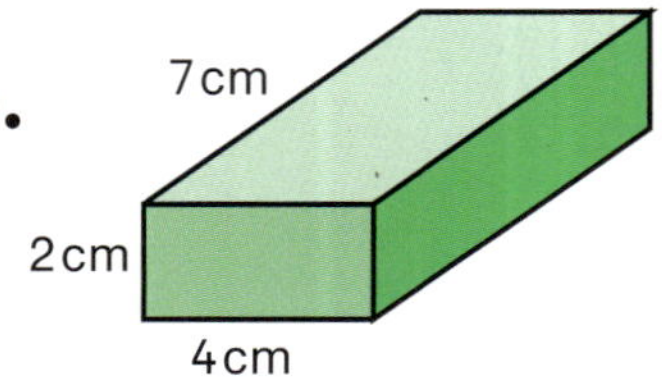

5.
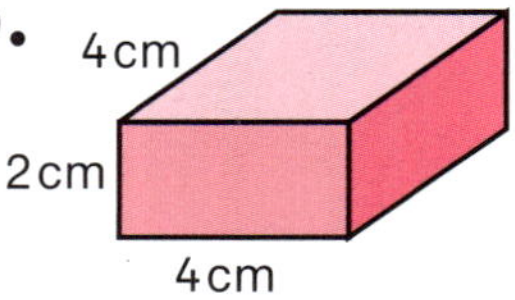

6.
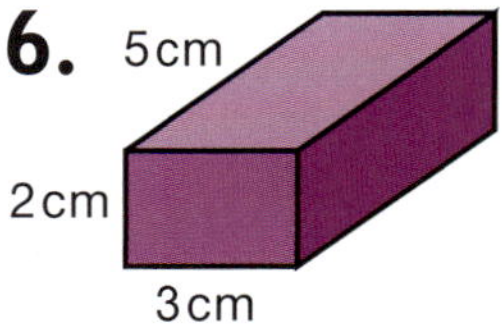

Volume = base area × height

In the exercise on page 129 you found the volume of the boxes by finding the number of cubes in a layer and the number of layers. In the example on page 130 we had:

Long side 4 cm Short side 3 cm Height 2 cm
Number of blocks in each layer $4 \times 3 = 12$
Number of layers $= 2$
Volume $12 \times 2 = 24\ \text{cm}^3$

Now compare these numbers.

Area of base $= 4\ \text{cm} \times 3\ \text{cm} = 12\ \text{cm}^2$ Height 2 cm
Volume $24\ \text{cm}^3 = 12\ \text{cm}^2 \times 2\ \text{cm}$

We can write

the volume of a box = area of the base × height.

Calculate the volumes of these boxes.

1. 24 x 1000

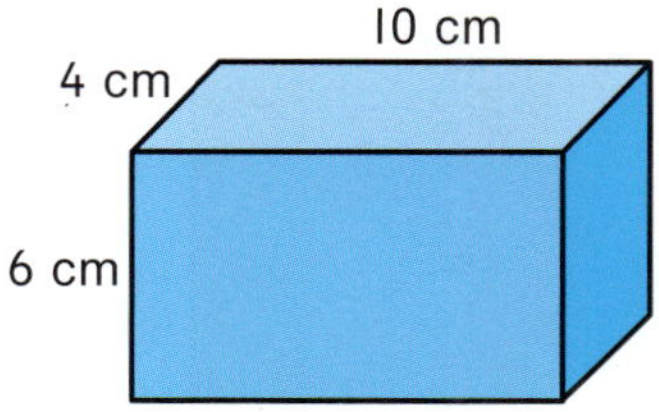

24000

2.

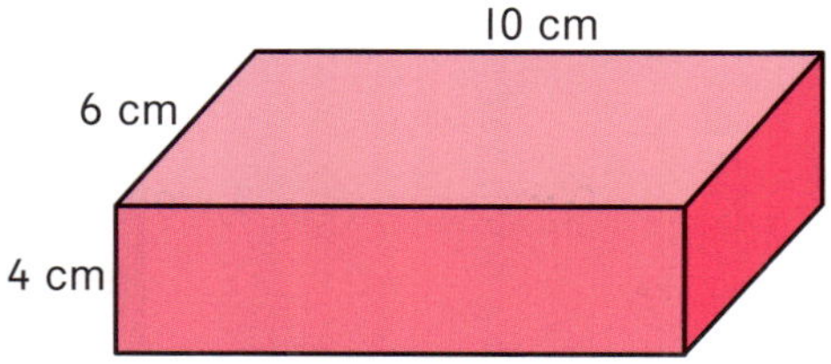

3.

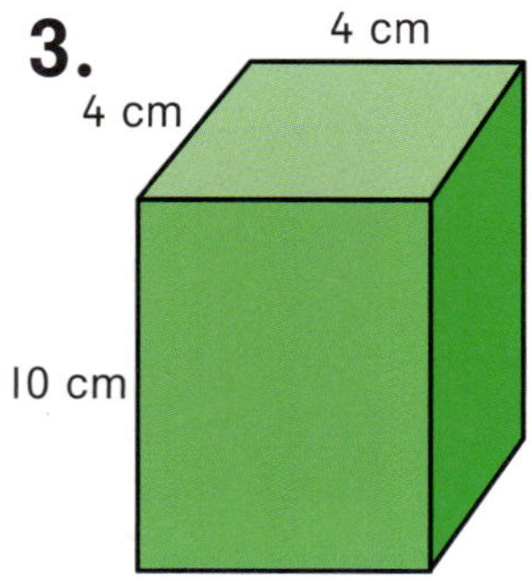

4.

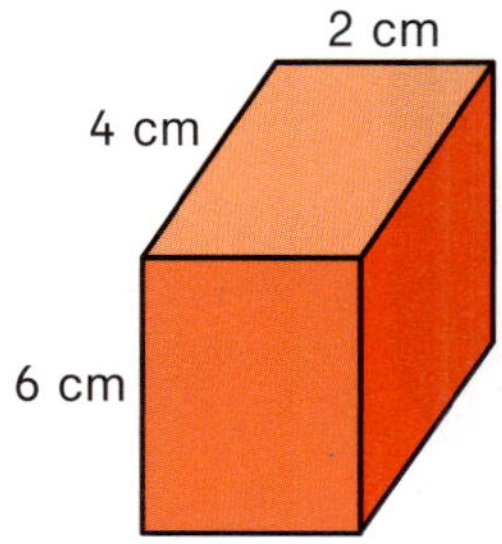

5.

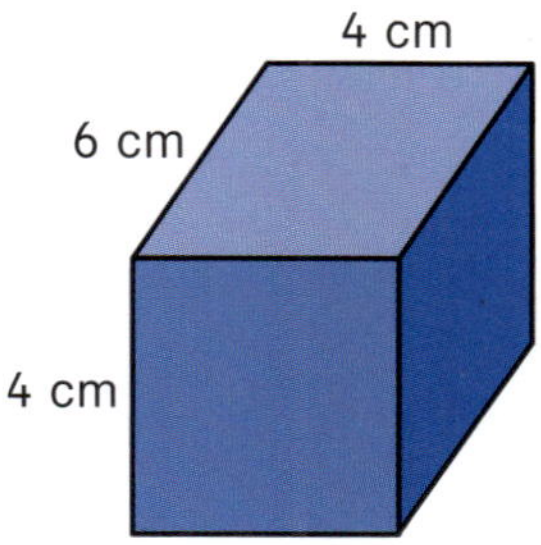

6.

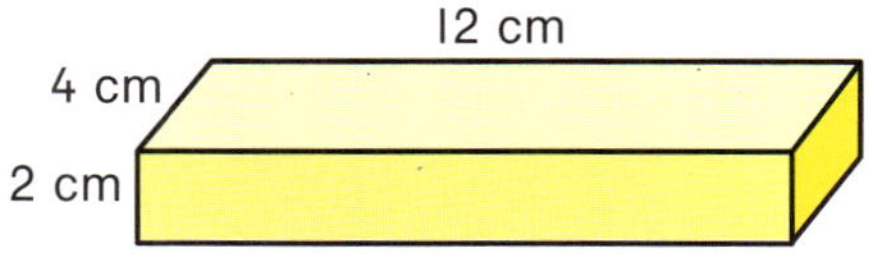

Assessment 7

Change to m and cm.

1. 125 cm **2.** 205 cm

Change to cm.

3. 3 m 1 cm **4.** 1 m 10 cm

5. What is the sum of 2 m 3 cm and 1 m 15 cm?

How many metres are there in

6. $1\frac{1}{2}$ km **7.** $2\frac{1}{4}$ km **8.** 3 km 50 m

Calculate the perimeters of these shapes.

9.

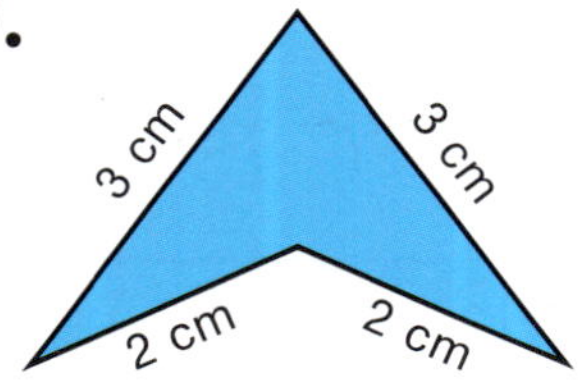

10.

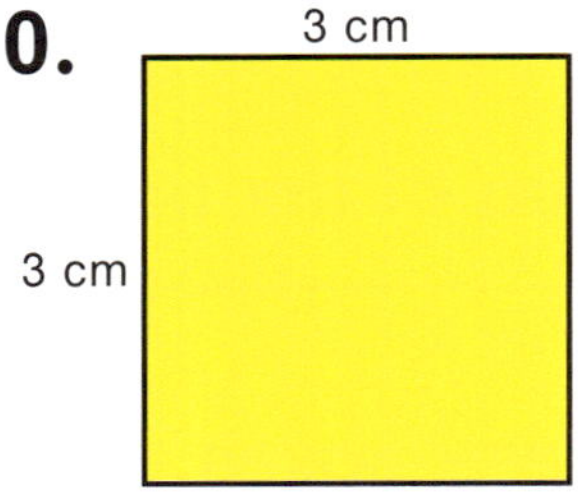

11.

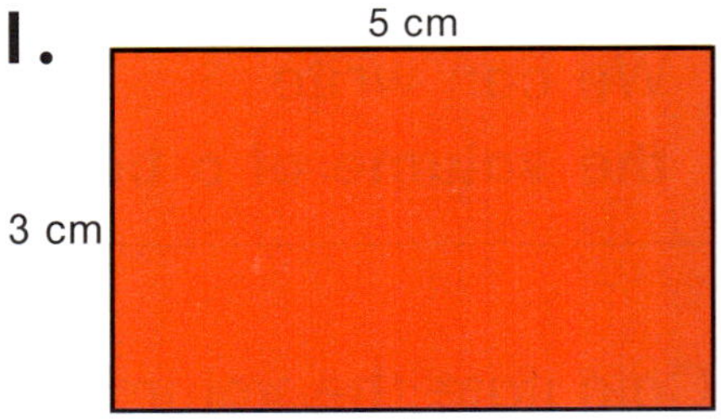

Calculate the areas of these shapes.

12.

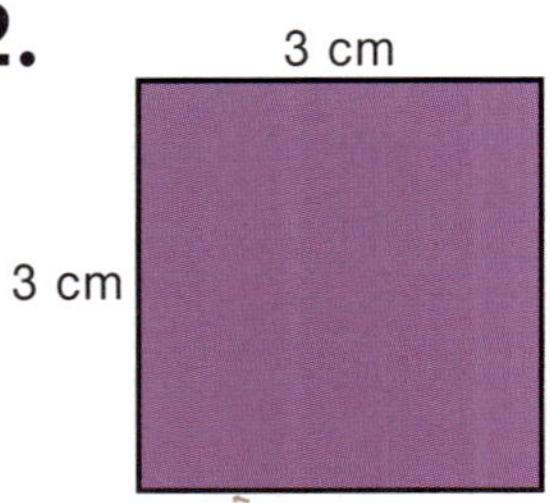

13.

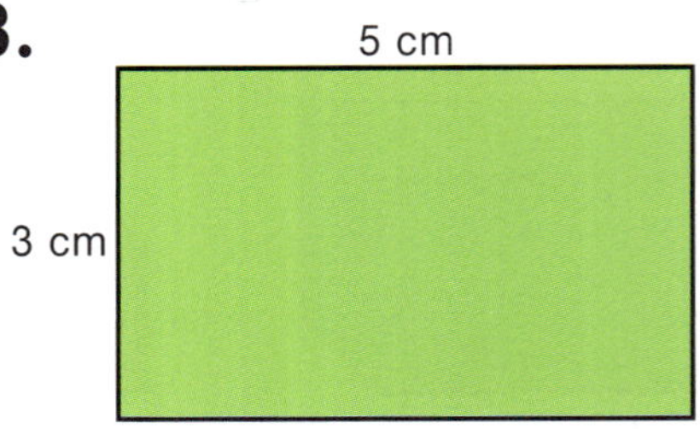

Calculate the volumes of these boxes.

14.

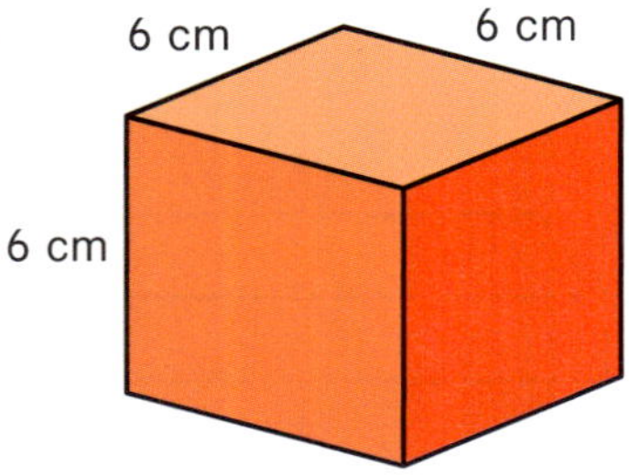

15.

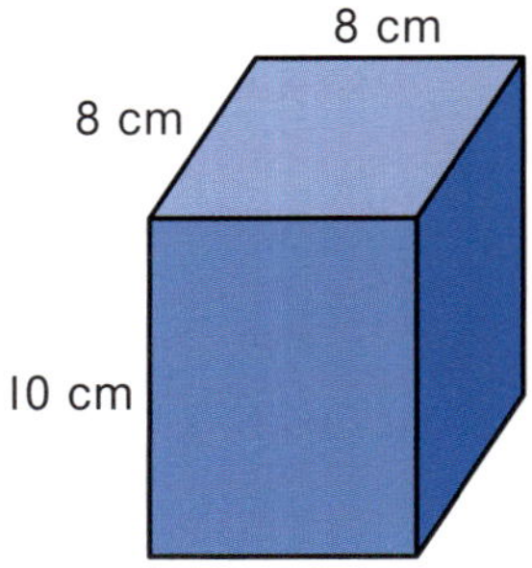

13 Weight and capacity

Kilograms and grams

Remember:
- the weight of a heavy object is measured in kilograms (kg)
- the weight of a light object is measured in grams (g)
- 1 kilogram (1 kg) = 1000 grams (1000 g)

Which unit would you use to measure the following, kg or g?

1. a friend in your class
2. an exercise book
3. a pencil
4. a frozen chicken
5. a bath soap
6. a tube of toothpaste
7. a packet of rice
8. a tub of margarine

Now try to find the real objects and check the weights.

Look at the pictures below. Which of the weights would be nearest to the correct weight?

9.

40 g, 400 g, 4 kg

10.

5 g, 50 g, 500 g

11.

10 g, 100 g, 1 kg

How many grams are there in the following:

12. $\frac{1}{2}$ kg
13. $1\frac{1}{2}$ kg
14. $\frac{3}{4}$ kg
15. $3\frac{1}{4}$ kg

What weights are shown on the scales below?

16.

17.

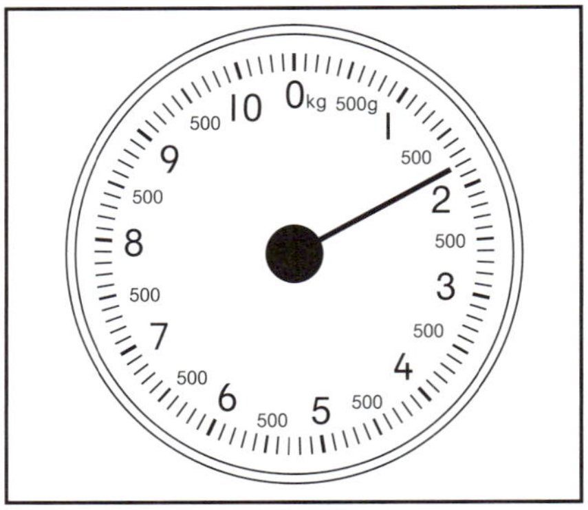

Look at these pictures. Write the weights in kg and g.

18.

2800 g

19.

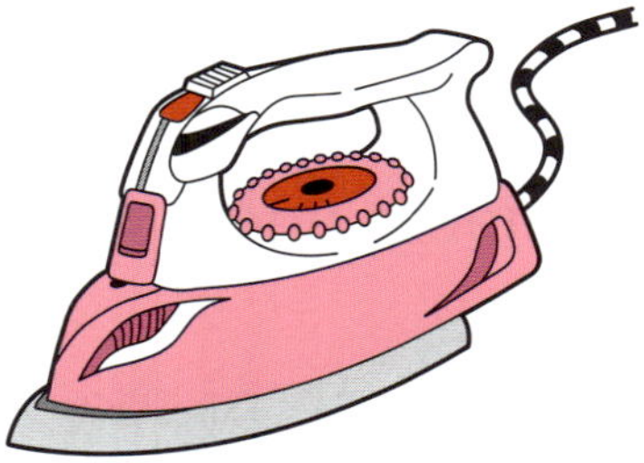

1350 g

20.

4960 g

21.

5500 g

22.

1950 g

23.

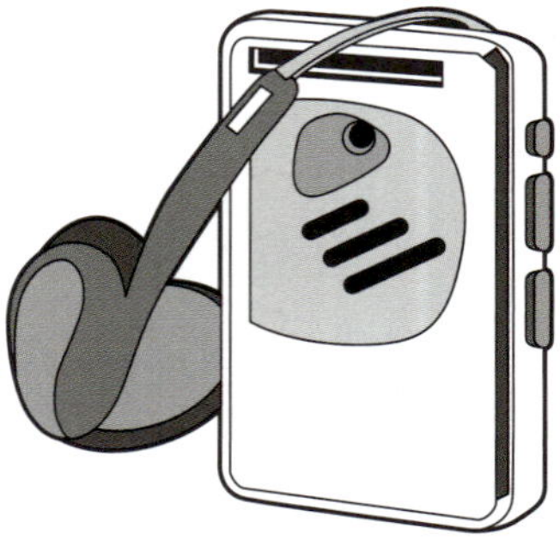

2200 g

Reading weights in kilograms

We can write lengths in metres and centimetres as lengths in metres only.
For example, 1 m 15 cm can be written as 1.15 m.

Very often weights in kilograms and grams are written as kilograms only.
Remember 1000 grams = 1 kilogram.
1·234 kg means 1 kg 234 g or 1234 g.

Look carefully at these numbers:
1 kg 5 g is written as 1·005 kg
1 kg 50 g is written as 1·050 kg
1 kg 500 g is written as 1·500 kg

There are always three digits after the decimal point. These digits show the number of grams, which are less than a kilogram.

Write these as grams:

1. 2·125 kg **2.** 3·015 kg **3.** 1·210 kg **4.** 2·300 kg
5. 2·005 kg **6.** 1·600 kg **7.** 2·010 kg **8.** 4·000 kg

Write these as grams:

9. 4 kg 15 g **10.** 1 kg 115 g **11.** 2 kg 50 g **12.** 1 kg 5 g
13. 2 kg 150 g **14.** 3 k 50 g **15.** 1 k 250 g **16.** 3 kg

Write these as kilograms and grams:

17. 1625 g **18.** 2035 g **19.** 1250 g **20.** 3050 g
21. 3003 g **22.** 3030 g **23.** 3300 g **24.** 3000 g

Comparing and approximating weights

Look at these weights: 2·125 kg   2 kg 85 g   2225 g
Which of these is the lightest, which the heaviest?

It would help if we wrote all the weights as grams:
2.125 kg = 2125 g   2 kg 85 g = 2085 g
The heaviest weight is 2225 g and the lightest is 2 kg 85 g.

Arrange each set of weights in order, lightest to heaviest.

1. 1·305 kg 1·035 kg 1·530 kg

2. 2·025 kg 2·205 kg 2 kg 520 g

3. 1·51 kg 1·15 kg 1·50 kg

4. 2·001 kg 2·010 kg 2·100 kg

5. 3400 g 3·04 kg 3 kg 4 g

6. $4\frac{1}{2}$ kg 4·51 kg 4·45 kg

Sometimes it is convenient to write weights to the nearest kg. We hardly ever weigh ourselves in kg and g. If you look at the bathroom scales you will not see any measurements in grams.
1000 g = 1 kg = 1.00 kg   500 g = 0 kg 500 g = 0.500 kg
Any weight that is 500 g or 0.500 kg or more is rounded up to the next kilogram.
So 2·512 kg is written 3 kg to the nearest kilogram.
2·215 kg is 2 kg to the nearest kilogram.

Write these weights to the nearest kilogram.

7. 1·134 kg

8. 1·635 kg

9. 2·015 kg

10. 3·5 kg

11. 18·55 kg

12. 10·610 kg

13. 6·006 kg

14. 5·59 kg

Adding and subtracting weights

Three parcels weighed 4·250 kg, 2·125 kg and 2.8 kg. What was the total weight?

(2·8 kg means the same as 2.800 kg)

$$\begin{array}{r} 4\cdot250 \\ 2\cdot125 \\ +\ 2\cdot800 \\ \hline 9\cdot175 \end{array}$$

Total weight is 4·250 kg + 2·125 kg + 2·800 kg = 9·175 kg
It is the same as adding all the weights in grams and then putting in the decimal point.

What is the difference in weight between the heaviest and lightest parcel?

4·250 kg – 2·125 kg = 2·125 kg

$$\begin{array}{r} 4\cdot250 \\ -\ 2\cdot125 \\ \hline 2\cdot125 \end{array}$$

It is the same as subtracting the weights in grams and then putting in the decimal point.

Copy and complete.

1.
$$\begin{array}{r} 3\cdot215\text{ kg} \\ 1\cdot038\text{ kg} \\ +\ 2\cdot104\text{ kg} \\ \hline \\ \hline \end{array}$$

2.
$$\begin{array}{r} 2\cdot205\text{ kg} \\ 1\cdot038\text{ kg} \\ +\ 4\cdot500\text{ kg} \\ \hline \\ \hline \end{array}$$

3.
$$\begin{array}{r} 6\cdot875\text{ kg} \\ -\ 3\cdot590\text{ kg} \\ \hline \\ \hline \end{array}$$

4.
$$\begin{array}{r} 3\cdot550\text{ kg} \\ -\ 1\cdot275\text{ kg} \\ \hline \\ \hline \end{array}$$

Work out the answers to these questions.

5. 2·451 kg + 3·185 kg + 5·002 kg

6. What is the weight of 4 boxes of candy each weighing 2·25 kg?

7. How much heavier is a parcel weighing 5·50 kg than one weighing 2·375 kg?

Capacity

Remember:
- large containers hold quantities measured in litres
- small containers hold quantities measured in millilitres
- 1 litre (1 l) = 1000 millilitres (1000 ml)

Which unit would you use to measure the following, l or ml?

1. a medicine glass
2. a drinking glass
3. a bath tub
4. a tablespoon
5. a teaspoon
6. a motor car petrol tank
7. your school water tank
8. a soft drink bottle
9. a milk carton
10. a teacup

How many millilitres are there in the following?

11. 2 litres
12. 5 litres
13. $1\frac{1}{2}$ litres
14. $2\frac{1}{4}$ litres
15. $1\frac{3}{4}$ litres
16. $3\frac{3}{4}$ litres

Look at these pictures. Which of the values given would be the best estimate?

17.

2 l
200 ml
20 ml

18.

10 l
100 l
100 ml

19.

60 l
6 l
600 ml

20.

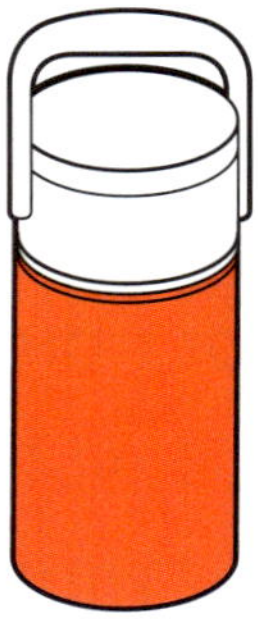

20 l
2 l
200 ml

Litres for litres and millilitres

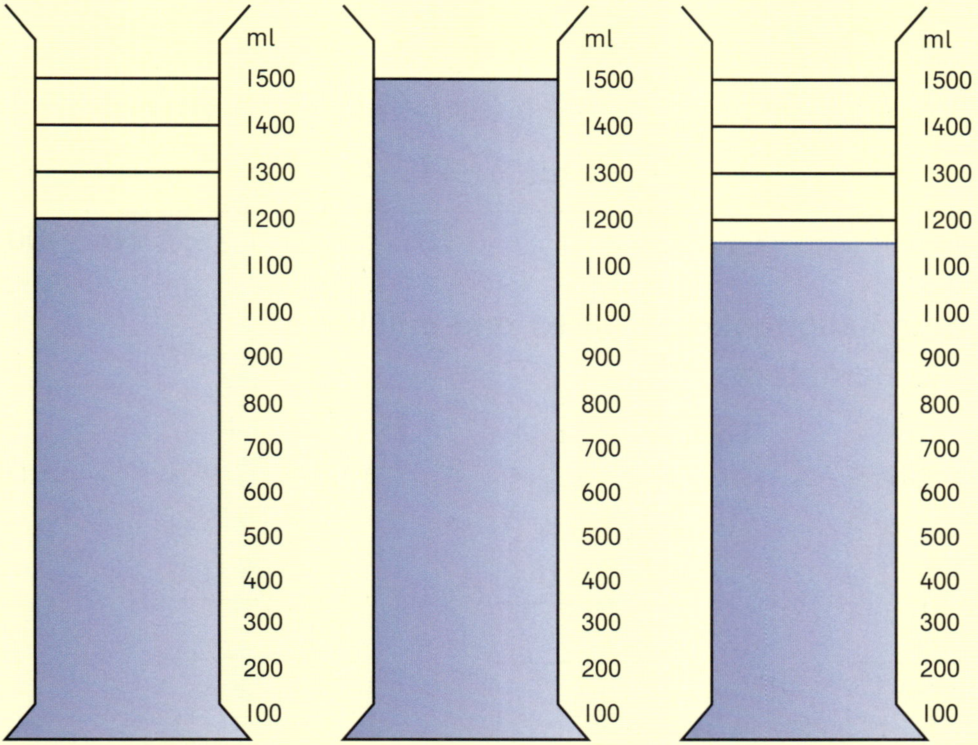

What quantities are shown in the measuring cylinders above?

We can write these quantities as l and ml.

1200 ml = 1 l 200 ml

1500 ml = 1 l 500 ml

1150 ml = 1 l 150 ml

We can also use the decimal point in writing l and ml just as in kg and g.

1200 ml = 1·200 l   1500 ml = 1·500 l   1150 ml = 1·150 l

It is important to write the quantity in ml first to be sure to put in the decimal point correctly.

For example 1 l 5 ml = 1005 ml = 1·005 l

and 1 l 50 ml = 1050 ml = 1·050 ml.

Write these quantities in l and ml.

1. 1545 ml **2.** 2325 ml **3.** 1065 ml **4.** 3106 ml

5. 2·235 l **6.** 4·105 l **7.** 5·005 l **8.** 6·075 l

Write these as l using the decimal point.

9. 2 l 155 ml **10.** 3 l 290 ml **11.** 4 l 50 ml **12.** 5 l 5 ml

13. 1565 ml **14.** 2005 ml **15.** 3230 ml **16.** 4000 ml

Addition and subtraction of litres and millilitres

Copy and complete.

17.
```
     ml
   3525
   1242
+  2600
  ______

  ______
```

18.
```
   l   ml
   3  525
   1  242
+  2  600
  ________

  ________
```

19.
```
      l
   3·525
   1·242
+  2·600
  _______

  _______
```

20. 2565 + 1220 + 2005

Look at the answer to question 20 and use this to write the answers to:

21. 2 l 565 ml + 1 l 220 ml + 2 l 5 ml

22. 2·565 l + 1·220 l + 2·005 l

Work out the answers to this word problem. Show all your working.

23. A motor car petrol tank holds 45 litres. After using the car for some time the owner needed 15·25 litres to refill the tank. How much petrol was in the tank before he filled up?

Comparing and rounding quantities

Problem Three containers were bought to store water for the class. One held 8·500l, another $8\frac{1}{4}$ l and the third 8·75 l. Which container held the most and which the least?

It will help us if we write each quantity as millilitres

8·500 l = 8500 ml $8\frac{1}{4}$ l = 8250 ml 8·75 l = 8750 ml

The largest container held 8·75 l and the smallest $8\frac{1}{4}$ l.

Arrange these quantities in order, largest to smallest.

1. 4025 ml 4205 ml 4250 ml

2. 5·130 l 5·310 l 5·013 l

3. 3 l 50 ml 3 l 5 ml 3 l 500 ml

4. $6\frac{1}{2}$ l 6·52 l 6·515 l

5. 1350 ml 1·530 l 1 l 35 ml

6. 1006 ml 1060 ml 1600 ml

7. 2 l 512 ml 2·215 l 2·521 l

8. 4·004 l 4·04 l 4·4 l

We can also write quantities to the nearest litre just as we did when working with kg and g.

We can write 3·312 l as 3 l and 2·625 ml as 3 l.
When the decimal part is ·500 or more, we round up to the next litre.

Write these quantities to the nearest l.

9. 1·125 l

10. 3·425 l

11. 5·500 l

12. 6·630 l

13. 6·005 l

14. 4·505 l

15. 3·035 l

16. 4 l 525 ml

17. 7 l 500 ml

18. 4 l 550 ml

19. 3 l 450 ml

20. 2 l 501 ml

14 Time

Write the times shown on these clocks.

1.

2.

3.

4.
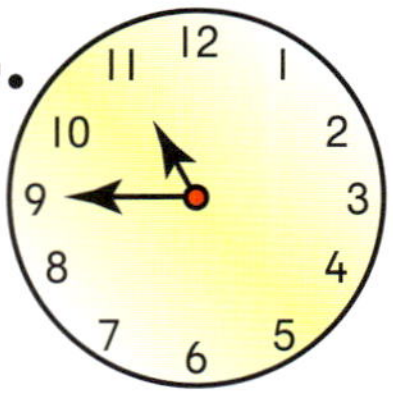

5.

6.

7.
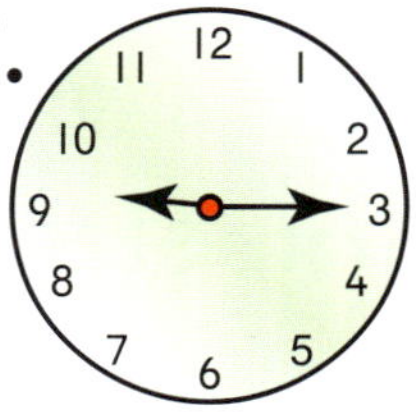

8.

9.

10.
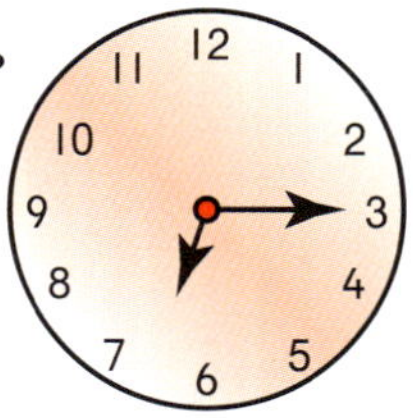

11.

12.
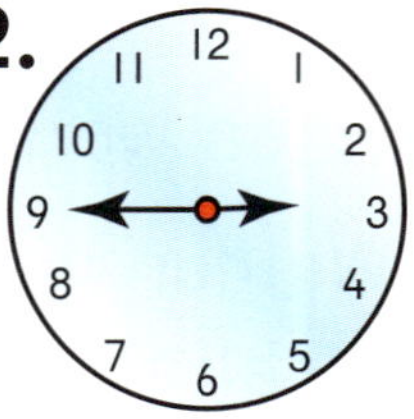

13.
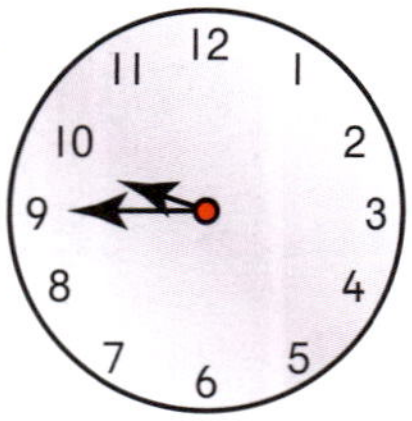

14.

15.

16.

Telling time at five-minute intervals

Clocks measure time in hours and minutes.
If you leave home at 2 o'clock and arrive in Port of Spain at 3 o'clock, then you have taken 1 hour or 60 minutes to get there.

A normal clock face only shows numbers for the hours.
Look at the clock face in the centre below.
The time is half past three.
How many minutes have passed since 3 o'clock?

The minute hand takes 5 minutes to move from one hour number to the next.
If you count in fives from the 12 o'clock mark you will reach 60 when you get back to the 12.
At half past 3 it is 30 minutes after 3 o'clock or 30 minutes before 4 o'clock.
The numbers in red show minutes past or minutes to the hour.
The clock on the right shows 20 minutes past 2; the one on the left says 20 minutes to 2.

Write the the times shown on the clocks below.

1. 
2. 
3. 
4. 
5. 
6. 
7. 
8. 

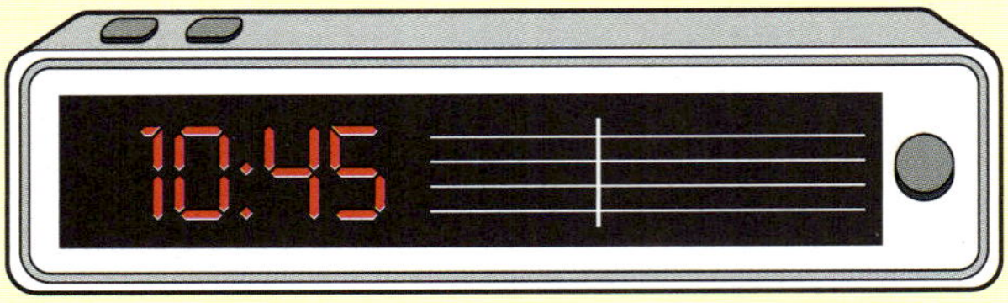

Both clocks show the same time.
10:45 means 45 minutes past 10 o'clock.
45 minutes past 10 o'clock means 15 minutes before 11 o'clock or quarter to 11.

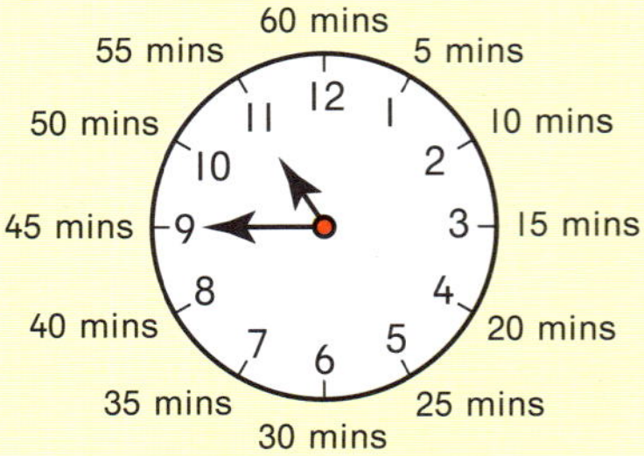

Look at the times shown below. The digital clock time is also shown.

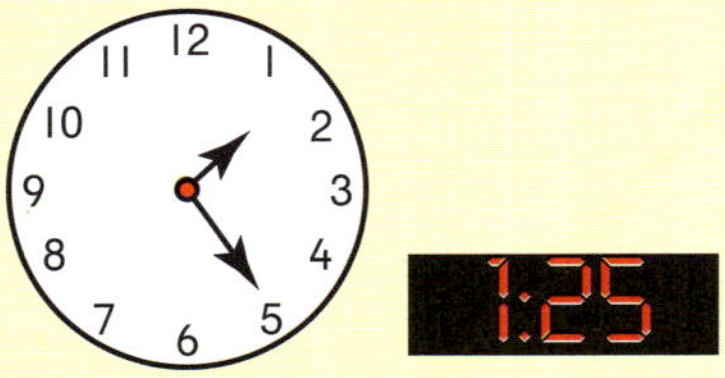

Twenty-five minutes past one

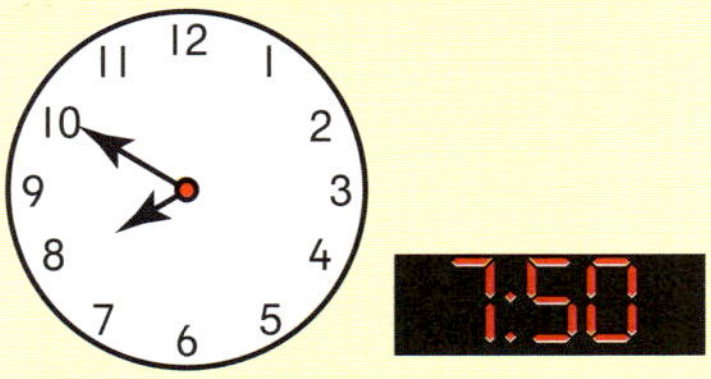

Ten minutes to eight

Five minutes past nine

Write times shown on the clock faces.

9. 

10. 

11. 

12. 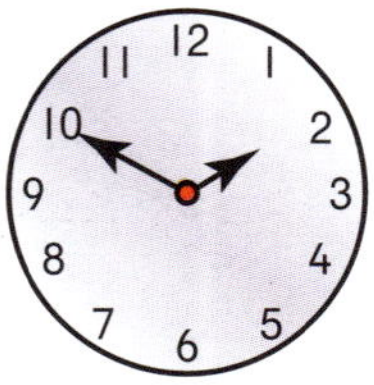

13. 

14. 

Draw clock faces to show these times.

15. 

16. 

17. 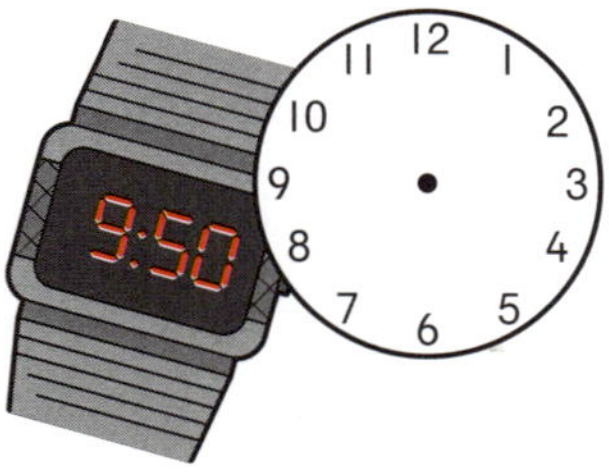

18. 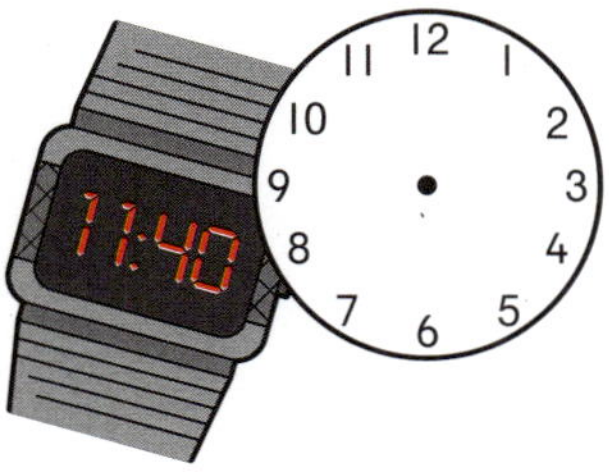

19. 

20. 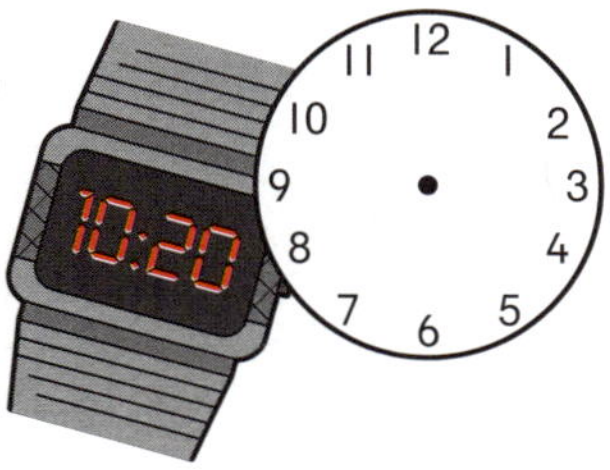

> Remember that a.m. means before midday, that is between midnight and the following midday.
> And p.m. means after midday, that is between midday and midnight.

Answer these questions.

21. How many hours are there between 6.30 a.m. and 11.30 a.m.?

22. How many hours are there between 10.15 a.m. and 12.15 p.m.?

23. How many hours are there between 11.45 a.m. and 2.45 p.m.?

24. What is the time 5 hours after 2.30 p.m.?

25. You go to sleep at 9.00 p.m. and wake up at 7.00 a.m.
How many hours do you sleep?

26. How many hours are there from midday today to midday tomorrow?

Word problems

Problem A man walks for 2 hrs 25 mins, rests for 30 mins, and then walks again for 1 hr 45 mins. How long does he walk altogether?
How long does the journey take?

First part of journey – 2 hrs 25 mins
Second part of journey – 1 hr 45 mins
Total time walking = 2 hrs 25 mins + 1 hr 45 min
= 3 hrs 70 mins
= 4 hrs 10 min

	hrs	mins
	2	25
+	1	45
	3	70

Time for journey = 4 hrs 10 mins + 30 mins
= 4 hrs 40 mins

	4	10
+		30
	4	40

Remember: **60 minutes = 1 hour**

Work out the answers to these word problems. Show all your working.

1. A bus takes 1 hr 25 mins for the first part of a trip and 1 hr 45 mins for the second part. How long does it take for the whole trip?

2. We spend 3 hrs in classes during the morning and 2 hrs 15 mins during the afternoon. How much time do we spend in classes?

3. Jimmy's father completes a bicycle ride in 2 hrs 45 mins. Jimmy takes 35 mins more. How long does Jimmy take?

4. A car takes 1 hr 40 mins to complete a journey. A bus takes 2 hrs 10 mins for the same trip. How much longer does the bus take?

Timetables

The school timetable shows when Class 3 has mathematics.

	Monday	Tuesday	Wednesday	Thursday	Friday
8.45 – 9.30 a.m.	maths	maths	maths	maths	maths
12.30 – 1.00 p.m.	maths	science	maths	science	maths

Use the timetable above to answer these questions.

1. How many times per week does Class 3 have mathematics?
2. How long does the mathematics lesson last in the morning?
3. How long does the mathematics lesson last in the afternoon?
4. How many hours and minutes does Class 3 have in mathematics every week?

The express bus from Port of Spain (P.O.S.) to San Fernando follows this timetable every day.

Depart	Arrive	Depart	Arrive
P.O.S.	Chaguanas	Chaguanas	San Fernando
6.00 a.m. 6.30 a.m. 7.15 a.m.	6.30 a.m. 7.00 a.m. 7.45 a.m.	6.40 a.m. 7.10 a.m. 7.55 a.m.	7.15 a.m. 7.45 a.m. 8.30 a.m.

Use the timetable above to answer these questions.

5. How long does the journey from Port of Spain to Chaguanas take?

6. How long does the journey from Port of Spain to San Fernando take?

7. How long does the bus stay in Chaguanas?

8. How long does the journey from Chaguanas to San Fernando take?

9. If the bus did not stop at Chaguanas how long would the journey from Port of Spain to San Fernando take?

10. If you missed the bus at Chaguanas at 7.10 a.m. how long would you have to wait for the next bus?

Assessment 8

How many grams are there in these?

1. $5\frac{1}{2}$ kg **2.** 3 kg 125 g **3.** 4·250 kg

How many millilitres are there in these?

4. $3\frac{3}{4}$ l **5.** 4 l 525 ml **6.** 2·505 l

Write these as kg and g.

7. 2255 g **8.** 6·505 kg

Write these as l and ml.

9. 5150 ml **10.** 3·345 l

11. What is the total weight of 2 parcels, one weighing 2 kg 125 g and the other 1 kg 350 g?

12. A bottle holds 1.5 litres of water. How much water will 3 bottles hold?

13. How much heavier is a box weighing 5 kg 400 g than one weighing 3 kg 850 g?

14. How many 250 ml bottles can you fill from a 2 litre can?

What time is shown on each of these clocks?

15.

16.

Draw clock faces to show the times written below.

17.

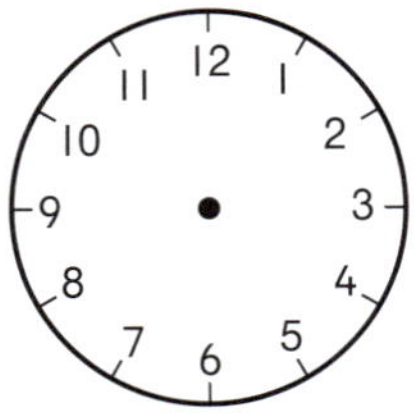

3.30

18.

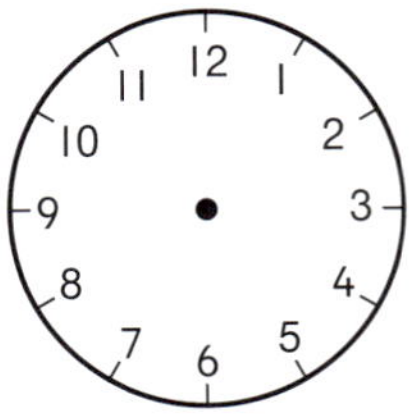

7.50

How many minutes are there in:

19. $\frac{3}{4}$ hour

20. 2 hrs 15 mins

How many hours and minutes are there between:

21. 1.30 p.m. and 2.45 p.m.

22. 11.15 a.m. and 2.15 p.m.

23. A man rides for 45 minutes, rests for 15 minutes, and then rides again for 30 minutes. What is the total time taken?

24. The winner of the race finished in 2 hours 20 minutes. The last placed runner finished in 3 hours 25 minutes. How much longer than the winner did the last runner take?

15 Handling data

Bar graphs

Children attending an art show were asked to state their favourite colour.
The information was presented in the form of a graph.
Look at the two graphs below.
The one on the left is a block graph. Numbers are shown as blocks.
The one on the right is a bar graph. Numbers are shown as bars.

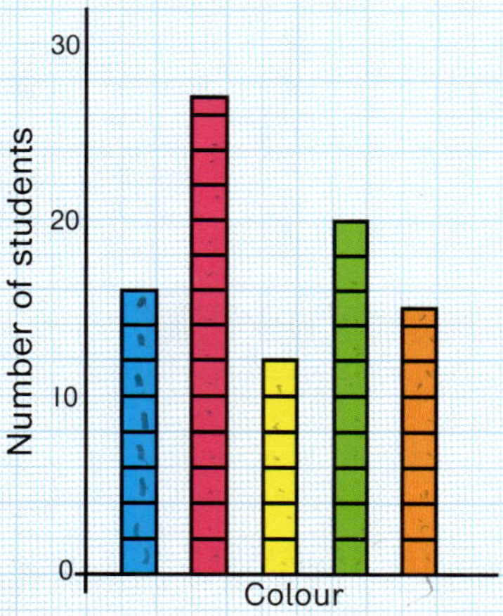

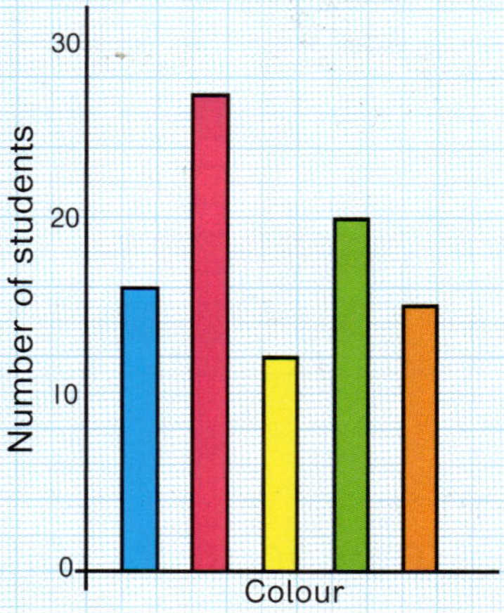

Use the information on the graphs above to answer these questions.

1. Which colour did most children like?

2. Which colour did children like least?

3. How many children liked green most?

4. How many children liked orange?

5. How many children chose blue as their favourite colour?

6. How many children gave answers to the question?

The horizontal bar graph

Sometimes the bars in the graph are drawn horizontally.
In the graphs on page 151 the bars were vertical.

At the end of the year party the pupils of Standard 3 were treated to ice cream.
The graph below shows the flavours the children chose.

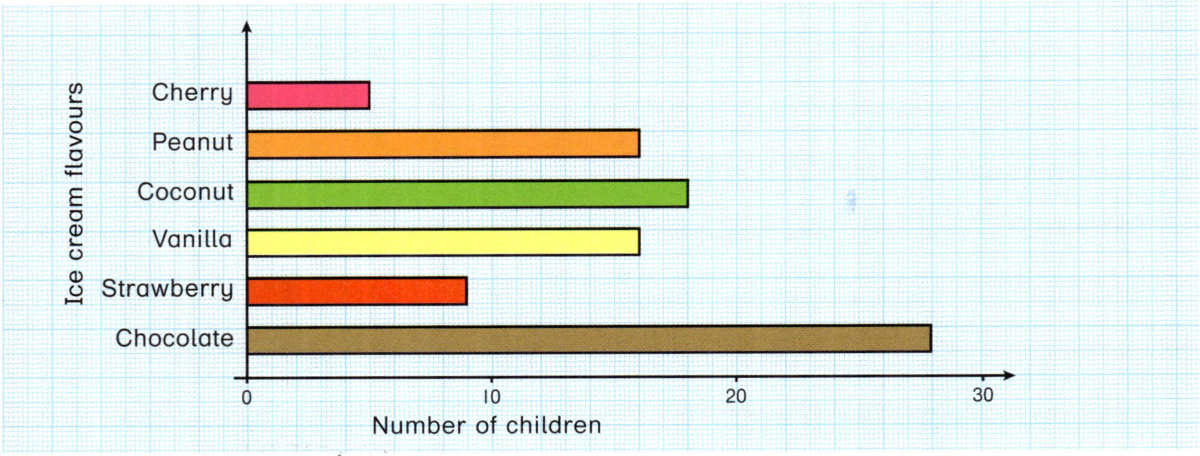

Use the information in the graph above to answer these questions.

1. Which was the most popular flavour?
2. Which was the least popular flavour?
3. Which two flavours were chosen by an equal number of children?
4. How many more children preferred coconut to peanut?
5. How many children chose peanut?
6. How many children chose either peanut or coconut?
7. How many children were treated to the party?

Using different scale factors

We asked the children in a school to say how many brothers and sisters they each had.
Their answers were tallied and the information is shown on the graphs below.
Can you say why the bars in one are taller than those in the other?

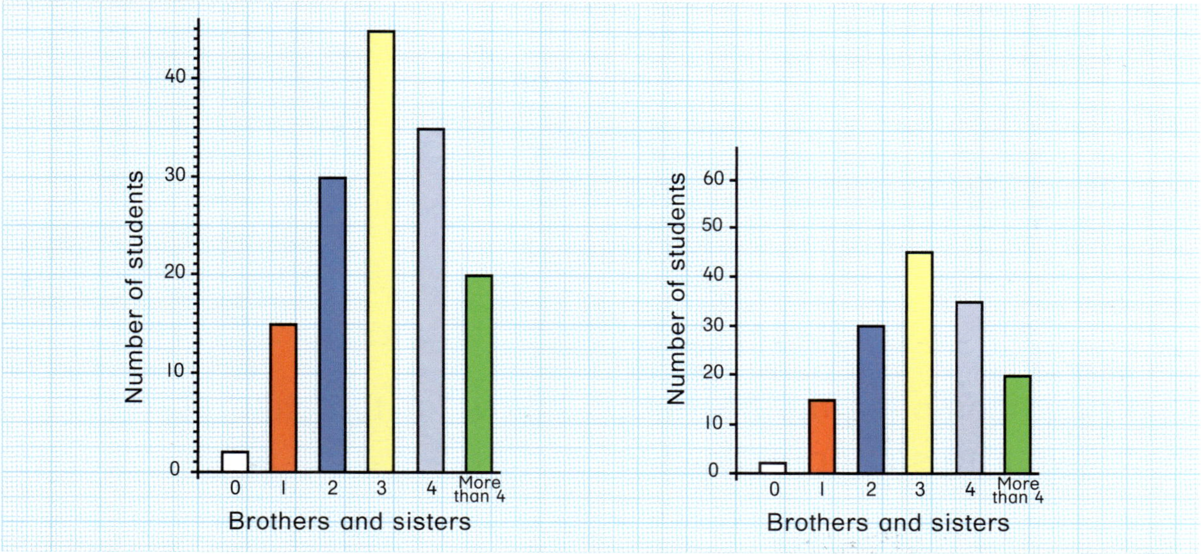

Answer these questions using the graph on the right.
Check your answers using the graph on the left.

1. How many children were counted in the school?
2. How many children had only 1 brother or sister?
3. How many children had more than 4 brothers or sisters?
4. How many brothers and sisters did the largest group of children have?
5. Which was the larger group, the group with 2 brothers and sisters, or the group with 4 brothers and sisters?
6. How many children were in the larger group in question 5?

Constructing bar graphs

Children in a school were asked to state their favourite soft drink flavour.

Their answers are shown in this table.

Children's favourite soft drink	
Soft drink	Number of children
Cola	25
Lemonade	16
Grape	30
Banana	24
Orange	12
Pear	26

Copy and complete the bar graph below for the children and their favourite soft drink flavours.

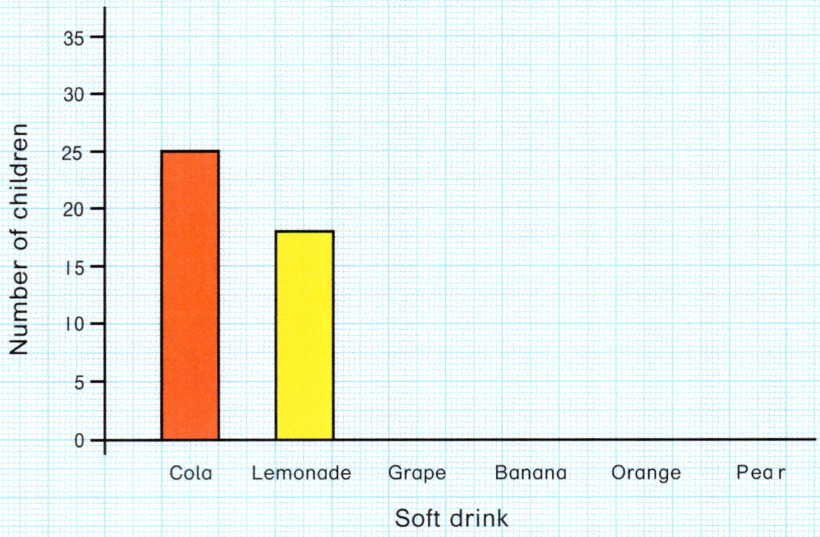

Children in one class were asked to state what pet animal they kept.

Copy and complete the frequency table to find out the number of children and the pets they kept.

Our pets		
Pet	Tally	Total
Dogs	𝍸 𝍸 𝍸	
Cats	𝍸 I	
Birds	𝍸 𝍸	
Rabbits	III	
Fish	𝍸 𝍸	

Copy and complete the horizontal and vertical bar graphs below, using the information presented in the frequency table above.

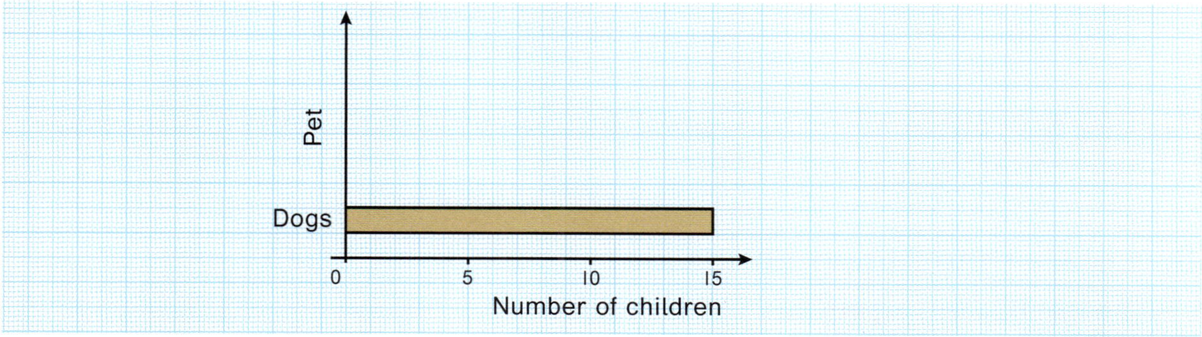

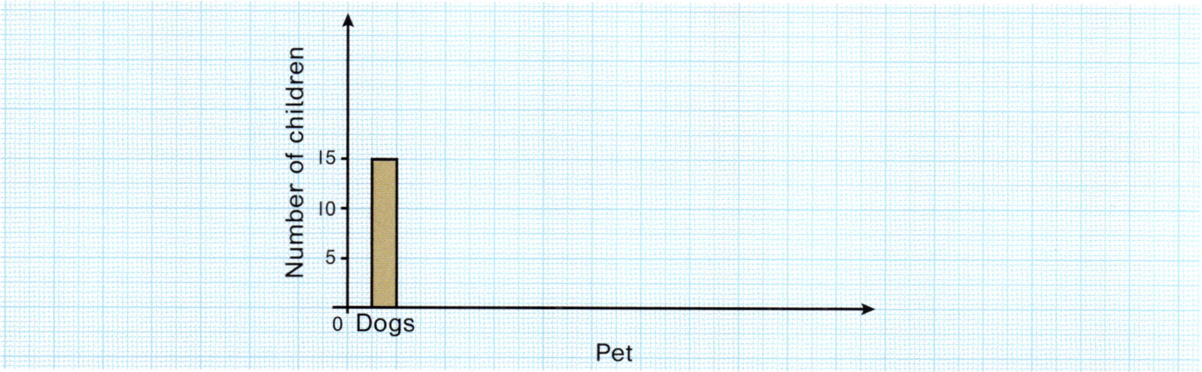

End of year test

1. Write the numeral for two thousand, three hundred and four.

2. Write the number 1023 in words.

3. Write the correct sign, $>$ or $<$, in the box to make the statement true.

   2153 ☐ 2513

4. Arrange these numbers in order, starting with the smallest.

   1423 1243 1342 1324

5. Write these numbers to the nearest hundred.

   (a) 224 (b) 467 (c) 312 (d) 194

6. On Friday 675 people went to a calypso show. On Saturday the number was 1024 and on Sunday 552. How many people attended the show on all three days?

7. From a stock of 1250 toys a dealer sold 936. How many toys remained unsold?

8. Look at the shape on the right. Write the number of

   (a) faces
   (b) edges
   (c) vertices

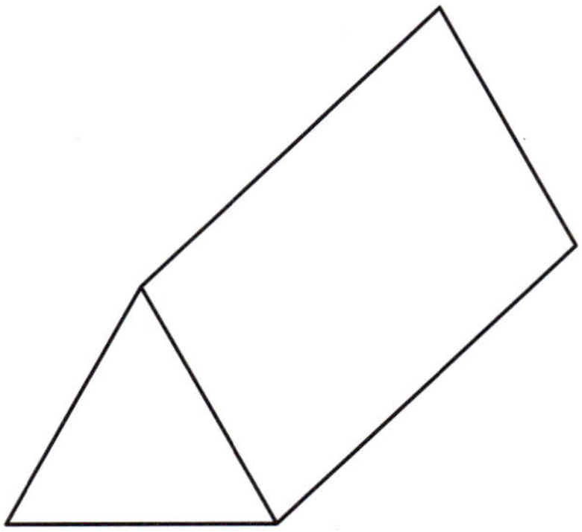

9. Name the solid that can be formed from this net.

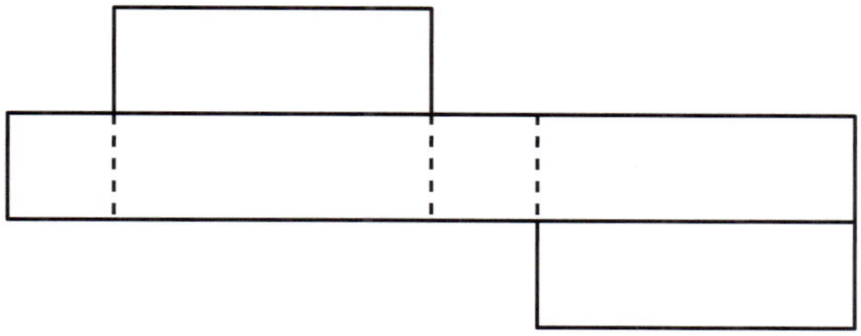

10. A storeworker is paid $9.50 an hour. How much does the worker earn for working 8 hours a day for 6 days?

11. A row in a football stand has 125 seats. How many people can sit in 24 rows?

12. Eighty-four chairs are arranged in 7 rows. How many chairs are in each row?

13. From a piece of ribbon $\frac{9}{10}$ of a metre long a piece $\frac{1}{2}$ m long is cut off. What is the length of the piece left?

14. Four children bought 5 cakes and wanted to share them equally. How much would each child get?

15. Two-thirds of a class of 24 children went on an outing. How many children did not go?

16. Write the number 15·1 in words.

17. Write the numeral for one hundred and six and seven-tenths.

18. A 5 litre bottle of cooking oil costs \$49.50. A 1 litre bottle of the same oils costs \$10.95. How much money do you save when you buy a 5 litre bottle?

19. What is the perimeter of a rectangle which measures 2 m 5 cm long and 1 m 25 cm wide?

20. How much carpet is needed to cover a floor which measures 6 m by 5 m?

21. What is the volume of a box which is 12 cm by 12 cm at both ends and is 20 cm long?

22. A traveller carried two suitcases, one weighing 29·4 kg and the other 30.2 kg. What was the total weight of the suitcases in kilograms and grams?

23. Three bottles contained $1\frac{1}{2}$ litres, 1 litre and $2\frac{1}{5}$ litres of drink that was left after a party. It was all then poured into a 5 litre bottle. How many more millilitres would be needed to fill this bottle?

24.

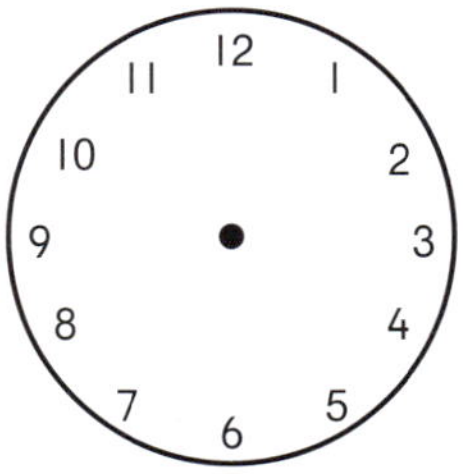

Draw the hands on the clock face to show the time on this radio clock.

25. The bar graph shows the colour of ribbons worn by some of the girls in a school.

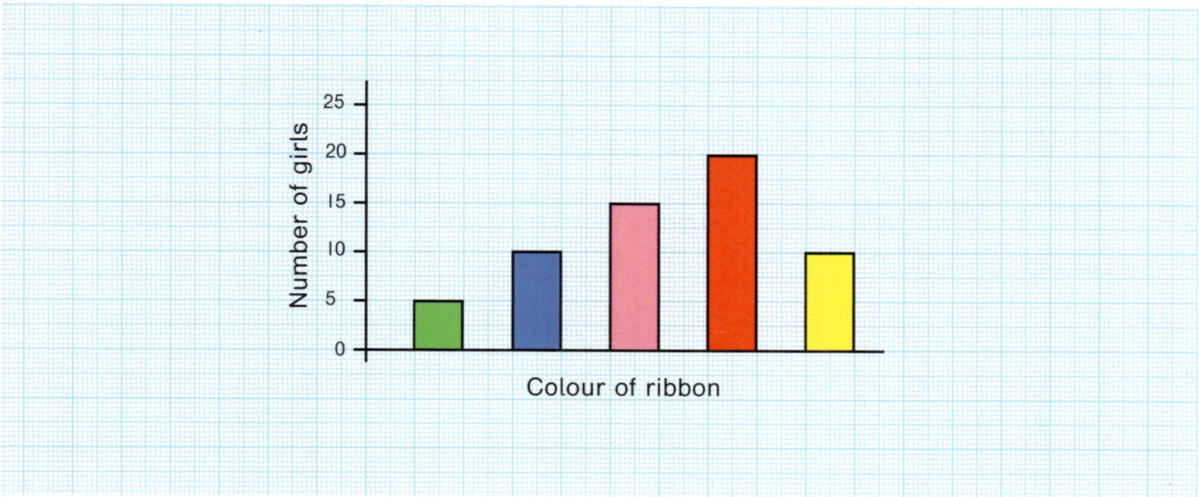

(a) How many girls were counted?

(b) Which was the most popular colour of ribbon?

(c) How many girls chose the most popular colour?

(d) How many girls chose the least popular colour?

(e) Which colours were chosen by an equal number of girls?